Palgrave Studies in Governance, Leadership and Responsibility

Series Editors
Simon Robinson
Leeds Business School
Leeds Beckett University
Leeds, UK

Jim Parry
Charles University
Prague, Czech Republic

William Sun
Leeds Business School
Leeds Beckett University
Leeds, UK

The fall-out from many high profile crises in governance and leadership in recent decades, from banking to healthcare, continues to be felt around the world. Major reports have questioned the values and behaviour, not just of individual organizations but of professionals, industries and political leadership. These reports raise questions about business corporations and also public service institutions. In response this new series aims to explore the broad principles of governance and leadership and how these are embodied in different contexts, opening up the possibility of developing new theories and approaches that are fuelled by interdisciplinary approaches. The purpose of the series is to highlight critical reflection and empirical research which can enable dialogue across sectors, focusing on theory, value and the practice of governance, leadership and responsibility.

Written from a global context, the series is unique in bringing leadership and governance together. The King III report connects these two fields by identifying leadership as one of the three principles of effective governance however most courses in business schools have traditionally treated these as separate subjects. Increasingly, and in particular with the case of executive education, business schools are recognizing the need to develop and produce responsible leaders. The series will therefore encourage critical exploration between these two areas and as such explore sociological and philosophical perspectives.

More information about this series at
http://www.palgrave.com/gp/series/15192

Marjan Marandi Parkinson

Corporate Governance in Transition

Dealing with Financial Distress and Insolvency in UK Companies

palgrave
macmillan

Marjan Marandi Parkinson
Centre for Governance, Leadership and Global Responsibility
Leeds, UK

Palgrave Studies in Governance, Leadership and Responsibility
ISBN 978-3-319-77109-0   ISBN 978-3-319-77110-6   (eBook)
https://doi.org/10.1007/978-3-319-77110-6

Library of Congress Control Number: 2018936795

© The Editor(s) (if applicable) and The Author(s), under exclusive licence to Springer International Publishing AG, part of Springer Nature 2018
This work is subject to copyright. All rights are solely and exclusively licensed by the Publisher, whether the whole or part of the material is concerned, specifically the rights of translation, reprinting, reuse of illustrations, recitation, broadcasting, reproduction on microfilms or in any other physical way, and transmission or information storage and retrieval, electronic adaptation, computer software, or by similar or dissimilar methodology now known or hereafter developed.
The use of general descriptive names, registered names, trademarks, service marks, etc. in this publication does not imply, even in the absence of a specific statement, that such names are exempt from the relevant protective laws and regulations and therefore free for general use.
The publisher, the authors and the editors are safe to assume that the advice and information in this book are believed to be true and accurate at the date of publication. Neither the publisher nor the authors or the editors give a warranty, express or implied, with respect to the material contained herein or for any errors or omissions that may have been made. The publisher remains neutral with regard to jurisdictional claims in published maps and institutional affiliations.

Cover credit: Andrey Danilovich/E+/Getty

This Palgrave Macmillan imprint is published by the registered company Springer Nature Switzerland AG
The registered company address is: Gewerbestrasse 11, 6330 Cham, Switzerland

Contents

Part I 1

1 Governance in Distress 3

2 Corporate Governance in Public Companies 9

3 Financial Distress, Insolvency and Business Rescue 43

4 Corporate Governance in Financial Distress 65

5 Corporate Governance in Insolvency 95

Part II 121

6 Corporate Governance Research: An Empirical Approach 123

7 Case Study 1: Stylo plc 145

8 Case Study 2: JJB Sports plc 163

9	Case Study 3: Waterford Wedgwood plc	185
10	Case Study 4: Woolworths Group plc	203
11	Case Study 5: Connaught plc	223

Part III — 245

| 12 | Insights from the Case Studies | 247 |
| 13 | Conclusions | 285 |

Index — 301

List of Tables

Table 1.1	New company insolvencies in England and Wales	5
Table 12.1	Sample overview	248
Table 12.2	Analysis of the sample based on mega insolvency criteria at the start of informal rescue process	250
Table 12.3	Board size and composition	251
Table 12.4	Analysis of assets and liabilities (millions)	252
Table 12.5	Informal rescue process: timeframe, and use of rescue options	255
Table 12.6	Board changes during informal rescue process	257
Table 12.7	Payment to unsecured creditors	272
Table 12.8	Unsecured creditor influence during administration	280

Part I

1

Governance in Distress

Overview

This book examines the impact of financial distress and insolvency on corporate governance. Whilst the book is written from a predominantly legal position, the review and analysis has been expanded to cover broader issues of business and strategic management that overlay director decision-making in such circumstances. It seeks to avoid normative prescription, choosing instead to illustrate its arguments with an empirical analysis of specific director decisions, revealed by a systematic review of five different case studies of large public companies that have experienced financial distress and ultimately insolvency.

In the UK, the law related to financial distress and insolvency focuses on specific director responsibilities, setting out how directors are expected to implement their legal duties in such circumstances to companies, shareholders and creditors. These duties have been established in common law and in statute, most notably through the Companies Act 2006, and the Insolvency Act 1986. In parallel, largely in response to prominent examples of business failure, codes of practice have been established to prescribe how public companies should behave in a range of different areas including determining the composition of the board of directors and ensuring its independence, financial reporting and the remuneration of senior executives—so-called governance codes. This latter development is a response to a perceived need for those charged with running a company to be more accountable and transparent in their decision-making.

This book examines the impact of financial distress and insolvency on governance structures and processes, taking a dual perspective that includes an investigation of the way in which directors discharge their legal responsibilities and the way in which they implement governance codes. This is a rapidly evolving agenda and the synthesis of these two areas in an approach that combines doctrinal, theoretical and empirical analysis should be of value to those responsible for interpreting, applying and developing statutory legislation and formulating and implementing appropriate codes.

Financial Distress: A Challenge for Governance

Most companies experience periods of financial distress, reflecting external environmental challenges such as new competition, changes in product technology, problems with labour supply or increasing capital costs—all of which have the potential to put pressure on the company's overall financial and economic viability. Companies can adjust to such problems in a variety of different ways including entry into new markets, new product development or diversification into new areas of business. Each of these business development options is likely to create a demand for more finance, at least in the short term, to successfully implement the business plan, putting pressure on cash flow in circumstances where resources may already be constrained. Alternatively (and potentially simultaneously) focus may be primarily placed on improving the flow of funds from existing business operations. In either situation, companies are likely to apply a range of different strategies to business financing and the management of cash flow, including cost reduction, equity/share issue, asset sale and/or new debt financing/debt renegotiation. Whilst such approaches to improving cash flow may resolve financial problems in the short term, ultimately the directors may run out of options and the company fails.

Business failure is an unfortunate but recurring corollary of business life. Table 1.1 shows that between 2013 and 2017, the number of new company insolvencies in England and Wales ranged from 14,658 to 17,243. The table also shows the relative frequency of different types of insolvency. Creditors' voluntary liquidations have been the most frequent, followed by compulsory liquidations, administrations, company voluntary arrangements and receiverships. There are no definitive statistics to indicate the number of companies that are experiencing financial distress at any particular moment; however, it would be reasonable to assume that the number is significantly higher than the number of company insolvencies.

Whilst Table 1.1 indicates the overall scale of the problem, over the last decade a series of high-profile business failures in the UK including JJB Sports plc, Waterford Wedgwood Group plc, Woolworths Group plc, Comet plc, HMV Group plc, British Home Stores Limited (BHS) and Carillion plc have created an increasing awareness of some of the key issues that business insolvency can create. The heightened attention paid to such failures is not difficult to understand. Large public companies are amongst

Table 1.1 New company insolvencies in England and Wales[a]

	Number of insolvencies					% change—2016 to 2017
	2013	2014	2015	2016	2017e	
Total new company insolvencies	**17,682**	**16,319**	**14,658**	**16,545**	**17,243**	**4.2**
Underlying total insolvencies	*17,682*	*16,319*	*14,658*	*14,749*	*15,112*	*2.5*
Compulsory liquidations	3632	3755	2889	2930	2799	−4.5
Creditors' voluntary liquidations (CVL)	11,453	10,401	9992	11,890	12,861	8.2
Underlying CVLs	*11,453*	*10,401*	*9992*	*10,094*	*10,730*	*6.3*
Administrations	2009	1587	1402	1374	1289	−6.2
Company voluntary arrangements	571	554	364	346	292	−15.6
Receiverships	17	22	11	5	2	−60.0

Source: Insolvency Service and Companies House, Jan. 2018

[a] For detailed interpretation see: The Insolvency Service. Insolvency Statistics - October to December 2017 (Q2017). Accessed February 1, 2018. https://assets.publishing.service.gov.uk/government/uploads/system/uploads/attachment_data/file/675931/Insolvency_Statistics_-_web.pdf

the most influential economic players in developed countries. Changes in the value of their assets and liquidity have a major impact on capital markets and they make major contributions in terms of employment and investment. Some employ large numbers of service sub-contractors or have a large number of suppliers that have extended credit to the company in different forms. Banks and other lenders may also have provided financial support through loans and other securities. Major institutional investment and pension funds may have significant shareholdings. Such companies may also have employee pension schemes that require continual funding. Where such prominent companies have failed, attention has increasingly been focused on corporate governance—specifically the way in which the directors of the company have met their responsibilities to shareholders, employees, creditors and the general public.

UK law has chosen to remain largely silent about the commercial decisions that are taken by the board of directors and the impact of such decisions on creditors and shareholders when the company enters a period of financial distress. The responsibility is typically left to the directors of such companies to resolve the debt problem before the company enters a formal insolvency regime. This informal rescue stage may frequently involve decisions that require approval by creditors and institutional shareholders. Once a formal regime is invoked directors see their control eroded as decisions are made by insolvency practitioners who maintain an independent role and do not necessarily require creditor or shareholder approval for such decisions. The governance pattern that takes shape during this stage is frequently vague and ill-defined from a legal perspective, partly due to a lack of detailed disclosure rules that would identify the influence of third parties (principally creditors). The precise nature of governance is also unclear. Governance codes do not directly address issues arising from financial distress and insolvency. It is not clear what impact financial distress or insolvency may have on the practical implementation of such codes.

This is a comparatively neglected area of research and analysis. The author has not found any systematic empirical research into the effects of financial distress and insolvency on corporate governance, that maps the evolving responsibilities and liabilities of each of the parties involved (directors, creditors, shareholders and ultimately insolvency practitioners) against the context of statute and common law responsibilities and governance codes. However, it is clear that this topic is becoming increasingly important in emerging doctrinal and empirical research in business, law and management. This is the gap that this book seeks to address.

Scope and Contribution

In summary this book focuses on:

- how UK law approaches financial distress and insolvency and the extent to which statutory legislation and current codes of governance acknowledge and accommodate both situations; the work should assist policy formulation by creating an increased awareness of the role of other key players—specifically creditors and institutional shareholders in the governance of financially distressed companies.
- the extent to which boards of directors continue to exercise their general duty to their company through effective business/commercial judgment during periods of financial distress, and how far their approach in such circumstances is consistent with statutory responsibilities and governance codes;
- the influence of shareholders and creditors on the board's choice of informal business rescue options and their subsequent success or failure;
- the influences of the decisions made by insolvency practitioners on creditor claims and the distribution of assets. The outcomes should provide further context for proposals to regulate for greater disclosure of secured creditor influence during administration, and the provision of more support for unsecured creditors.

Narrative

Chapter 2 of this book examines the emergence of codes of corporate governance and the scope of directors' legal duties to the company. It also considers the role of external markets and credit rating agencies as indirect governance mechanisms. Chapter 3 considers the main causes of financial distress and its impact on business activity. The chapter compares legal and managerial perspectives and ambiguities arising from a shift in directors' perceived duties from shareholder to creditor interests. Chapter 4 then looks at each of the major informal rescue mechanisms in detail, highlighting the change in focus of director priorities when the board deems it necessary to implement specific rescue activities including changes to the membership of the board, cost reduction, asset sale, equity/share issue and new debt financing/debt renegotiation.

Chapter 5 discusses formal insolvency regimes. In the UK, the Insolvency Act 1986 provides four formal insolvency procedures: administration, company voluntary arrangement (CVA), administrative receivership and liquidation. The chapter reviews each of these regimes, focusing on the diminishing role and responsibilities of the board of directors and the increasing importance of secured creditors and insolvency practitioners.

Having set the scene discussion then moves to an analysis of the impact of financial distress and insolvency on governance in practice in five case studies of major UK plc's that encountered a period of financial distress resulting ultimately in business failure. This approach follows an emerging trend in legal research towards the greater use of empirical research to supplement doctrinal analysis. Chapters 7 to 11 set out each case in detail.

The case studies examine corporate governance and the debt structure of each company prior to entry into an informal rescue process. They also examine the apparent internal and external causes of financial distress at the start of the informal rescue process, and the causes of insolvency at the time of appointing an insolvency practitioner. The influence of shareholders and creditors (secured and unsecured) on directors' attempts to resolve financial distress is also examined as well as governance patterns during administration and CVA.

Readers may choose to skip these chapters initially and move directly to a synthesis of the main findings in Chap. 12. However, each of the case studies merits detailed consideration in their own right, providing multiple insights into the issues raised in this book. Chapter 13 then concludes the discussion and sets out a future research agenda.

2

Corporate Governance in Public Companies

Overview

The corporate governance agenda can be summarised as follows: when ownership of a company is separate from control and professional managers are employed to direct a company, mechanisms are needed to ensure that decisions are ultimately made in the interests of the shareholding investors. A broader view of governance also includes the interests of other stakeholders including employees, suppliers and the general public. Such mechanisms (governance processes) should work collectively to ensure that shareholder interests (and potentially the interests of a wider range of stakeholders), rather than managerial interests, are the primary focus of decision-making. This chapter reviews the governance mechanisms that have emerged to protect such interests. These include specific direct obligations prescribed by common law and statute, and recommended in governance codes as well as indirect influences such as those exerted by external markets and credit rating agencies (CRAs).

The scope of this review is necessarily narrow, and is largely concerned with the governance of large UK-based public companies, the primary focus of this book. It does not discuss governance models in other countries in detail, nor does it consider governance in small private companies.

The review has also deliberately taken an applied perspective rather than reviewing and comparing alternative emerging theoretical models of governance. Such analyses are widely reported elsewhere. Finally, whilst the discussion of statutory obligations is relevant to companies of all sizes, the discussion of the indirect influence of external markets and CRAs in the later sections of this chapter is also most relevant to such large public companies.

Early Perspectives of Corporate Governance

Early perspectives of the nature and role of governance in large public companies are dominated by American interpretations. These interpretations can be divided into three basic categories: the implications of the separation of ownership and control of the enterprise, the company as a nexus of contracts and the development of the concept of professional managers as contractual agents acting on behalf of shareholders. Much of the discussion of current issues in governance can be categorised into one or more of these areas.

Berle and Means' "separation of ownership and control" theory is generally regarded as one of the most significant early contributions to our understanding of corporate governance. This theory, published in 1932 at the time of the Great Depression in the USA that followed the stock market collapse of 1929, distinguishes between the ownership and managerial control of a company. The authors argued that in private companies, ownership and control are combined giving investors an incentive to manage capital carefully since their decisions impact directly on themselves as owners of the company. However, in public companies, the diffuse ownership of shares is a barrier to direct control. Ownership and control may well be in different hands and those who manage the company may seek to maximise their own personal interests at the expense of the company's owners. Shareholder economic interests are potentially damaged as a result (Hessen 1983, 277). The consequent need for effective information disclosure and appropriate checks and balances to prevent management acting in their own self-interest rather than in the interests of shareholders is an important theme which has been reflected in the emergence of governance codes.

A second influential theory focuses on the role of firms in reducing the costs of transactions. The theory of the "nature of the firm" advocated by Coase stresses the role of companies as intermediaries between supply and demand. Coase's analysis observes that in perfect markets, where firms do not exist as intermediaries, individual market transactions between buyer and seller determine costs and prices. However, when product technology becomes more complex and mass production drives down costs thereby opening up new markets (e.g. in the early stages of development of the market for motor vehicles), the role of intermediaries becomes increasingly critical. In such circumstances intermediaries eliminate or at least reduce the costs of pure "market transactions". "Manager-entrepreneurs" take on an increasingly important role, adding value through the management of the resources of the firm in line with changing customer requirements (Coase 1937, 388). Coase's theory views the firm as a "system of relationships which comes into existence when the direction of resources is dependent on an entrepreneur [manager]". The implication is that such entrepreneur-managers require sufficient compensation for the value that they add, and should also be given sufficient freedom of action to exercise their judgment in pursuing the interests of the firm. Discussion about the limitations on the exercise of such director judgment is a debate that continues today.

The agency theory of the firm provides a third perspective, defining firms as "legal fictions that serve as a nexus for a set of contracting relationships among individuals" (Jensen and Meckling 1976, 310). Agency theory proposes a contractual principal-agent relationship between shareholders and managers, arguing that shareholders have delegated the power of decision-making to such agent-managers. The agency role of managers requires them to use corporate resources for the maximisation of shareholder gain, avoiding any harmful decisions that will divert resources or destroy shareholder interests.

These areas of analysis (separation of ownership and control, company as a nexus of contracts, the rise of the professional manager and managers as contractual agents) are fundamental albeit abstract representations of corporate governance themes. Such themes have come increasingly into practical focus as a result of a series of high-profile corporate scandals in the USA (e.g. Enron) and the UK (e.g. Robert Maxwell and Polly Peck), which heightened public concern about the accountability of directors to shareholder and broader stakeholder interests. This concern was reflected in increasing attention being paid to the role and duties of directors in UK companies, primarily through the formulation and introduction of the initial UK Corporate Governance Code in 1992 and the formulation of a new Companies Act in 2006.

Origins of Modern Corporate Governance

In May 1991 the Committee on Financial Aspects of Corporate Governance was set up by the Financial Reporting Council (FRC), the London Stock Exchange and the accountancy profession. The Committee's membership included senior members of major British financial, business and legal institutions. After 20 months of deliberation, evaluation and consultation, the report of the Committee titled *Financial Aspects of Corporate Governance*, (widely known as the Cadbury Report, reflecting the name of the Chair, Sir Adrian Cadbury) was published. The Report pointed to a general growing concern with standards of accounting practice, the failure of directors to "review controls in their business" and a corresponding failure of external auditors to report objectively on the behaviour of some boards of directors. The Committee also cited "unexpected failures of major companies" and "the lack of effective board accountability for such matters as directors' pay". In the Committee's view all of these problems could be traced back to a fundamental breakdown in corporate governance—specifically a failure of directors to act in the interests of the owners of the company (i.e. shareholders).

The Cadbury Report set out a series of recommendations (the Code) on the governance of public companies, covering directors' roles in terms of leadership, effectiveness and accountability as well as their remuneration and relationship with shareholders. Companies were required to demonstrate how they complied with each of the elements of the Code or explain why they were not in compliance. These recommendations have been widely adopted elsewhere, albeit frequently in a modified form. The Code has been enhanced since its original introduction reflecting inputs from different committees set up to review different aspects of governance.[1] The core principles have remained relatively constant and still serve as governance guidelines for companies seeking to demonstrate how they comply with the Code.

Cadbury defined corporate governance as "the system by which companies are directed and controlled. The board of directors is responsible for the governance of their companies". In an alternative definition, the UK Chartered Institute of Internal Auditors (IIA) defines corporate governance as "the combination of processes and structures implemented by the board in order to inform, direct, manage and monitor the activities of the organisation toward the achievement of its objectives". Both of these definitions appear to be relatively narrowly focused on the role of governance in securing shareholder interests. The Organisation for Economic Co-operation and Development (OECD) takes a broader view defining corporate governance as a set of "procedures and processes according to which an organization is directed and controlled. The corporate governance structure specifies the distribution of rights and responsibilities among the different participants in the organization – such as the board, managers, shareholders and other stakeholders – and lays down the rules and procedures for decision-making".

Combining these different elements, in its broadest sense governance can be viewed as both a system and a set of processes designed to ensure that business decisions are made in an appropriate way to maximise the long-run benefit of a specific class(es) of investors. This book is focused more narrowly on the influence of key parties on the decisions of the board of directors of large public companies as well as director liabilities for those decisions at the time of financial distress and insolvency. Adapting Cadbury's definition of corporate governance, this book's terms of reference define corporate governance as "The systems *and processes* by which companies are directed and *influenced*". The addition of "processes" makes explicit the potential existence of a range of different processes through which the decisions of the board of directors are made. The balance of discussion in this chapter considers the main elements of such systems including the board of directors, shareholders, markets and credit rating agencies and the way in which they contribute to corporate governance. The addition of "influenced" makes explicit the role of key parties other than the board of directors in the governance of companies potentially including investors, creditors (such as lenders and suppliers) and independent entities such as insolvency practitioners. Later chapters in this book examine the impact of such third parties on the core director-shareholder relationship, specifically in the context of financial distress and insolvency.

Models of Corporate Governance

Two dominant models of corporate governance have developed which appear to reflect the influence of the social, legal and economic contexts of the countries in which they operate. The first is the Anglo-American governance model based in advanced economies with common law jurisdictions. The model is applied in different variations in countries such as the UK, USA, Canada, Australia and New Zealand. It emphasises the maximisation of shareholder wealth as a corporate objective, relying on the principle of the divorce of ownership and control.

The Anglo-American corporate governance model is based on a one-tier board of directors. The exercise of shareholder rights and other internal governance structures provides checks and balances on management decision-making. The model also relies on codes and regulations that have been formulated by independent regulatory bodies. A series of statutes may have also been enacted in parallel as further safeguards. Financial markets and CRAs may also play a role as external structures that monitor management decision-making by reviewing corporate performance. There are differences in the emphasis given to statutory law and voluntary codes in different countries although such codes all apply the same basic principles.

The two most widely discussed of these models are the UK Corporate Governance Code (UK Code) and the US Sarbanes-Oxley Act 2002. The UK Code is based on a set of prescriptions for effective governance. Companies are required to demonstrate whether and how they comply with the different elements of the Code. By contrast, Sarbanes-Oxley introduces a series of statutory requirements for company directors and auditors which they are obliged to observe. Detailed comparison of the similarities and differences between the UK Code and the Sarbanes-

Oxley Act is beyond the scope of this book. However, both emphasise similar principles including the need for external unambiguous financial auditing, and relevant, up-to-date and sufficient information provision by directors to shareholders.

An alternative model operates in many countries with a civil law heritage including Germany, Japan and France. The core German-Japanese model focuses on the prioritisation of stakeholders' long-term interests rather than short term, potentially high-risk decisions that might bring a higher immediate return for shareholders. In such settings corporate governance may also include the interests of a broader range of stakeholders such as employees, suppliers, customers and wider society. Such interests may frequently conflict.

The German model prescribes mandatory two-tier boards consisting of a management board and a supervisory board. In Japan the unitary board system is used. In France companies can choose between unitary and dual boards. Banks are encouraged to have representatives on the management board, sharing confidential information and having the right to vote, as a result potentially increasing their sense of ownership and responsibility for the financial sustainability of the company (Du Plessis 1996, 25–26). The German-Japanese model also encourages the role of employees in assisting company directors in decision-making (a process known as co-determination). This role is frequently exercised through representation of employees on supervisory boards. For instance, in Germany the Betriebsrat, or Works Council, is a statutory secondary board that includes the workforce, trade unions and other stakeholders, through which board decisions may be reviewed, modified and ratified.

In the UK, the significance of non-shareholding parties is now reflected in section 172(1) of the Companies Act 2006 that links director duties to other stakeholder interests, although it does not prescribe any specific enforcement mechanisms. Lack of worker representatives on UK unitary boards does not necessarily mean neglect of their interests as statutory law also protects the rights of employees. Although the Anglo-American corporate governance model and the German-Japanese corporate governance model are different from each other, international or regional efforts have attempted to provide paths for convergence of governance models. For example, the European Union has taken progressive measures to persuade member states to harmonise their rules and laws relating to certain aspects of corporate governance and corporate law, including directives relating to shareholder voting rights, financial auditing and reporting. Public companies including those in the UK are currently required to show their compliance with such relevant directives.

Corporate Governance in the UK: The Primacy of Directors

Since the publication of the Cadbury Report in 1992, every company listed on the London Stock Exchange has been obliged to demonstrate how it meets the requirements of the governance code. Although compliance with the Code is not mandatory for unlisted companies, the concept of good corporate governance has been more widely accepted and an increasing number of such companies have included annual statements about their compliance for the benefit of shareholders and other parties.

The current version of the Code (2016) recommends that public companies determine a "sufficient size" for the board that meets "the requirements of the business" and at the same time avoids "unwieldy" boards. Board size is commonly specified in a company's articles of associations in terms of a minimum and maximum number of directors. However, the size of the board may vary depending on business conditions and demands on board members. For example, an empirical study by Lehn et al. of 82 US companies concluded that the size of the board is positively correlated with the size of the company and inversely correlated with its business growth (Lehn et al. 2009, 775).

The composition of the board is more than a cosmetic arrangement. Baysinger and Butler (1985) share Williamson's view that "the composition of the board is as important to the theory of corporate governance as the structure of organizations to the theory of the firm". This perspective includes the dynamics of change in board membership over time, with new members, resignations and dismissals, and changing roles. Members are usually required under the company's articles of association to seek re-appointment on a regular basis, typically between one and three years. The appointment or re-appointment of directors may be a significant issue, especially if it relates to the choice of the chair as s/he leads the board and has the potential to persuade board members to challenge chief executive decisions, and suspend or dismiss them. These board dynamics are likely to feature extensively in times of financial distress, and the topic is explored in detail in later chapters. The case studies forming the empirical research in this book illustrate how board membership can change rapidly, even within comparatively short timeframes.

The presence and participation of non-executive directors on boards is seen as one of the central pre-conditions for effective governance. In 2003, the Higgs Review made a recommendation on the proportion of non-executive and executive directors on the board, as part of an independent enquiry into the role of non-executive directors. The Code was revised to include a provision that at least half of the members of the board should be independent non-executive directors. This recommendation applied to UK one-tier boards of medium- and large-sized companies.

In practice, there may be considerable differences in the extent to which executive and non-executive directors may be involved in business decision-making. Non-executive directors may not necessarily have access to the detailed information that is often available to executive directors. Asymmetry of information between the two groups may become a barrier for informed judgment by the board as a whole, for instance where major strategies are presented for approval. Senior management may seek to exploit such asymmetry to persuade the board to approve their preferred strategies (Eisenberg 1997, 245). This is one of the potential weaknesses in governance that the Code has identified and sought to address, particularly in the stress that it places on the importance of education and training for non-executive directors and the provision of timely and relevant business and accounting information.

Initially Cadbury (1992) made it the responsibility of the chair of the board to ensure that the information which is given to non-executive directors is sufficient and timely for them to exercise their role. In 1998 the Hampel Report took the view that the information should be of the required "form and quality" to help the board's collective discharge of its obligations. It also stressed the importance of a clear division of the role of chair from the role of chief executive as the combination of the two could "represent a considerable concentration of power". The Report suggested that if such a separation is not achieved, at least one independent non-executive director should be appointed and the board should "justify and explain" its reasons to shareholders for the combination of the two roles. However, this provision applies only to public companies that operate in the London Stock Exchange (LSE). Those companies that operate in the Alternative Investment Market (AIM) are not obliged to comply with these recommendations.

The extent to which non-executive directors are likely to be informed about strategic issues will depend on the experience and knowledge of such directors, the demands which non-executive directors make for information, the spirit of trust and collaboration between members of the board and the expected reporting standards set out in any internal governance code. These issues become particularly important in times of financial distress where business conditions may be rapidly changing.

The current Code (The UK Corporate Governance Code 2016) does not provide detailed guidelines on changes in board composition with the exception that the Code stresses the importance of a "rigorous review" for the appointment and re-appointment of members of the board, particularly those non-executive directors who stay in the company for more than six years. Non-executive directors should preserve an independent status in terms of their financial interests and decision-making. Directors' previous employment with the company, their individual "material business relationship", any additional personal financial gains from the company, "close family ties", "relationship with other company directors and advisors" and "significant shareholding" as well as duration of membership of the board are indicators that may be used to determine the level of their independence.

By stressing these principles the Code addresses the perceived need to create an environment that prevents any potential conflict of interest that might affect director decision-making. Such an environment is not always easy to maintain. The choice of non-executive directors is made at the discretion and authority of the board, and the chair may choose to ignore the recommended criteria for determining the independence of non-executive directors provided that they disclose the reasons for their decisions to shareholders when recommending the appointment (Baysinger and Butler 1985, 103–104). With such broad powers and influence, the selection of new chairs is a critical issue, particularly for a chief executive if s/he is concerned about a conflict of views amongst board members, a potential coup in the boardroom or if s/he plans to retire and is anxious to find the right "successor" (Shen and Cannella 2002).

Some members of the board may leave at their own initiative before the end of their period of appointment. Some may leave at the request of the majority of other board members or the chair or may shift role from executive to non-executive. The chair can also be expected to play a significant role in the selection of non-executive directors.

In contrast with the coverage in the Code, there is very little discussion of the composition of the board, the role of executive and non-executive directors and the chair and changes in board membership in legislation. The minimum number of directors in public companies is stipulated as two persons. UK legislature does not differentiate between the roles and responsibilities of executive or non-executive directors. The Act does not address the issue of the appropriateness of the reasons for changes in board composition. It does give authority to shareholders to approve or decline such changes. However, the Act does not require shareholder approval as a prerequisite for director employment and allows the election of directors to be registered with Companies House before shareholder approval is obtained, potentially giving directors considerable discretion in changing the composition of the board since shareholder approval is not immediately required.

Three Major Board Sub-Committees

The monitoring role of the board in public companies is facilitated through three main sub-committees that are likely to be most closely linked with governance issues: the nominations committee, the remuneration committee and the audit committee. Nominations committees typically consider senior-level appointments, including the appointment (and dismissal) of chief executive and other senior executive board members. The remuneration committee is typically concerned with the salary and other rewards of senior staff, and the audit committee is primarily concerned with the company's current and future financial position (potentially including issues related to solvency and financial distress). Nominations and remuneration committees are typically led by the chair of the board, whilst the audit committee is frequently chaired by a non-executive director with sufficient financial background and expertise.

The appointment and remuneration of the chief executive and senior members of the board is ultimately subject to shareholder approval at an Annual General Meeting (AGM) or Extraordinary General Meeting (EGM), providing a potential safeguard for shareholder interests. In the UK since 2013, shareholders of public companies listed on the London Stock Exchange (LSE) have new rights to a binding vote on directors' remuneration and the other benefits of senior staff, increasing the accountability of such managers to shareholders for their decisions.

The monitoring role of the board is underpinned in the Code by a mandate that requires the board to establish and maintain a framework of "prudent and effective [internal] controls" that helps the assessment and management of different forms of risks. Such a framework should facilitate a systematic and comprehensive review of "financial, operational and compliance controls" and risk management that can be "reported to shareholders" through a "formal and transparent arrangement". The responsibility for this role is delegated to an audit committee that should "consist of at least three independent non-executive directors one of which should have recent and relevant financial experience". The report on the results of any review requires approval by the whole board.

An independent audit committee provides an opportunity for non-executive directors to check that executive management is behaving appropriately and has robust plans for managing the financial affairs of the company. This process can be effective only when regular progress reports are provided against which performance can be monitored. Arguably, if a company enters a period of financial distress, this should become evident to an audit committee as soon as actual performance begins to deviate from planned. The process can also be effective only when the company's external auditors are also able to provide timely, full and objective reviews of the company's financial situation, a point made in the original Cadbury Report. The case studies in Chaps. 7 to 11 examine the extent to which this appears to happen in practice.

The Code also prescribes that the audit committee should not take over the responsibility for producing the company's annual report. Much of the discussion in the original Cadbury Report focuses on the role of this committee, and in particular the role of the external auditor as a separate and independent monitor of the company's financial position. The issue of how much information should be provided to shareholders on the company's performance and the frequency of such information provision is also considered. Whilst the Report recognised that on balance information on the company's financial position should be provided to shareholders on a regular basis, and more frequently than in an annual report, it also recognised that there are issues of commercial sensitivity that would preclude wider distribution of such information.

The role of an audit committee is also to check that management uses appropriate accounting methods. The audit committee's prescribed role in this capacity is to ensure that management does not make potentially fraudulent financial transactions or commitments and detect orchestrated expropriation of corporate wealth by individuals or groups of managers. The audit committee should also ensure that the board can confidently approve the company's annual report and accounts on the basis that it is "as a whole, fair, balanced and understandable". Where fraud is disguised in sophisticated international transactions, it may be hard for the board to identify unless a third party comes forward and claims the assets that have been transferred. More importantly, where such a fraud is identified, the company may find it too difficult to recover the assets.

Whilst many companies now appear to have put in place their own governance codes, in line with the recommendations of the Code of Corporate Governance, the question remains as to the extent to which such codes actually influence director behaviour in managing the day-to-day business of the company. There is also a further question of the extent to which compliance with such codes is modified or withdrawn entirely in times of financial distress. This issue has been highlighted in a series of relatively recent business failures including BHS and Carillion. The detailed case studies in Chaps. 7 to 11 explore this issue in depth.

Common Law and Statutory Aspects of Governance

The previous section examined how corporate governance codes have emerged to safeguard shareholder interests. In addition to such codes, the actions of company directors can be viewed in the context of legal obligations, established both in common law and statute. The following section looks at the implications of such constraints, focusing specifically on two critical dimensions: the status of companies as independent legal identities and director duties.

UK public companies operate in an environment where the landmark case of *Salomon v Salomon & Co Ltd.* establishes companies as "legally independent personalities" making them responsible for their own acts and omissions, including fixing mutually binding contracts with employees, banks and other stakeholders (Hansmann and Kraakman 2001, 439–440). The Companies Act 2006 identifies shareholders as members of the company, owning shares, and thus legally entitled to receive dividends, if any are declared.

A company is formally incorporated when a certificate of registration is issued by Companies House, following submission of a proposed memorandum and articles of association (Companies Act 2006, ss. 7–9). Under sections 540–546 of the Act, the individual economic interest of shareholders is determined by the number of shares each shareholder owns, proportionate to the total volume of issued shares. In general, there is no limit on the number of shares one person may have. Public and private companies differ in terms of the extent and diversity of share ownership. Each is able to alter their status (from private to public and vice versa) subject to meeting certain statutory requirements. Private companies tend to have fewer shares (potentially as low as one), each of which has limited nominal value, whilst public companies must meet a certain threshold before they can offer their shares to the public. Unlike most private companies, public companies have a large number of shareholders, both individual and institutional, with potentially little or no attachment to the company other than their shareholding.

When a company makes a public offering of shares, the Companies Act 2006 places no restriction on the pattern of shareholding that emerges. In private businesses that become public companies, control may still be concentrated in the hands of a small number of shareholders, including the original founders of the company who may be family members. Directors are effectively left to run the company, subject to shareholder rights established by legislation, and shareholders have no statutory right to directly control directors' day-to-day actions.

In recent years greater attention has been given to shareholder value, following a review of the need for a reform to company law commissioned by the Department of Trade and Industry (DTI) and conducted by the Company Law Review Steering Group (CLRSG). This review resulted in two White Papers, Modernising Company Law (White Paper, Cm 5553, 2002) and Company Law Reform (White Paper, Cm 6456, 2005), leading ultimately to new legislation in the form of the Companies Act 2006. The CLRSG identified shareholder value and pluralism as potential parallel corporate objectives. The concept of "enlightened shareholder value" was also proposed to take account of the interests of both shareholders and other stakeholders.

The nature of a director's duties is established under sections 171–177 of the Companies Act 2006. These sections determine that directors must act within powers, promote the success of the company for its members, exercise independent judgment reasonable care, skill and diligence, avoid conflicts of interest, not accept benefits from third parties and declare interests in any proposed transaction or arrangement. There are no specific legislative prescriptions on the decisions that directors should implement to perform their duties. Breach of such duties by directors has significant consequences, exposing them to civil liabilities and a potential obligation for civil remedies.

Section 172 of the Companies Act 2006 (the duty to promote the success of the company) is the most relevant obligation of directors in terms of corporate governance. Section 172(1) of the Companies Act 2006 mandates company directors to focus primarily on shareholder interests; however, they are also required to take into account the interests of stakeholders, including, inter alia, employees, suppliers, customers, the community and the impact of decisions on the environment. This provision highlights the significance of stakeholders, but it does not prescribe any specific change in directors' primary focus or duties.

Section 172(1) appears to reflect government concern that director duties to those other than shareholders should receive a degree of legislative acknowledgement in company law and ultimately prevent the "abuse of limited liability" by company directors (Walters and Davis-White 2011). The provision is mainly informative and requires directors to adopt "a good faith" approach that promotes the success of the company having "regard" to such non-shareholders. It does not offer any guidelines for directors on what business decisions they must either take or those that they must avoid in order to show their "regard to" creditor interests. Nor does it appear to make any change to the scope of discretionary and fiduciary powers that are reserved to company directors because it does not provide any "objective criteria" that might be used to gauge directors' success or failure in performing their specific duty under the provision (Keay 2007).

Section 172(1) also seems to acknowledge the shareholders' primary position compared to that of other stakeholders and treat their interests as the end and the interests of others as the means. Further, the secondary position of other stakeholders is confirmed by the lack of any *locus standi* for such stakeholders throughout the whole of the legislation with no detail on their rights or interests. The provision does single out "suppliers" as one category of creditor, but there is no detailed inclusion of other creditor interests (such as those of lenders). Section 172(1) appears to indicate that "shareholder value" rather than stakeholder value remains the core focus in company law and there is no real prospect of this position changing substantially, at least in the short term. This provision can be set against that in section 172 (3) which refers to a form of directors' liability that could hold company directors responsible for a breach of their responsibility, where the company is "factually" insolvent but continues to operate outside of a formal insolvency regime. In such circumstances directors may be held personally liable to creditors for maintaining a company as a going concern despite insolvency (Walters and Davis-White 2011). Chapter 4 examines this aspect of director responsibilities in more detail.

Boards of directors of medium and large companies are legally subject to a reporting requirement designed to ensure that shareholders can develop an informed view of the board's overall performance. The annual report should include a review of the company's development and position in the previous financial year and its plans and forecast for the years ahead (Companies Act 2006, s. 414C). This review should include a balanced assessment of the company's position in terms of its business, challenges and opportunities, key financial performance indicators and other indicators of the directors' performance of statutory duties under s. 172 of the Companies Act 2006.

Such information could in theory be of use not only to shareholders in large public companies but also for new investors, lenders and other creditors. However, the content of such a report can be moderated by director discretion on what is to be included or omitted, and concerns related to commercial confidentiality and the report may present an optimistic view of the future rather than a negative one. If the company faces serious financial distress, the board may not present a complete picture of the actual risks and liabilities that the company is facing, fearing the potential consequences for their own position as directors in terms of loss of the trust and approval of shareholders. Some boards may downplay the assessment of risks, limit the scope of a business review or not produce one at all if the company is planning to adopt a formal insolvency procedure. Ultimately, in practice, the decisions of potential investors especially institutional shareholders are typically informed by detailed information and analysis, that goes well beyond the information that is required in the public report and accounts, making such reports a minor or inconsequential part of decision-making, particularly in periods of financial distress.

Significantly perhaps, there is an overlap between the specification of director duties in the Companies Act 2006 and the standards for effective governance set out in the UK Governance Code, implying that some of the issues leading to the formulation of the original governance code may have been considered when prescribing the statutory duties of directors. Chapters 4 and 5 explore this issue in more detail considering the particular challenges that financial distress and insolvency can pose to directors in fulfilling such duties.

Shareholder Influence on Governance

Shareholders' investment in a company through the purchase of at least one share brings with it specific rights and liabilities. Their influence on corporate governance is potentially exercised through two mechanisms: legal rights that are attached to share ownership, including the right to vote on matters presented for approval at the AGM or an EGM, as well as the right for minority shareholders to pursue claims on behalf of company interests (derivative claims) and ultimately the threat of sale of shares should performance not match expectations.

The threat of shareholder exit is likely to have greater impact on management decisions when such shareholders are long-term investors holding a large number of shares in the company. These shareholders are typically financial institutions such as hedge funds, mutual funds and pension funds which frequently hold significant percentages of the shares of a specific company on behalf of clients, giving them considerable influence over the company's decision-making through proxy voting. Private negotiations with major shareholders are an ongoing feature in such situations, with institutional investors being able, on occasions, to persuade boards to change course (Carleton et al. 1998). Such shareholders may have privileged access to financial information before it is disclosed to existing dispersed shareholders and outside investors (Admati and Pfleiderer 2009, 2647). Shleifer and Vishny (1986, 463) refer to the potential influence of major shareholders in supporting third party takeovers, in exchange for a share of profits with the bidder. Institutional shareholders typically acquire a large volume of shares and may become major shareholders in the company. Their exit may be a significant problem for the board, making management more sensitive to their demands. However, such shareholders may not actually sell their shares, due to concerns about the substantial losses that share disposal might cause (Admati and Pfleiderer, 2676).

In the UK, institutional shareholders seem to have shown less willingness to play an active role, at least in public, although informal negotiations may influence management decisions (Bainbridge 2011, 104). Such negotiations may lead to greater support for specific resolutions at shareholder meetings and shareholder proposals are likely to "receive significantly more votes" if they are sponsored and co-ordinated by institutional shareholders (Gillan and Starks 2000, 303). The formulation and adoption of a Stewardship Code, recommended in the Walker Report (2009), was intended to persuade institutional shareholders to take a more active role in the context of large UK public companies.

The company's AGM provides a focus for regular communication between company directors and the members of the company. In the UK shareholder rights to information about the operations of the company are formally set out in the Companies Act 2006. Directors have a formal duty to prepare an annual set of accounts for the company (s. 394) that provide a true and fair view of the assets, liabilities, financial position and profit or loss (s. 393). They are also required to produce a strategic report for each year of the company setting out how they have performed their duty under section 172 (duty to promote the success of the company). They are required to "lay" these reports before the AGM.

Other formal business will typically include proposals for the payment of dividends, the appointment of new directors and the re-election of existing directors, the remuneration of members of the board, discharge of retiring members of board from director liabilities, the re-appointment of auditors and any other relevant matters. Shareholder voting rights on specific board proposals are prescribed by the Companies Act 2006, and vary depending on the type or category of share, the company's articles of association and any specific agreements between shareholders.

Shareholders' ability to contribute to the business of the meeting is restricted to information provided by management in any reports, financial statements and supplements or individual briefings. Although the law allows shareholders to seek prescribed information from the board, their access is limited by management discretion, as an earlier section of this chapter has commented. Whilst directors are obliged to provide an annual strategic report that sets out a "a fair review of the company's business, and a description of the principal risks and uncertainties facing the company", they are also given a great deal of discretion on the disclosure of commercially sensitive information in the provision that "nothing in this section requires the disclosure of information about impending developments or matters in the course of negotiation if the disclosure would, in the opinion of the directors, be seriously prejudicial to the interests of the company" (CA 2006, s 414c).

Where information is provided, dispersed shareholders with relatively small shareholdings frequently face the problem of assessing the consequences of management decisions and may need to incur costs in order to seek advice from others. The costs of expert advice and the asymmetry of information between dispersed shareholders and management may discourage shareholders from voting and in effect leave decisions to well-informed institutional or major shareholders or management.

In principle, shareholders show their collective governance power by voting for or against proposals or abstaining. An empirical study by Bottomley (2003) of 217 Australian public companies in 2003 indicates that shareholders' active participation at AGMs may be relatively low—in the companies covered in their study only 20% of shareholders or their proxies attended AGMs and voted. This appears to be a more general feature of AGMs and EGMs. A low level of participation may be due to a variety of factors including practical issues such as the costs of attendance, especially where distances are large. It may also reflect a situation where the bulk of shares are held by a relatively few major shareholders who did attend and vote.

The problem of shareholder apathy has been addressed through "proxy" voting. Those shareholders who are not willing or able to take part in the voting process themselves are entitled to appoint a legal or real entity called a "proxy" who can vote on their behalf. For those shareholders who choose a proxy outside the company, such proxy could be a broker. However, for those shareholders who are not willing to pay the costs of a proxy, management may solicit their proxy for general meetings and any adjourned meetings with the promise that voting will be confidential. In such cases management uses the proxy to vote for the resolutions that it is putting forward so that it facilitates unchallenged implementation of those resolutions.

Whilst the main business of an AGM may be determined by several prescribed matters, the balance of the content is typically left to the senior management team, with the discretion to include or exclude specific topics unless they are required by a specific proportion of shareholders to include such items by special resolution. The terms under which special resolutions may be included are typically defined by the articles of association of the company. Complex issues that relate to the business operations of the company including regular commercial transactions are rarely drawn to the attention of shareholders in such formal meetings, and ultimately delegated to the business judgment of directors.

Individual shareholders can propose agenda items for general meetings. However, it is frequently difficult and expensive for such shareholders to contact all the other shareholders and provide sufficient information prior to formal voting. Legislation does not prohibit informal communication between individual shareholders who wish to co-ordinate opposition against specific management proposals. Shareholders may find it more cost efficient to use social media to co-ordinate their actions ahead of attending shareholder meetings and voting on specific proposals. Use of internet tools such as Facebook, YouTube and Twitter has reduced the costs of forming and shaping informal coalitions amongst such shareholders.

Shareholders may also seek more general market information independently of the information they receive from the board and make their own assessment of directors' performance, especially where the board of directors seeks prior approval for specific actions to avoid personal liability. Shareholders could exercise their collective power to challenge board decisions. For example in 2011, Easyjet's shareholders contested the board's decision to pay an "undeserved and unjustified" consultancy fee to a former chief executive who had accepted an interim appointment. In this situation the board used a common defence that shareholders would find difficult to argue against, stating that "these arrangements were a one-off and agreed in unusual and difficult circumstances".

Derivative Claims

Common law offers help to those shareholders who believe that their company has suffered from the "injurious", "abusive" actions of majority shareholders and company directors, although the rule in *Foss v Harbottle* puts primary responsibility on the company to challenge those wrongs. Part 11 of the UK Companies Act 2006 provides members of a company with a statutory right to obtain judicial relief from previous and prospective decisions and proposals of company directors and majority shareholders if such decisions have been based on "an actual or proposed act or omission involving negligence, default, breach of duty or breach of trust".

A shareholder may use a derivative claim for various reasons. The claim allows the shareholder to challenge company directors over an alleged wrong through a legally enforceable process. Such an action also allows the shareholder to retain his shareholding status in the company if he wishes to, without any pressure to transfer equity. An out-of-court settlement may also be achieved before or during the proceedings. The derivative claim may also increase collective shareholders' wealth indirectly through an increase in share prices when the litigation becomes public and future improved dividends are declared. The claimant can also use a derivative claim as a legal platform to obtain disclosure of information to modify the decisions that directors have taken in diverting wealth from the company to ineligible parties.

Use of a derivative claim by shareholders is difficult especially in public companies. Minority shareholders are likely to experience cumbersome procedures and evidential rules that may frustrate them from pursuing their claims. In the UK, the claimant goes through a procedural sequence that includes a threshold test prior to the main proceedings. A favourable court order at the threshold test stage gives the claimant the right to continue the action. The main proceedings allow the shareholder to support the claim with detailed information that relates to the nature of the wrong and its adverse consequences on the company. The relevance and credibility of this information can be rebutted by the defendants who are assumed to have privileged access to information and greater financial resources than the claimant. Minority shareholders face further challenges since courts have avoided making judgments on the commercial correctness of a decision.

Whether a derivative claim can operate as an effective governance mechanism is a matter of debate. From a conceptual perspective, the derivative claim has developed strong roots in common law pursuant to the court-sanctioned exceptions to the rule in *Foss v Harbottle* that applied before the enactment of the statutory derivative scheme. Under the rule, a minority shareholder is obliged to yield to the decisions of a majority of shareholders on corporate matters unless he or she believes that the company has suffered harm. In effect, the minority shareholder takes the action on behalf of the company to remedy the losses. The main ground for a derivative claim in common law is fraud but other reasons may include "acts that are ultra vires the company, transactions requiring approval by a special majority and where the individual holds the majority of votes in the company".

Statutory derivative schemes now apply in many common law jurisdictions. The provisions allow the courts to take into account the decisions of majority shareholders and hypothetical company directors. If the contested decision is seen to meet with general shareholder approval through the process of ratification, the claim loses its merit. However, as illustrated in the case *Franbar Holdings Ltd v Patel and others*, UK common law has prevented the potential wrongdoer from exerting control over the ratification process and allowed shareholders to bring claims based on the view that the ratification "improperly prevented the shareholder from bringing a claim on behalf of the company".

Under the UK's statutory scheme, claimant shareholders must be able to demonstrate good faith. Those shareholders that have not contributed to the wrong committed, and have intended to benefit the company, have received the leave of the court to pursue their claims. However, courts may refuse leave to those shareholders who have shown their intention to benefit a third party (*Lesini v Westrip Holdings Ltd*), have failed to show the prima facie status of a claim, contributed to the wrong subject to the litigation, have demonstrated a motive based on a "vendetta" (*Barrett v Duckett*) with defendant directors or have failed to produce sufficient evidence. In the USA, where a claimant shareholder who has purchased shares with the knowledge of the wrong, may find his good faith is challenged (Wells 2004).

The credibility of the claim is also subject to investigation. For instance, UK law demands a prima facie status for the claim, allowing the court to refuse leave to a claim that does not demonstrate a high potential prospect for success. This then may require a "virtual trial within a trial" (Keay and Loughrey 2010, 154). The courts have allowed some cases based on the benefit of doubt at least at the prima facie stage, although in general they have set a high threshold for such claims. Ultimately it seems that the economic costs of derivative claims may deter shareholders from initiating such actions reducing the likelihood that directors might be challenged in this way, especially in large public companies.

External Governance Mechanisms

The proponents of agency theory argued that the market in general may operate as an efficient institution for corporate control (Gilson and Kraakman 1984, 551). Financial markets are well-developed mechanisms that provide access to capital from a wide range of investors. Such markets typically have highly regulated, internally moderated standards. In the London Stock Exchange compliance with such standards was regulated and monitored by the Financial Service Authority (FSA), an independent self-regulatory body until April 1, 2013, when a new regulatory body, the Financial Conduct Authority (FCA), took over the responsibility to ensure that directors in public companies comply with listing rules.

Stock market prices typically reflect perceptions of the performance of the board and are therefore a major indirect controlling factor. An increase in share price reflects a positive perception of the board's actions. Positive factors may include the appointment of new company directors with previous outstanding performance records elsewhere, or an increase in turnover and profits. Strong share price performance may also reflect financial and economic stability. On the other hand, when conflict between the board and senior managers becomes public or institutional shareholders announce their sale of shares, share prices may plummet. As Easterbrook and Fischel (1996) state, "the mechanism by which stocks are valued ensures that the price reflects the terms of governance and operation, just as it reflects the identity of the managers and product the firm produces".

Managing market perceptions is an important issue for the boards of publicly owned companies particularly when the company shows signs of financial distress. The perceived quality of a company's performance may result in an increase or decrease in a company's cost of finance, reflecting the degree of risk assessed by potential lenders. In such circumstances the board may decide to postpone mandatory disclosure of financial information or provide partial financial reports that portray a positive picture of the financial and economic position of the company. If the management of a listed company seeks to avoid market rules relating to disclosure of information, it may be obliged to suspend or delist its shares, or move its shares from the London Stock Exchange to the Alternative Investment Market (AIM).

In the UK management must comply with a takeover framework regulated by the Takeover Panel, the relevant supervisory and regulatory authority. Potential takeovers can have a variety of different impacts. The threat of takeovers may focus management's attention on maximising current dividend payments to shareholders, keeping share prices higher in the short term at the expense of strategies that support long-term business growth and overall improvement in shareholder wealth (McCahery, Picciotto and Scott 1995). Management is forced in such circumstances to focus on enhancing shareholder value and shareholders do not need to resort to costly legal action to protect their interests. If management anticipates the threat of hostile takeovers, it may adopt a "poison pill" strategy that commits it to pay dividends to existing shareholders or issue ordinary shares at some future date to be purchased by existing shareholders at a discount rate (Macey 2008), again potentially benefitting existing shareholders.

Credit rating agencies (CRAs) can provide another external governance mechanism. Such agencies are independent organisations that have an exclusive regulatory licence granted by the government or a regional regulatory body. They provide capital markets with an evaluation of the level of risk associated with investing in specific public companies. Existing shareholders can also use credit ratings to determine whether to stay in, or exit public companies.

Public companies may employ a CRA to produce an assessment of their creditworthiness. In such circumstances, they are given direct access to financial information that is typically confidential and exclusive to insiders. The agency then uses this information to develop an independent assessment of the company's "ability and willingness" to honour its promises to investors. The outcome is typically then made publicly available.

CRAs take no liability for the impact of the final rating of the company. They do not benefit financially if the company receives a high rating and borrows at low cost, nor are they liable for any potential or actual loss that shareholders or bondholders may face as a result of any downgrading of the rating of that public company. They are not compromised by any conflict of interest that may arise due to their service contract with the public company (Pinto 2006, 345). As Pinto suggests such strong protection means that they can be independent in setting their own standards and are not regulated. The role of CRAs goes beyond offering services to specific clients. They may frequently produce analyses of the position of specific companies that are then made available by public subscription.

The board of directors cannot ignore the impact of a credit rating on their competitive position. They cannot improve a credit rating overnight but this is likely to appear on the medium- to long-term agenda of most companies (Sinclair 1994, 142). Members of the board may feel uncomfortable or perhaps see it as the time to resign if a credit rating is downgraded badly or even withdrawn, reducing the options for securing or attracting new capital.

CRAs are dependent on the information that is provided by company directors and lenders. Any over-estimation or under-estimation of the company's financial strength can affect its credit score. CRAs may lack proper mechanisms to evaluate a company's financial position as it enters financial distress. They are also unable to exert any penalty on those company directors who report erroneous information. Enron had a very good credit score shortly before it collapsed, demonstrating the difficulty of obtaining an accurate assessment of a company's financial position when directors fail to fulfil their duties.

Concluding Remarks

This chapter has reviewed the different mechanisms that can be considered as part of the corporate governance environment of modern large public companies. Codes of corporate governance provide the most explicit guidelines for directors in terms of exercising their powers in the interests of shareholders. Legal and statutory obligations also limit the actions of directors particularly in terms of the duties and responsibilities that are set out in the Companies Act 2006, and in the tradition of common law that has established many precedents that govern director behaviour. Shareholders have a range of rights and responsibilities that are established by statute, which can be exercised in support of their rights as owners of the company. However, the traditional passivity of shareholders means that this element of governance is less likely to be effectively exercised, except by large institutional shareholders. The only exception to this is where minority shareholders may choose to pursue a derivative claim to seek redress for an action by directors that has damaged the interests of the company. Finally, financial markets and CRAs may also indirectly influence director decision-making.

The following chapters examine the extent to which such governance mechanisms survive, are modified or become less useful in periods of financial distress and insolvency. As we move into this discussion it becomes evident that significant new players emerge, specifically secured creditors and administrators. Each of these actors can play a major role in changing governance patterns. The next chapter begins this discussion with a review of the main elements of financial distress and insolvency and the role of the key parties.

Note

1. A history of the UK Corporate Governance Code setting out the stages in its development, and the inputs from various enquiries between 1992 and 2017, is available from the Financial Reporting Council at https://www.frc.org.uk/directors/corporate-governance-and-stewardship/uk-corporate-governance-code/history-of-the-uk-corporate-governance-code

Bibliography

Admati, Anat R. and Paul Pfleiderer. 2009. "The "Wall Street Walk" and Shareholder Activism: Exit as a Form of Voice." *Review of Financial Studies* 22(7): 2645–2685.

Allen, Matthew. 2010. "Shareholders Hold UBS Ex-bosses Accountable." *Swissinfo.ch,* April 14. Accessed 21 December 2013. http://www.swissinfo.ch/eng/business/Shareholders_hold_UBS_exbosses_accountable.html?cid=8672112

Bainbridge, Stephen M. 2011. *Corporate Governance after the Financial Crisis.* New York: Oxford University Press.

Baysinger, Barry D. and Henry N. Butler. 1985. "Corporate Governance and the Board of Directors: Performance Effects of Changes in Board Composition." *Journal of Law, Economics & Organization* 1(1): 101–124.

BBC News. 2004. "M&S Rejects Philip Green Offer." *BBC*, July 8. http://news.bbc.co.uk/1/hi/business/3875859.stm

BBC News. 2010. "Cadbury Agrees Kraft Takeover Bid." *BBC*, January 19. http://news.bbc.co.uk/1/hi/8467007.stm

Berle, Adolf A. and Gardiner C. Means. 1933. *The Modern Corporation and Private Property.* New York: The Macmillan Company.

Bhagat, Sanjai and Bernard Black. 2002. "The Non-correlation Between Board Independence and Long-Term Firm Performance." *Journal of Corporate Law.* 27(2): 231–273.

Bottomley, Stephen. 2003. *The Role of Shareholders' Meetings in Improving Corporate Governance.* Centre for Commercial Law, Faculty of Law, Australian National University.

Butler, Sarah et al. 2013. "Angela Ahrendts Leaves Burberry for New Job at Apple." *Guardian*, October 15. https://www.theguardian.com/business/2013/oct/15/burberry-angela-ahrendts-new-job-apple

Cadbury, Adrian. 1992. *Report of the Committee on the Financial Aspects of Corporate Governance*. London: Gee.

Carleton, Willard T., James M. Nelson, and Michael S. Weisbach. 1998. "The Influence of Institutions on Corporate Governance through Private Negotiations: Evidence from TIAA-CREF." *Journal of Finance* 53(4): 1335–1362.

Chartered Institute of Internal Auditors (IIA). 2017. "Corporate Governance." Last Modified July 26, 2017. https://www.iia.org.uk/resources/ippf/international-standards/glossary/

Cheffins, Brian R. 2013. "The Undermining of UK Corporate Governance?" *Oxford Journal of Legal Studies* 33(3): 503–533.

Clark, Pilita. 2011. "Sir Stelios Leads Investor Revolt over EasyJet Directors' Pay-Outs." *Financial Times*, February 18.

Coase, R. H. 1937. "The Nature of the Firm." *Economica* 4(16): 386–405.

Du Plessis, Jean J. 1996. "Corporate Governance: Reflections on the German Two-Tier Board System." *Journal of South African Law* 1: 20–46.

Easterbrook, Frank H. and Daniel R. Fischel. 1996. *The Economic Structure of Corporate Law*. Cambridge, MA: Harvard University Press. 18.

Eisenberg, Melvin A. 1997. "The Board of Directors and Internal Control." *Cardozo Law Review* 19(1–2): 237–264.

Enrich, David, Suzanne Kapner, and Dan Fitzpatrick. 2012. "Pandit Is Forced Out at Citi; Clash with Board Followed Stumbles over Pay and Rejected Plan for Buybacks." *Wall Street Journal (online)*, October 17.

European Central Bank (ECB). 2004. *Annual Report*. Frankfurt: ECB. Accessed July 17, 2017. http://stats.oecd.org/glossary/detail.asp?ID=6778

Gillan, Stuart L. and Laura T. Starks. 2000. "Corporate Governance Proposals and Shareholder Activism: The Role of Institutional Investors." *Journal of Financial Economics* 57(2): 275–305.

Gilson, Ronald J. and Reinier H. Kraakman. 1984. "The Mechanisms of Market Efficiency." *Virginia Law Review* 70(4): 549–644.

Grant, Kevin and Andrew P. Marshall. 1997. "Large UK Companies and Derivatives." *European Financial Management* 3(2): 191–208.

Hansmann, Henry and Reiner Kraakman. 2001. "The End of History for Corporate Law." *Georgetown Law Journal* 89(2): 439–468.

Hessen, Robert. 1983. "The Modern Corporation and Private Property: A Reappraisal." *Journal of Law & Economics* 26(2): 273–289.

Hoi, Chun-Keung and Ashok Robin. 2010. "Labor Market Consequences of Accounting Fraud." *Corporate Governance: The International Journal of Business in Society* 10(3): 321–333.

Jensen, Michael C. and William H. Meckling. 1976. "Theory of the Firm: Managerial Behavior, Agency Costs and Ownership Structure." *Journal of Financial Economics* 3(4): 305–360.

Keay, Andrew. 2007. "Section 172(1) of the Companies Act 2006: An Interpretation and Assessment." *Company Lawyer* 28(4): 106–110.

Keay, Andrew R. 2011. *The Corporate Objective*. Cheltenham: Edward Elgar Publishing.

Keay, Andrew. 2013. *The Enlightened Shareholder Value Principle and Corporate Governance*. Oxon: Routledge.

Keay, Andrew and Joan Loughrey. 2010. "Derivative Proceedings in a Brave New World for Company Management and Shareholders." *Journal of Business Law* 3: 151–178.

Kirkbride, James and Steve Letza. 2005. "Can the Non-executive Director Be an Effective Gatekeeper? The Possible Development of a Legal Framework of Accountability." *Corporate Governance: An International Review* 13(4): 542–550.

Kollewe, Julia. 2012. "Shareholder Rebellions over Executive Pay: Timeline." *Guardian*, May 8. Accessed August 29, 2017. http://www.theguardian.com/business/2012/may/08/shareholder-rebellions-executive-pay-timeline

Lehn, Kenneth M., Sukesh Patro, and Mengxin Zhao. 2009. "Determinants of the Size and Composition of US Corporate Boards: 1935–2000." *Financial Management* 38(4): 747–780.

Long, Tracy, Victor Dulewicz, and Keith Gay. 2005. "The Role of the Non-executive Director: Findings of an Empirical Investigation into the Differences Between Listed and Unlisted UK Boards." *Corporate Governance: An International Review* 13(5): 667–679.

Macey, Jonathan R. 2008. *Corporate Governance: Promises Kept, Promises Broken*. Princeton: Princeton University Press.

McCahery, Joseph, Sol Picciotto, and Colin Scott. 1995. Corporate Control: Changing Concepts and Practices of the Firm' in *Corporate Control and Accountability: Changing Structures and the Dynamics of Regulation*. Oxford University Press.

Milani, Lisa M. 1986. "The Continuous Ownership Requirement: A Bar to Meritorious Shareholder Derivative Actions?" *Washington and Lee Law Review* 43(3): 1013–1035.

Murphy, Kevin J. 1986. "Incentives, Learning, and Compensation: A Theoretical and Empirical Investigation of Managerial Labor Contracts." *RAND Journal of Economics* 17(1): 59–76.

Nolan, Richard C. 2005. "The Legal Control of Directors' Conflicts of Interest in the United Kingdom: Non-executive Directors Following the Higgs Report." *Theoretical Inquiries in Law* 6(2): 413, 428.
Oakley, David. 2013. "FirstGroup's Chairman Martin Gilbert Knew It Was Time to Go." *Financial Times*, May 21. Accessed August 29, 2017. https://www.ft.com/content/3898e894-c15c-11e2-9767-00144feab7de
Payne, Jennifer. 2002. "'Clean Hands" in Derivative Actions.' *Cambridge Law Journal* 61(1): 76, 83–85.
Pinto, Arthur R. 2006. "Control and Responsibility of Credit Rating Agencies in the United States." *The American Journal of Comparative Law* 54: 341–356.
Reisberg, Arad. 2006. "Theoretical Reflections on Derivative Actions in English Law: The Representative Problem." *European Company and Financial Law Review* 3(1): 69–108.
Robinson James and Mark Sweney. 2010. "David Montgomery Leaves Mecom." *Guardian.com*, September 9. http://www.theguardian.com/media/2010/sep/09/david-montgomery-leaves-mecom
Shen, Wei and Albert D. Cannella. 2002. "Revisiting the Performance Consequences of CEO Succession: The Impacts of Successor Type, Post-Succession Senior Executive Turnover, and Departing CEO Tenure." *Academy of Management Journal* 45(4): 717–733.
Shleifer, Andrei and Robert W. Vishny. 1986. "Large Shareholders and Corporate Control." *Journal of Political Economy* 94(3): 461–488.
Shleifer, Andrei and Robert W. Vishny. 1997. "A Survey of Corporate Governance." *The Journal of Finance* 52(2): 737–783.
Simpson, Tom. 2011. "Update 1-Big US Funds Join List Voting Against Voting Against BP at AGM." *Reuters.com*, April 12. Accessed August 29, 2017. http://www.reuters.com/article/bp-agm-idUSLDE73B1ZK20110412
Sinclair, Timothy J. 1994. "Passing Judgment: Credit Rating Processes as Regulatory Mechanism of Governance in the Emerging World Order." *Review of International Political Economy* 1(1): 133–159.
Sterling, M. J. 1985. "Personal Bars to Shareholder Actions." *Oxford Journal of Legal Studies* 5(3): 475–485.
Talbot, Lorraine. 2013. *Progressive Corporate Governance for the 21st Century*. Oxon: Routledge.
Trojanowski, Grzegorz and Luc Renneboog. 2002. *The Managerial Labor Market and the Governance Role of Shareholder Control Structures in the UK*. Tilburg University Working Paper No. 2002–68. doi: https://doi.org/10.2139/ssrn.389002

United Kingdom. Department of Trade and Industry. 2002. *Modernising Company Law* (White Paper, Cm 5553).
United Kingdom. Department of Trade and Secretary. 2005. *Company Law Reform*. Cmnd 6456. London: HMSO.
Walker, David. 2009. *A Review of Corporate Governance in UK Banks and Other Financial Industry Entities: Final Recommendations*. 1–175.
Walters, Adrian and Malcolm Davis-White. 2009. *Directors' Disqualification and Insolvency Restrictions*. 3rd ed. London: Sweet & Maxwell.
Wells, Sarah. 2004. "Maintaining Standing in a Shareholder Derivative Action." U.C. *Davis Law Review* 38(1): 343–374.
Williamson, Oliver. 1984. "Corporate Governance." *Yale Law Journal* 93(7): 1197–1230.

Legislation

Canada Business Corporation Act 1985, s 241.
Companies Act (CA) 2006, ss 7–9, 112, 171–176, s 154, 160, 168, ss 215–222. 260–269, 281, 282, 283, 328, 361, 284, s 414, 417, 540–546, 544, 829, 830, 544, 829 & 830., 763. 324–331.
US Fed. R. Civ. P. 23(1).

Cases

Barrett v Duckett [1995] 1 BCLC 243, [1995] BCC 362.
Continental Assurance Co of London plc (in liquidation) (No 4), Re [2007] 2 BCLC 287.
Foss v Harbottle (1843) 2 Hare 461, 67 ER 189.
Franbar Holdings Ltd v Patel and others [2008] EWHC 1534 (Ch), [2009] 1 BCLC 1.
Iesini v Westrip Holdings Ltd [2009] EWHC 2526 (Ch), [2011] 1 BCLC 498, [2010] BCC 420.
McDougall v Gardiner (1875) 1 Ch D 13.
Mozley v Alston (1847) 1 Ph 790, 16 LJ Ch 217, 11 Jur 315, 317, 41 ER 833, 9 LTOS 97.
Prudential Assurance Co Ltd v Newman Industries Ltd (No 2) [1982] Ch 204, [1982] 1 All ER 354, [1982] 2 WLR 31.
Salomon v Salomon [1897] AC 22.

Directives

Directive 2006/43/EC of 17 May 2006. For a list of relevant EC legislations see: *Community Accounting Legislation.* 2009. http://ec.europa.eu/internal_market/accounting/docs/legal_framework/cal_2009_en.pdf. Accessed December 21, 2013.

Directive 2007/36/EC (Shareholders' Rights Directive) (Exercise of certain rights of shareholders in listed companies).

3

Financial Distress, Insolvency and Business Rescue

Overview

This chapter introduces the concepts of financial distress and insolvency and sets out alternative approaches to the resolution of the problem. Discussion begins with an examination of legal and business perspectives. The chapter then identifies the potential external and internal causes of financial distress and the informal rescue processes that might be put in place. It also considers how and when companies might choose a non-rescue regime, that is, receivership and liquidation. The chapter introduces the history and nature of the formal rescue regimes that are available to all companies in the UK within the framework of insolvency legislation, specifically administration and company voluntary arrangement (CVA). This discussion provides the context for the discussion of the impact of informal and formal rescue processes on governance in Chaps. 4 and 5.

Legal Definitions of Financial Distress

There is no specific definition of financial distress in UK statute. The legislature has used the term "inability to pay debt" to describe a situation where the company can be subject to a formal insolvency procedure such as winding up following judicial intervention. Under section 123 of the Insolvency Act 1986, a corporate debtor may be deemed to be unable to pay its debt if it fails one of two tests: a cash flow test or a balance sheet test. In determining a company's cash flow insolvency, the statutory provision focuses on the company's present capacity demonstrated by its possession of cash or cash equivalent, to pay current or overdue liabilities per se, excluding any other assets that may take time to be liquidated. The test does not reflect the debtor's potential future income should it continue in business. This test is relatively straightforward and is typically used by courts in practice.

English case law has added some complexity to the statutory cash flow test by introducing future liabilities into the equation (*Re Cheyne Finance plc (In Receivership) (No 2)*). In *BNY Corporate Trustee Services Ltd v Eurosail-UK 2007-3BL plc*, the Supreme Court took the view that the cash flow test includes current debts as well as those that fall due "from time to time in the reasonably near future … [which] will depend on all the circumstances, but especially on the nature of the company's business". Previously, the Court of Appeal, in considering the case, had taken the view that English law as "a commercially sensible legal system" does not allow a future or contingent creditor to use the cash flow test to trigger winding up. This is partly because creditors with immediate and short-term claims will have less difficulty in recovering their claims whereas long-term creditors are more likely to face the prospect of no payment (Goode 2011, 114).

The balance sheet test provided for under section 123(2) of the Insolvency Act 1986 uses a more detailed examination of the company's total assets and total liabilities. Judicial discretion is also applied to determine debtor insolvency. The balance sheet test focuses on the overall economic viability of the corporate debtor, potentially triggering a formal insolvency regime if, on the balance of probabilities, liabilities are assessed to be substantially more than the liquidated value of the assets. Common law has taken the view that the balance sheet test "is not the production of an annual balance sheet but a comparison of the value of assets with the amount of liabilities in order to ascertain solvency". It is not "a snapshot of the affairs of a company at any particular point in time". The situation of each company, including the maturity date of prospective liabilities, the source and type of currency to be used to pay debt as well as assets and compensation for losses should be considered. However, the test is not "a mechanical assets-based test" and the circumstances of each case including its normal trading activities affect its balance sheet solvency. Arguably, the decision of the Supreme Court in *Eurosail* puts less informed and less resourceful creditors in a difficult position if they wish to prove the debtor's inability to pay debt and trigger administration by applying a balance sheet test (Walton 2013), which may explain why it is rare for companies with complex balance sheets (particularly large companies) to be placed into a formal insolvency procedure through a court order.

Business Definitions of Financial Distress

The business perspective of financial distress and insolvency is typically addressed within the broader context of management of the going concern. Burke and Cooper (2004) reflect the generally held view that all businesses encounter challenges, including cash flow and solvency problems and business leaders must be ready to react when such problems arise. Financial distress is likely to become a matter of major concern when a company's trading position substantially deteriorates, costs increase or other major changes occur in the business environment triggering major problems with cash flow. Hendel (1996) defines financial distress as a situation where "bankruptcy (insolvency) is likely depending on the level of liquid assets and credit availability". Platt and Platt (2002, 184–185) define financial distress as "a late stage of corporate decline that precedes more cataclysmic events such as bankruptcy or liquidation". In research carried out by Franks and Sussman into one specific bank lending to a range of corporate customers, a company identified as being in financial distress would be one whose account had been transferred into "the bank's Business Support Unit" on the advice of "the local bank branch or the regional credit officer" (2005, 74).

Whilst legal interpretations of financial distress may include a range of different considerations, business definitions typically focus on cash flow (net income adjusted for non-cash charges) relative to current liabilities. Whitaker defines financial distress as the situation where a company's cash flow is insufficient to cover the current debt obligations that are a consequence of long-term debt (1999, 124). Wruck adopts the same definition (1990, 421), believing it to be comparable with Altman's definition of technical insolvency where the company is unable to meet its current obligations due to lack of liquidity. This definition is similar to the cash flow test under the Insolvency Act 1986, s. 123(1)(e) with its focus on current assets and liabilities.

Reports on liquidity are an integral part of corporate financial reporting where companies are required to report cash flow from operating activities, investment and business financing decisions. Whilst such reports tend to be a universal requirement, actual approaches to cash flow measurement have been found to vary from country to country and between companies operating in the same country. This makes any process of intercompany comparison difficult.

Financial distress may also be detected through changes in the balance sheet, as liabilities increase and assets are used as securities for loans or sold to meet debt. Such changes may reflect the result of compromises between creditors and management, including informal arrangements and new financial commitments. Taken to its extreme, this process of gradual compromise may lead to corporate bankruptcy (insolvency)—a chronic condition where the company's total liabilities exceed a fair valuation of its total assets and the net worth of the firm is negative (Altman and Hotchkiss 2006). Altman (2000) considers that changes to liquidity, profitability and solvency are important "predictors" of a company's likely bankruptcy. Similarly, Lasfer, Sudarsanam and Taffler (1996) suggest that the balance sheet of financially distressed companies may suddenly show unexpected reductions in the value of corporate assets, linked to the sale of such assets to cover debt liabilities or to pay dividends to shareholders in an attempt to positively influence share prices.

Some financial analysts have observed that the balance sheet of a distressed company may differ from the one that might be presented by the same company in a non-distressed status. For instance, those companies that have low bond ratings or high levels of gearing are more likely to use structured financing arrangements that are not included as debt liabilities in their balance sheet (Mills and Newberry 2005, 251–253). Alternatively, liabilities may be extended in terms of maturity date through a process of "reclassification" allowing the company to have more time to pay its short-term debts (Gramlich et al. 2001, 283–284). The effect would be to reduce financial pressure on the company, increase liquidity and prevent a breach of contract. The authors suggest that such changes can be reversed as the company gets back to a stable financial position.

Barton and Simko (2002) have shown that companies frequently attempt to present an over-optimistic view of the company's financial status to avoid the consequences of being perceived as being in a financially distressed position. This can take the form of an overstatement of assets or an understatement of liabilities in financial disclosure, subject to any previous reporting of "net asset values". Mills and Newberry (2005) also suggest that technical improvements can be made to the balance sheets of distressed companies to achieve similar results. They cite off-balance-sheet techniques that include showing loan interest on tax reports but excluding it from financial reports, where it is treated as part of dividends.

A deliberate decision to present the balance sheet in this way may be initiated by management, acting independently or with the mutual agreement of creditors. The importance of a positive corporate financial reputation—especially if this explicitly or implicitly results in performance rewards for company directors—may lead to attempts to present a favourable balance sheet position even in times of financial distress (Maydew 2005, 284–285). Nevertheless, such companies are likely to face higher levels of scrutiny from external bodies, including Her Majesty's Revenues and Customs (HMRC), and face legal sanctions if the behaviour of directors could be seen as misleading or deliberately fraudulent. In such circumstances, obtaining a clear picture of a company's solvency solely based on balance sheet information may be a difficult process. This problem was recognised in the work of the

Cadbury Committee which recommended an independent audit of a company's financial position on a regular basis as part of an effective governance process, and incorporated this recommendation into the proposed UK Governance Code. Such an audit would identify where companies might be deliberately producing misleading information. The question posed in later chapters of this book is the extent to which financial distress and insolvency might lead to a breakdown in the regular provision of such an independent audit for shareholders and other stakeholders.

Causes of Financial Distress

Lingard has suggested that internal factors including poor production quality, poor marketing and weak financial controls can contribute to corporate insolvency (1989, 1–3). Anything that prevents a company from manufacturing (processing or delivering) efficiently is a potential cause of such insolvency. This can happen at any stage in the supply chain, from purchasing and operations management, to logistics and quality control. Lack of balance in the number of employees, over- or under-production and lack of awareness of customer needs leading to an inappropriate advertising and communications strategy are all possible contributory factors. Building up a business without creating a contingency for injecting cash into the company as it expands also indicates inadequate financial planning which may create future problems.

Finch links corporate insolvency with the "mismanagement" of company resources, inappropriate processes and structures and the overall performance of the board of directors and other senior managers (2002, 129–132). She suggests that incompetence or disinterest of company directors or other employees is likely to lead to inefficient and ineffective corporate performance and potential financial difficulties for the company. Similarly, Whitaker (1999) associates financial distress with a lack of efficient management and a decline in firm performance compared to that of the industry or market in which it operates. These perspectives are reflected in the Cork Report (see discussion below) that blames management for many of the problems that ultimately lead to corporate failure.

Whilst a company may be able to do something about internal factors it is only able to monitor and adapt to new external conditions such as changes in consumer confidence or a new trading environment. It cannot change such conditions. Its continuing survival depends on its ability to forecast and respond effectively to such changes, subject to its own resources. When there is a general business downturn the potential impact of financial distress may be more acute unless the company has strong financial viability. Opler and Titman argue that in an industry-wide recession, the performance of companies and consequently their solvency is very much influenced by their existing level of debt; that is, the more debt a company has, the more vulnerable it is to hostile market conditions and competition from industry rivals (Opler and Titman 1994, 1016–1017).

Corporate insolvency is directly linked to economic cycles. The 2008 sub-prime mortgage storm that hit US and European financial markets resulted in the total collapse and insolvency of a large number of companies. A forecast by KPMG at the time stated that corporate insolvencies were likely to double as a result of external factors including "declining consumer confidence, lack of credit insurance for companies and the soaring cost of importing goods to the market". Equally, where a company is highly dependent on one client, the sudden loss of the client's business or the insolvency of that client can lead to the collapse of the company. Those companies selling products or services to the public sector are particularly vulnerable to fluctuations in purchasing behaviour caused by declining budgets as a result of political decisions, exemplified by Connaught plc (see the case study in Chap. 11), and more recently Carillion plc.

Regardless of the cause of financial distress, a board of directors has a responsibility to maintain the company's position as a going concern and respond to financial distress as soon as it appears. A potential financial liability for the company, reflected in a balance sheet contingency or a pending court order, may not threaten the ongoing viability of the company, provided that there are plans in place to deal with such situations when they arise. There are likely to be more options to solve the potential problem if action is taken at an early stage than if management takes no action whilst financial distress worsens and no contingency plans are made.

The business and management literature uses such terms as "turnaround" or "business restructuring" to describe the recovery process. This book uses the phrase "informal business rescue", distinguishing this phase from the formal business rescue processes that are put in place when such informal processes do not succeed. The general aims of informal rescue may include minimising losses and modifying or developing new business relationships, which may improve profitability and revenue (Slatter and Lovette 1999, 5). Rescue strategies can also include cost reduction, asset sale, equity/share issue in public companies and new debt financing/debt renegotiation. The composition of the board of directors may also be changed to bring in new members with appropriate skills or exit those directors who are seen to have contributed to the original problem. The likelihood of successful rescue is likely to depend on the scale of financial distress, corporate resources, confidence in the senior executive team and the effectiveness of implementation (Smith and Graves 2005, 305–307). Chapter 4 discusses how the implementation of each of these informal rescue strategies has the potential to change the nature of corporate governance.

Formal Non-Rescue Procedures

Ultimately despite the best efforts of directors to rescue a company, a formal insolvency procedure may be instigated by secured creditors, by the company (or its directors) or by a court order (usually as a result of the presentation of either a winding-up petition or an administration application). A formal insolvency regime is typically instigated as a last option. At this stage management may have run out of ideas and resources and/or a deterioration in its credit rating may have alarmed creditors sufficiently to end any financial confidence. The company may have overwhelming debts and liabilities with no prospect of future earnings to cover debt repayments. The initiation of a formal insolvency process may have also been triggered by a breakdown of informal discussions with creditors (debt workouts), when one or more major creditors have withdrawn from negotiations with the intention of achieving a better deal. Since such workouts require the consent of all major creditors, a challenge by one or more of such creditors is sufficient to cause negotiations to cease.

The UK's formal non-rescue process is characterised by a focus on creditor interests. This focus may be traced back to medieval days when social, economic and cultural norms empathised with creditors' financial losses and entitled them to act individually to recover their financial interests in whatever way possible. Significant changes to insolvency law have been embedded in legislation, starting with the Joint Stock Companies Act 1844, originally designed to facilitate company incorporation. This was followed by over 150 years of legislation on different elements of company law. The Insolvency Act 1976 reflected the cumulative findings of a series of parliamentary reports published between 1906 and 1976. In the Act receivership and liquidation were identified as recognised insolvency procedures. Both of these procedures were intrinsically creditor-focused rather than being designed to support the rescue of companies in financial distress.

Receivership is a well-established procedure available only to secured creditors. Prior to the enactment of the Insolvency Act 1986, the procedure was available to institutions that operated as an "integral part of the national economy" and ignored the interests of unsecured creditors. Receivership could be commenced by a private application made by a secured creditor under a debenture or by a court order. Appointment of a receiver in such circumstances often led to the sale of secured assets.

The Insolvency Act 1986 established administrative receivership as an insolvency procedure available to debenture holders of a company, where a floating charge existed. The floating charge was a type of security that could crystallise upon any default of payment by the debtor. The holders of a floating charge were able to appoint an administrative receiver provided the charge deed permitted changes to control of the business, and the receiver was entitled to sell the assets of the company that were subject to charge. The debtor was also threatened by potential litigation on behalf of the floating charge holder if the proceeds of sale were not sufficient to repay the debt. The procedure was entirely unilateral, typically ignored the prospects for rescue of the company and did not benefit unsecured creditors. The Enterprise Act 2002 limited the powers of floating charge holders, removing their right to appoint a receiver for charges created after September 15, 2003. Charge holders are now only able to appoint an administrator, but may do so without any court intervention. For those creditors who have secured interests (fixed charges) on tangible assets of the corporate debtor such as machinery and real estate, the Law of Property Act 1925 defines a process of receivership that keeps assets outside the scope of insolvency law. This form of receivership continues to be used today.

The alternative process, liquidation or winding-up is the oldest and fastest insolvency procedure in UK insolvency. The procedure was created in the Winding-Up Act 1844 and modified in the Bankruptcy Act 1883. The latter introduced the concept of insolvency as a civil issue. Unlike receivership, liquidation can be initiated by different interest groups. Where a company is solvent, the shareholders' right to invoke liquidation may be exercised through a resolution voted on at general meetings. A declaration of solvency by company directors is a prerequisite to such meetings. The scope of shareholder-invoked liquidation is outside the scope of this book as insolvency is not an issue in such circumstances. In circumstances where the declaration of solvency cannot be issued due to critical financial distress, or such a declaration is successfully challenged by unpaid creditors, creditors can initiate liquidation as a right as soon as the necessary court order is issued (compulsory winding-up). Liquidation can also be initiated following a creditors' meeting where the majority have approved winding up the business (creditors' voluntary winding-up).

It is also possible for an insolvency practitioner to initiate liquidation following a court order if he no longer believes that other insolvency procedures such as administration can satisfy the demands of creditors. Regardless of the nature of liquidation, commencement of the procedure transfers the control of unsecured assets and affairs of the company to an insolvency practitioner who, as the liquidator, is the agent of the company and has no commitment to fulfil the demands of individual creditors. His or her responsibility is to the general body of creditors. Speedy sale of assets through auction and distribution of the proceeds amongst creditors are the main objectives of the liquidator.

Dissolution of the company usually follows liquidation, which means that the company as a legal entity no longer exists unless liquidation is brought to standstill or termination as a result of a court order, where a court finds valid grounds for a CVA, scheme of arrangement, or even resumption of business activities (see below).

Formal Business Rescue Regimes

In 1982 the Cork Committee, named after its chair Sir Kenneth Cork, published a comprehensive overview of insolvency legislation in common law countries including the UK, the United States, Canada, Australia, New Zealand, Germany and France. The Cork Report proposed substantial "radical reforms" to the existing "unsatisfactory" insolvency law in the UK, focusing on a debtor-oriented approach that "increase[d] the survival chances" of financially distressed companies. The Report offered a comprehensive review of insolvency law in the UK that overtly involved the courts and focused on pre-insolvency creditor bargains mainly for the full benefit of secured creditors. It made seven detailed recommendations which were aimed at "a radical reform" of UK insolvency law. These recommendations included: restriction of formal non-rescue procedures to potentially serious cases especially where there was an element of financially unlawful conduct; development of "simplified" insolvency procedures that could be debtor invoked; promotion of a rescue culture that allowed the preservation of jobs and avoided the immediate sale of debtor's assets; time-specified deferment of creditor-centred enforcement of claims and qualification requirements for insolvency practitioners.

The Cork Report could be regarded as the first cautious step towards the development of a formal rescue regime that was willing to address the imbalance of power between financial institutions and debtor companies. A debtor-focused insolvency regime was a new departure in the UK, with its traditional reputation for protecting the interests of powerful financial institutions. The Report's recommendations were also motivated by the lessons learned from changes to American bankruptcy law where a culture of corporate rescue had been introduced through the enactment of Chapter 11 of the US Bankruptcy Code. Whilst the recommendations made in the Cork Report reflect a lack of satisfaction with previous approaches, the Report still assured secured creditors that pre-insolvency rights would not be eroded and preserved the role of security as a risk protection mechanism.

A formal rescue regime focuses on the potential for business recovery. This difference in emphasis is due to the potential social and economic impact that business failure may cause, and the costs to society that may go beyond those costs to the business community narrowly defined (Baird 1989, 577). A formal rescue regime is designed to allow the debtor to retain a viable business position, with a reduced burden of debt and smaller-than-before volume of assets. Such a recovery is facilitated through a new set of rules that allow departure from the pre-insolvency contractual obligations of the parties, on the basis that the freedom of parties to enter into a contract is restricted by their inability to foresee future problems (McCormack 2003).

A formal rescue regime also relies on the prospective income that may be earned by keeping business opportunities open for the debtor and valuing the business as a going concern. It creates a time shield that in principle allows the debtor to reconstruct its weakened financial structure, with less concern about the immediate legal enforcement of its creditors' claims. The corporate debtor has the opportunity to change its business model, potentially increasing the pool of assets available to creditors. The debtor can also establish new contractual relationships with both new and existing creditors although some sort of priority may have to be offered. The possibility of extending the time shield may help a corporate debtor to repair its damaged financial structure.

A formal rescue regime uses security interests as the means of creating a priority ranking between creditors, and adds other categories including preferential and unsecured creditors. It puts unsecured creditors as residual claimants at the bottom of its priority ranking, only just above shareholders, but entitles them to have a say on how they collectively wish their interests to be treated. It also gives employees preferential status with the effect that their claims are paid ahead of unsecured creditors, and possibly some secured creditors, and provides for the interests of unsecured creditors to be determined on a pari-passu basis (Mokal 2001). Similar to a formal non-rescue regime, secured creditors maintain their status but various limitations are imposed on the way that such creditors can recover their losses from the total pool of assets.

A formal rescue regime does not necessarily leave the power and status of the management team intact. Depending on the norms of society and the relative novelty of the local rescue culture, those leading the rescue might regard management as the cause of business failure and replace them with external insolvency professionals who are totally independent and act as the officers of the court. When the management team is kept in place the power of decision-making is shared between management and all pre-insolvency creditors. Management will be held responsible for any unlawful conduct that has purposely benefited management at the expense of creditors.

Administration and Company Voluntary Arrangement

The government's response to the Cork Report came initially in the Insolvency Act 1985. The Act introduced a formal rescue regime that offered two insolvency procedures: Administration and Company Voluntary Arrangement (CVA). The Act was replaced almost immediately by the Insolvency Act 1986. The acceleration of the legislation towards a more debtor-oriented approach increased in the enactment of the Enterprise Act 2002, which placed mandatory restrictions on the power of secured creditors to invoke administrative receivership and effectively replaced the procedure with administration.

Administration was originally created as a formal procedure under Part II of the Insolvency Act 1985. However, it was actually enforced as part of the Insolvency Act 1986. The initial structure of administration under this Act reflects the early thoughts of the legislature on a rescue procedure that does not violate the security rights of banks and financial institutions. Administration discharges management from its powers and responsibility for control and replaces management with an insolvency practitioner who is qualified to act as the officer of the court and lead the company through the rescue process, settling claims based on statutory provisions as s/he deems necessary. Administration entitles the insolvent company to a flexible moratorium in terms of duration. It provides for a priority ranking amongst creditors that gives preferential status to employees.

Despite comprehensive rescue features, administration as originally prescribed had some limitations and was not an attractive option to companies. The original form of administration was regarded as expensive, complex, formal and time consuming. The small number of insolvency cases using administration was an important indicator for government that the regime was not going to be practical without further improvement. To improve the rescue features of administration, the legislature had to gradually reform the law, reconfiguring rescue into a more efficient procedure. It repealed the use of administrative receivership, but was also reluctant to change administration for those debtors and creditors that had previously relied on it. As a result, the process of receivership in relation to debentures created prior to September 15, 2003 was not repealed.

The Enterprise Act 2002 introduced a new route to administration that was essentially a reconfiguration of the old procedure. The new powers of administration that were added to the Insolvency Act 1986 in Schedule B1 tightened the powers of the administrator. These changes remove veto power from debenture holders and allow companies to appoint an insolvency practitioner without obtaining a court order unless there are exceptional circumstances. A percentage of the proceeds of the assets subject to floating charges can be paid to unsecured creditors. A company can now be put into administration without seeking a court order. The appointment of an administrator signifies the exercise of a right reserved for company directors or a qualifying charge holder to rescue the company within a legal framework. The appointment can still be made by the court, although in practice this rarely now happens.

Under the administration process a formal notice is sent to all creditors to inform them of the new circumstances and ask them to submit their claims. An automatic stay (moratorium) brings the enforcement of all claims to a halt and allows creditors, especially unsecured creditors, to determine whether they would prefer to continue their business with the company. A moratorium may be a desirable feature of administration for those companies that are overwhelmed with the creditors' persistence in recovering their claims. A moratorium can be up to a year with the possibility of extension, with either creditors' consent or the leave of the court. Unlike the US Bankruptcy Code, there is no obligation on creditors to continue their business with the insolvent debtor. During administration, the assets subject to security can be used to keep the business going but unlike unsecured assets, any sales of secured assets are subject to administrator or court approval. The face value of the assets determines whether the administrator has to hold a creditors' meeting. Priority ranking amongst creditors requires the administrator to follow a systematic rule in terms of payment of debt. Creditors' claims are settled under the priority ranking which requires the costs of administration to be paid ahead of all creditors, and the floating charge holder will be paid from the proceeds from the sale of relevant assets. Any claims should be proved before they can be paid.

Entry into administration will not necessarily lead to proposals for business rescue. Administration has to be followed by an arrangement such as a CVA if the company is to be rescued as a going concern. Otherwise, administration may result in winding up or straight dissolution if the company cannot be rescued. One alternative route to rescue is a pre-packaged administration (pre-pack) which provides the possibility of a rapid exit from insolvency. In a pre-pack the sale of corporate assets is negotiated with potential buyers and the consent of major creditors to the sale is also sought, before entry into administration. The commencement of administration precedes the formal sale of assets. After administration commences the company's business is transferred under a sale contract to the acquiring company.

A CVA provides a debt payment arrangement that is exclusively binding on unsecured creditors. The arrangement offers a safety net for unsecured creditors that puts primary focus on their interests in a formal rescue procedure. As a legally backed procedure, the requirements of an enforceable CVA have many similar features to those already provided under the Companies Act 2006 for both solvent and insolvent companies—known as a scheme of arrangement.

Some academics suggest that such arrangements are "unattractive" and "complex" for insolvent companies. However, it is viewed as a practical solution for distressed companies that take a realistic approach towards the potential threat of liquidation. It could also be argued that the intention of the legislature is to improve the impact of the rescue regime by reducing the difference between the position of solvent and financially distressed companies who apply an arrangement under the Companies Act or the Insolvency Act. This may cause the market to moderate its negative response to the CVA as an insolvency procedure.

Unlike administration that comes with an automatic stay, a CVA offers the possibility of a moratorium only if it is desired by those who inform the court of their intention. Even then, such an option is available only for small companies under the Insolvency Act 2000. The CVA in its early form was criticised for its lack of moratorium. The legislature has shown its support for a moratorium-based CVA that requires a different process compared with the moratorium-less CVA but has left it to the skills and expertise of insolvency practitioners as well as company directors to determine which form of CVA suits their case best. Parry regards the CVA as an English version of the US debtor in possession where the company achieves a better outcome when facing a difficult financial problem (2008, 131).

There is no legislative requirement as to who should prepare the initial CVA proposal. The assumption is that it is the responsibility of the initiator of the CVA, namely the directors, to draft the proposal. It is usually done in consultation with an insolvency practitioner who becomes the nominee. Similarly, legislation does not provide a great deal of information on what a proposal should include. The legislation does stipulate that a proposal should provide detailed information on how the company is going to settle the claims of its unsecured creditors, and its plan for payment of future claims for those creditors who wish to continue their contracts with the company after the CVA. The proposal must also nominate someone who will be in charge of all matters relating to the implementation of the CVA including the pre-voting and post-voting stage.

After the proposal is drafted, it is the responsibility of the initiator of the CVA to submit it to a nominee, the insolvency practitioner, to draft and submit a feasibility report for court consideration within a maximum 28 days' time limit. A creditors' meeting must be convened, and the nominee is required to invite all known creditors to attend the meeting. The meeting should take into account all of the creditors' views and modify the proposal where appropriate. The proposal will be approved if it receives the support of those creditors who take part in the voting, and who are owed 75% of the total debt owed to voting creditors, and if at a separate meeting a simple majority of the members agree to the proposal.

Otherwise, the proposal will be dismissed and no CVA formed. The Chairman of the meeting should inform the court in writing of the results of both meetings; he should also inform creditors of the outcome as they will be bound by the result of the votes unless the results are challenged. The enforcement of the CVA will be supervised by the insolvency practitioner for the duration of the CVA, unless it is terminated prematurely.

As soon as the CVA is formed, no other insolvency procedure can replace the arrangement unless a decision is made by the creditors to terminate the CVA. The supervisor is empowered to wind up the company. Unfair prejudice or material irregularity, if proven, can be reasonable grounds for minority creditors asking for the termination of the CVA and a winding-up of the company.

The CVA has been described as a cost-effective process for a company and its creditors. This may be due to the fact that the continuation of a small-scale trust through a straightforward approved proposal may result in better dividends for creditors than liquidation. There is also no requirement to seek the satisfaction of the court on the proposals and the performance of the trust. Another reason could be that since the supervisor controls the assets, as soon as the flow of assets ceases, the supervisor can inform the creditors and propose to wind down the trust. Since the scope of the CVA only applies to the body of creditors who have input their views on the adjustment of their claims at the pre-voting stage, the probability of litigation by an unsecured creditor is low.

Concluding Remarks

This chapter has demonstrated that the interpretation of financial distress and insolvency depends on variables that are not clear-cut or transparent. Financial distress is a threshold position for company directors, although there is unlikely to be one absolute threshold that is consistently experienced across all companies. What is perceived to be financial distress in one company may be perceived to be "business as usual" in another. The chapter also examined how formal processes to deal with business insolvency in the UK have gradually evolved from a predominantly creditor-oriented system to a more debtor-oriented approach that might favour business rescue rather than business closure. Decisions that are made by directors during financial distress and ultimately insolvency are likely to lead to substantial changes in the way in which the company is managed and impact directly on corporate governance. Chapters 4 and 5 explore this potential impact.

Bibliography

Altman, Edward I. 1968. "Financial Ratios, Discriminant Analysis and the Prediction of Corporate Bankruptcy." *Journal of Finance* 23(4): 589–609.

Altman, Edward I. 2000. "Predicting Financial Distress of Companies: Revisiting the Z-Score and Zeta Models." *Stem School of Business, New York University*, 4. Accessed December 22, 2013. http://citeseerx.ist.psu.edu/viewdoc/download?doi=10.1.1.25.1884&rep=rep1&type=pdf

Altman, Edward I. and Edith Hotchkiss. 2006. *Corporate Financial Distress and Bankruptcy: Predict and Avoid Bankruptcy, Analyze and Invest in Distressed Debt.* 3rd ed. New Jersey: John Wiley & Sons.

Aminoff, Nicholas A. 1989. "The Development of American and English Bankruptcy Legislation – From a Common Source to a Shared Goal." *Statute Law Review* 10(2): 124–134.

Armour, John and Sandra Frisby. 2001. "Rethinking Receivership." *Oxford Journal of Legal Studies* 21(1): 73–102.

Asquith, Paul, Robert Gertner, and David Scharfstein. 1994. "Anatomy of Financial Distress: An Examination of Junk-Bond Issuers." *Quarterly Journal of Economics* 109(3): 625–658.

Aziz, Abdul and Gerald H. Lawson. 1989. "Cash Flow Reporting and Financial Distress Models: Testing of Hypotheses." *Financial Management* 18(1): 55–63.

Baird, Douglas G. 1998. "Bankruptcy's Uncontested Axioms." *Yale Law Journal* 108(3): 573–599.

Barth, Mary E., Donald P. Cram, and Karen K. Nelson. 2001. "Accruals and the Prediction of Future Cash Flows." *Accounting Review* 76(1): 27–58.

Barton, Jan and Paul J. Simko. 2002. "The Balance Sheet as an Earning Management Constraint." *Accounting Review* 77: 1–27.

BBC News. 2013. "BP Wins Reprieve over Gulf of Mexico Oil Spill Payouts." *BBC*, December 3. Accessed November 8, 2017. http://www.bbc.co.uk/news/business-25196879

Beaver, William H. 1966. "Financial Ratios as Predictors of Failure." *Journal of Accounting Research* 4: 71–111.

Bose, Trina. 2004. "Resolving Financial Distress—Justice as Fairness and Reciprocity." *UCL Jurisprudence Review* 230–251.

Burke, Ronald J. and Cary L. Cooper. 2004. "Leading in Turbulent Times: Issues and Challenges." in *Leading in Turbulent Times: Managing in the New World of Work*, edited by Ronald J. Burke and Cary L. Cooper. Massachusetts: Blackwell Publishing Ltd.

Casey, Cornelius and Norman Bartczak. 1985. "Using Operating Cash Flow Data to Predict Financial Distress: Some Extensions." *Journal of Accounting Research* 23(1): 384–401.

Dahiya, Sandeep, Anthony Saunders, and Anand Srinivasan. 2003. "Financial Distress and Bank Lending Relationships." *Journal of Finance* 58(1): 375–399.

Doyle, Louis and Andrew Keay. 2009. *Insolvency Legislation: Annotations and Commentary*. Bristol: Jordan Publishing Ltd.

Financial Accounting Standard Board. "Summary of Statement No. 95," Accessed November 8, 2017. http://www.fasb.org/jsp/FASB/Pronouncement_C/SummaryPage&cid=900000010365

Finch, Vanessa. 1997. "The Measures of Insolvency Law." *Oxford Journal of Legal Studies* 17(2): 227–252.

Finch, Vanessa. 2002. *Corporate Insolvency Law: Perspectives and Principles*. Cambridge: Cambridge University Press.

Franks, Julian and Oren Sussman. 2005. "Financial Distress and Bank Restructuring of Small to Medium Size UK Companies." *Review of Finance* 9(1): 65–96.

Gentry, James A., Paul Newbold, and David T. Whitford. 1985. "Classifying Bankrupt Firms with Funds Flow Components." *Journal of Accounting Research* 23(1): 146–160.

Gilbert, Lisa R., Krishnagopal Menon, and Kenneth B. Schwartz. 1990. "Predicting Bankruptcy for Firms in Financial Distress." *Journal of Business Finance & Accounting* 17(1): 161–171.

Goode, Roy. 2011. *Principles of Corporate Insolvency Law*. 4th ed. London: Sweet & Maxwell.
Gramlich, Jeffrey D., Mary Lea McAnally, and Jacob Thomas. 2001. "Balance Sheet Management: The Case of Short-Term Obligations Reclassified as Long-Term Debt." Journal of Accounting Research 39(2): 283–295.
Hendel, Igal. 1996. "Competition under Financial Distress." *Journal of Industrial Economics* 44(3): 309–324.
Jensen, Michael C. 1989. "Eclipse of the Public Corporation." *Harvard Business Review* 67(5): 61–74.
Keasey, Kevin and Robert Watson. 1991. "Financial Distress Prediction Models: A Review of Their Usefulness." *British Journal of Management* 2(2): 89–102.
Keay, Andrew and Peter Walton. 2008. *Insolvency Law: Corporate and Personal*. 2nd ed. Bristol: Jordan Publishing Ltd.
Lasfer, M. Ameziane, Puliyur S. Sudarsanam, and Richard J. Taffler, 1996. "Financial Distress, Asset Sales, and Lender Monitoring." *Financial Management* 25(3): 57–66.
Lin, L. and J. Piesse 2006. "Identification of Corporate Distress in UK Industrials: A Conditional Probability Analysis Approach." *Applied Financial Economics* 14(2): 73–82.
Lingard, James R. 1989. *Corporate Rescues and Insolvencies*. 2nd ed. Butterworth-Heinemann.
Maydew, Edward. 2005. "Discussion of Firms' Off-Balance Sheet and Hybrid Debt Financing; Evidence from Their Book-Tax Reporting Differences." *Journal of Accounting Research* 43(2): 283–290.
McCormack, Gerard. 2003. "The Priority of Secured Credit: An Anglo-American Perspective." *Journal of Business Law* 389–419.
McCormack, Gerard. 2007. "Control and Corporate Rescue – An Anglo-American Evaluation." *International & Comparative Law Quarterly* 56(3): 515–551.
Mills, Lillian F. and Kaye J. Newberry. 2005. "Firms' Off-Balance Sheet and Hybrid Debt Financing: Evidence from Their Book-Tax Reporting Differences." *Journal of Accounting Research* 43(2): 251–282.
Milman, David. 2013. *Governance of Distressd Firms*. Cheltenham: Edward Elgar Publishing Limited.
Mokal, Rizwaan Jameel. 2001. "Priority as Pathology: The *Pari Passu* Myth." *Cambridge Law Journal* 60(3): 581–621.
Opler, Tim C. and Sheridan Titman. 1994. "Financial Distress and Corporate Performance." *Journal of Finance* 49(3): 1015–1040.

Parry, Rebecca. 2008. *Corporate Rescue*. 1st ed. London: Sweet & Maxwell.
Pearce, John A. and D. Keith Robbins. 1994. "Retrenchment Remains the Foundation of Business Turnaround." *Strategic Management Journal* 15(5): 407–417.
Platt, Harlan D., and Marjorie B. Platt. 2002. "Predicting Corporate Financial Distress: Reflections on Choice-based Sample Bias." *Journal of Economics and Finance* 26(2): 184–199.
Rasheed, Howard S. 2005. "Turnaround Strategies for Declining Small Business: The Effect of Performance and Resources." *Journal of Developmental Entrepreneurship* 10(3): 239–252.
Sakoui, Anoushka. 2009. "New Insolvency Risk for Companies in Crisis." *Financial Times*, September 2. 4.
Scherrer, Philip Scott. 2003. "Management Turnarounds: Diagnosing Business Ailments." *Corporate Governance: The International Journal of Business in Society* 3(4): 52–62.
Sealy, Len, David Milman, and Peter Bailey. 2018. *Sealy & Milman: Annotated Guide to the Insolvency Legislation*. 21st ed. 2 vols. London: Sweet & Maxwell.
Slatter, Stuart and David Lovette. 1999. *Corporate Turnaround: Managing Companies in Distress*. 2nd ed. London: Penguin Group.
Smith, Malcolm and Christopher Graves. 2005. "Corporate Turnaround and Financial Distress." *Managerial Auditing Journal* 20(3): 304–320.
United Kingdom: Cork Review Committee. 1982. *Insolvency Law and Practice: Report of the Review Committee*. Cmnd. 8558. London: HMSO.
Wallace, R. S. Olusegun, Mohammed S. I. Choudhury, and Maurice Pendlebury. 1997. "Cash Flow Statements: An International Comparison of Regulatory Positions." *International Journal of Accounting* 32(1): 1–22.
Walton, Peter. 2013. ""Inability to Pay Debts": Beyond the Point of No Return?" *Journal of Business Law* 2: 212–236.
Ward, Terry J. 1994. "Cash Flow Information and the Prediction of Financially Distressed Mining, Oil and Gas Firms: A Comparative Study." *Journal of Applied Business Research* 10(3): 78–86.
Webb, David C. 1991. "An Economic Evaluation of Insolvency Procedures in the United Kingdom: Does the 1986 Insolvency Act Satisfy the Creditors' bargain?." *Oxford Economic Papers* 43(1): 139–157.
Whitaker, Richard B. 1999. "The Early Stages of Financial Distress." *Journal of Economics and Finance* 23(2): 123–132.

Wilner, Benjamin S. 2000. "The Exploitation of Relationships in Financial Distress: The Case of Trade Credit." *Journal of Finance* 55(1): 153–178.

Wruck, Karen Hopper. 1990. "Financial Distress, Reorganization, and Organizational Efficiency." *Journal of Financial Economics* 27(2): 419–444.

Legislation

Insolvency Act 1986 (IA 1986).

Cases

BNY Corporate Trustee Services Ltd v Eurosail-UK 2007-3BL plc [2011] 2 BCLC 1 (Morrit J).

BNY Corporate Trustee Services Ltd v Eurosail-UK 2007-3BL Plc [2011] BCC 399, 416 (Lord Neuberger).

BNY Corporate Trustee Services Ltd v Eurosail-UK 2007-3BL plc [2013] UKSC 28.

Cheyne Finance plc (in receivership) (No 2), Re [2008] 1 BCLC 741.

4

Corporate Governance in Financial Distress

Overview

This chapter focuses on corporate governance during periods of financial distress. It reviews the changing roles of directors, shareholders and creditors as alternative informal rescue mechanisms are implemented. The review highlights the governance implications of the increasing importance of secured creditors as an influence on director decision-making. It also examines how the implementation of different informal rescue approaches may challenge or compromise the way in which directors fulfil their legal responsibilities.

This chapter and the following are presented in a more structured format than previous chapters. The format has been chosen to enable readers to make a direct link between the individual elements and the structure of the case studies of companies facing financial distress and insolvency presented in Chaps. 7 to 11 and discussed in Chap. 12. The first part of the chapter investigates five board-led approaches to resolving financial distress and reviews potential shareholder and creditor response to these options. Discussion then focuses specifically on directors' personal responsibilities and potential liabilities in situations of financial distress.

Informal Rescue Processes

Chapter 3 identified five broad options as informal rescue processes, namely board change, cost reduction, asset sale, equity/share issue and new debt financing/debt renegotiation. The use of each of these mechanisms has the potential to disrupt existing governance structures, dilute the board's primary fiduciary duty to shareholders and give secured creditors a greater say over the direction of the company. The following discussion explores these themes examining the role of each of the major parties in informal rescue.

Board of Directors' Role

Board change: Changes to membership may be seen as a reaction to financial distress as the board, potentially influenced by shareholders and creditors, brings new skills into the company to deal with the emerging problem, and manages out those individuals who may be seen to be the cause. Such changes may be necessary to reassure shareholders and stakeholders—secured creditors in particular—that the company has recognised the scale of any issue and is taking positive steps to address it. In other instances, members of the board may decide to leave at their own discretion before the problem becomes widely known and their own future careers and reputation are potentially damaged. The same factors are likely to apply to both executive and non-executive directors.

The board may not necessarily have total control over the process of director appointment and remuneration, especially in situations of financial distress. Shareholders and creditors may play a significant role by seeking the appointment of their representative to the board of directors and the dismissal of those who they may perceive to have been the primary contributors to the problem. An example of the appointment of a secured creditor representative is given in the Stylo plc case study in Chap. 7.

Those executive directors who survive the scrutiny of the board, investors and creditors may be obliged to renegotiate the terms of their employment contract including salary and other aspects of remuneration. New terms of contract may also require bonuses or annual increases in salaries to be linked to successful debt management or restructuring.

An empirical study of 381 large US public companies by Gilson (1989) showed that board changes were significantly more likely in companies experiencing financial distress (52%) than in solvent companies (19%). Reasons for leaving the board included pressure on ineffective directors, poor financial performance, retirement, termination of contract, health problems, new employment opportunities or inability to cope with pressure and loss of confidence.

The departure of existing members of the board may then be followed by attempts to recruit new members with relevant expertise, particularly in areas such as financial restructuring or debt management. The board may also appoint new members to the board from existing staff. Examples of such changes can be seen in all of the case studies examined in detail in Chaps. 7 to 11.

As Chap. 2 discussed, the UK Companies Act 2006 requires that a public company has at least two non-executive directors. Non-executive directors should in theory enrich the resources of the company and enhance the skills of management bringing "external [resourceful] influence" to the company (Langevoort 2004). It would be reasonable to expect that in a financially distressed company, the non-executive directors might adopt a more hands-on approach if they believe that shareholder interests are at risk, and move from an advisory role to a position where they become actively involved in business restructuring and recovery and the renegotiation of existing obligations.

Non-executive directors who are recruited in times of relatively prosperous trading may not be comfortable in distress situations. It may be difficult to recruit suitable non-executive directors with appropriate experience who are capable of dealing with such situations. Whilst governance codes require equal numbers of executive or non-executive directors regardless of the financial stability of the company, an empirical study by Elloumi and Gueyie (2001) of 92 Canadian public companies suggests that the number of non-executive directors on the board of financially distressed companies is likely to be "significantly fewer" than that of solvent ones. The authors comment that

CEOs change quickly in such companies and it is unlikely that a new CEO would also be appointed as Chairman at the same time. An examination of the case studies in Chaps. 7 to 11 supports this view.

As Chap. 2 indicated, non-executive directors have by definition advisory roles. Typically they have relatively limited access to details of the company's business operations and limited time available to spend on monitoring the performance of executive directors. At the beginning of any period of distress the members of the board may show their support for senior management, especially the CEO, through public announcements. However, as the scale of the problem emerges, non-executive directors might be more interested in the successful resolution of the debt problem than in keeping those who they originally appointed or endorsed in post. This may involve pressing for the termination of appointments of those executives who had created the problem or appeared to be incapable of dealing with it.

Cost reduction: Companies might be expected to focus on cost reduction as part of the day-to-day management of the business as a going concern. Financial distress appears to focus attention more sharply on cost efficiency (Pearce and Robbins 1993, 616), through increased productivity, staff redundancies, termination of expensive contracts, sourcing new suppliers that provide products or services at a cheaper price, reducing stock levels and work-in-progress, and the closure of loss-making business units. Such measures are the easiest and most straightforward way to address cash flow problems. They are also under the immediate direct control of management and although they may require consultation and discussion with employees, major shareholders and suppliers before they can be implemented, management has the ultimate decision over the implementation of such strategies. However, there is a finite limit on the capacity of such strategies to return the company to solvency, particularly when the external environment that the company operates in deteriorates and competition increases. At some point the company is likely to be faced with the need to implement more significant major restructuring of its operations. Chapters 7, 9, and 10 give examples of the implementation of such strategies in three companies, Stylo plc, Waterford Wedgwood plc and Woolworths Group plc.

Asset sale: Asset sale is a significantly greater step change in attempts to resolve a situation of financial distress. Asset sale may be substantial, involving the sale of a complete business or may be limited to piecemeal sale. All of the case study companies described in Chaps. 7 to 11 attempted to use asset sale to resolve financial distress, with varying outcomes.

Directors should exercise as much discretion and care in dealing with company assets during financial distress as they do during solvency. Directors' general fiduciary duty requires that they take sufficient care during the sale of assets to avoid shareholder or liquidator/administrator actions against them for transactions that appear to have undervalued assets. Creditor influences become particularly significant where there are fixed or floating charges in place to secure existing borrowings (see the discussion below) as company directors cannot sell assets that are subject to security without the prior consent of the lender. In such circumstances, piecemeal sale of assets may be the only choice for company directors. An example of such a sale can be seen in the Woolworths Group plc case in Chap. 10. The deployment of specialists and professional advisors by the board for asset valuation and marketing has become an essential part of such sales.

Equity/Share issue: Equity/share issue is an alternative route to resolving problems of financial distress. Under section 617 of the Companies Act 2006, the board may initiate an increase in share capital, and/or the sub-division or consolidation of share capital in part or total. New shares may be issued as ordinary shares or divided into "units", a combination of ordinary shares with income shares that guarantee payment of dividends at a fixed rate. The new share issue in the Waterford Wedgwood plc case study in Chap. 9 in such an example. Alternatively, new shares could be preference shares. Changes to share capital have major implications for existing shareholders, potentially changing the locus of power and influence of existing shareholding and leading to a dilution/increase in the value of shareholder capital. There is also no guarantee that new shareholders will take the same approach to corporate governance as those who previously owned shares. For example, whilst previously shares may have been held by a small group of shareholders who were also board directors, the decision to raise funds by increasing share capital may bring new shareholders into the company who take a more aggressive, challenging approach to the decisions of the board of directors.

Public companies have two options to increase share capital. New shares may be sold through stock markets (public offering), in which case existing shareholders and new investors will be equally entitled to purchase shares. The company may also attempt to use a private placement which allows it to sell a fixed percentage of shares to one or more investors (Wruck and Wu 2009), in which case specific agreements between the board and the private investor may be negotiated and finalised. The initiation and choice of the form of share issue and choice between public offering and private offering is at the discretion of company directors following any advice from financial advisors on shareholder structure, the urgency of the funding requirement and the company's ability to bear the associated costs (Burton et al. 2005, 172).

Directors may choose a public offering as the preferred option. A public offering allows company directors to retain control whilst the number of dispersed and institutional shareholders increases with no change to statutory rights. Although a public offering requires advanced planning, compliance with listing rules and disclosure of statutory information, the costs should be outweighed by the benefits if the company receives a positive response from potential investors and raises the cash required to resolve its financial distress. However, in situations of financial distress such an offering may have less chance of succeeding as the Waterford Wedgwood case study in Chap. 9 illustrates.

Markets are not perfect and the prevailing asymmetry of information between company directors and existing or potential shareholders creates different responses from different types of investors reflected in the outcome of any share offering (Dierkens 1991). Markets are likely to treat any equity issue as an unfavourable signal about the status of the company as a going concern and downgrade its future prospects (Asquith and Mullins 1986). Boards of directors may face a negative market response as they offer shares to the public, reflected in a drop in share price and therefore a reduction in the firm's value (Dierkens 1991). In such circumstances informed investors are likely to respond negatively to public offerings.

Those companies that do issue equity may be relying on irrational or ill-informed investors who do not adjust their valuation to reflect the potential implications of the share issue (Dittmar and Thakor 2007). A more extreme response may be seen in large companies where insiders and major shareholders may decide to sell their shares in advance of implementation of such strategies (Kim and Purnanandam 2006).

The possibility of a negative response to public offerings may be avoided, or at least minimised, by private placements where a company uses professional financial advisors as agents, and targets professional investors. Shares offered in private placements, which may include preference shares and/or share units, are typically considered as securities. A company's success in finding investors typically depends on the specialised skills of professional advisors and agents who can identify potential buyers in "a relatively small group of investors" including rival companies in the same industry, private equity investors and banks, and expedite the sale of "a block of shares" (Wruck and Wu 2009). The decision of the board of directors of JJB Sports plc to use a private placement, which allowed Sports Direct to become one of its investors (discussed in Chap. 8), is an example of such an action.

Wruck (1989) believes that the sale of equity securities through private placement increases shareholder wealth by improving a company's market value, but public offerings have the opposite effect on the firm's value. She asserts that those who have bought shares in such a way (private placers) might not support the existing shareholder/manager relationships and priority of their interests. Such new investors are unlikely to take an active public role in managing the performance of the company (Barclay et al. 2007). Those who take up private placements are aware that their public involvement including the appointment of their representative on the board of directors is likely to have a negative effect on the value on the firm (Wruck 1989). Therefore, they are not likely to challenge management in public, nor support the takeover of these companies (Barclay et al. 2007). Given the sophisticated nature of such investments and the investor's commercial rationale, it is likely that any communication or negotiation with the management of companies where they have invested takes place behind closed doors with an implicit promise from company management that everything should remain confidential (Short and Keasey 1999). It has been suggested that these investors often have a previous relationship with the company and use their investment as an opportunity to be represented on the board of directors (Wruck and Wu 2009). There is currently little or no research on the role that lenders may play in promoting or preventing equity issue when the company is in financial distress.

New debt financing/debt renegotiation: Finally companies may seek to use new debt financing/debt renegotiation as an alternative source of funding when encountering a period of financial distress. As Chap. 3 discussed, solvent non-distressed companies by definition have positive balance sheets and access to cash reserves. It has been suggested that such companies may maintain "an emergency reserve of unused borrowing power" (Modigliani and Miller 1963) which can be used to resolve cash flow problems. In such circumstances, the board may use debt renegotiation in an attempt to extend the maturity of existing debt, or alternatively seek new unsecured or secured borrowings (or a combination). In a financially distressed company, unsecured borrowing is unlikely and the costs of such borrowing even when available are likely to be excessively high, particularly if the company's credit rating has been downgraded (Mann 1997).

Where new debt financing on a secured basis is an option, the ownership of secured assets remains with the company as long as it continues to make repayments when due. This form of financing has potentially significant implications for existing creditors depending on the securities offered to secure new borrowings. Security interests have been defined as "a right given to one party in the assets of another party to secure payment or performance by that party or by a third party" (Goode 1988). Since there are no legal restrictions on directors or lenders on the use of security interests, lenders are free to seek a grant of security interests such as mortgages, charges and/or lien over a debtor's assets as a condition for new lending or refinancing.[1] Each type of security interest provides different rights for secured creditors which become important if the debtor defaults.

When the board confers security interests in the form of a commercial mortgage, it confers to the secured creditor—often a bank—interests over tangible assets such as premises and building, in return for a fixed loan at a specified rate of interest. The size of the loan available depends on the extent of equity in such assets. Debtor costs include interest, and legal and administrative fees as mutually agreed. During the currency of the mortgage, the lender/mortgagee maintains an interest in the property that prevents the corporate debtor (mortgagor) from making any changes to ownership rights without the consent of the security holder (Mann 1997). Property rights are "redeemed" when the grantor of security interests, that is, debtor, has fully performed its obligations under the security transaction and repurchases its assets (Harpum, Bridge and Dixon 2012). Should the debtor default or enter a formal insolvency regime such as administration, the lender is expected to receive the highest priority ranking amongst creditors.

Alternatively the board of directors may use a fixed or floating charge to give a secured creditor one of two different "preferential rights" (McCormack 2004). A fixed charge allows the lender to obtain security interests over "ascertained and definite property or property capable of being ascertained" (*Illingworth v Houldsworth*) without the need to transfer their ownership rights. A floating charge allows the lender to obtain security interests over "circulating assets" (*Re Spectrum Plus Ltd*) that is "ambulatory and shifting in its nature, hovering over … [and takes effect] until some event occurs or some act is done which causes it to settle and fasten on the subject of the charge within its reach and grasp" (*Illingworth v Houldsworth*). The two charges create different rights for lenders should the debtor become formally insolvent. A lender with a combined fixed and floating charge is entitled to enforce its security interests on the debtor's default and be placed at the highest priority ranking above other creditors when the company enters administration. Registration of a charge gives the lender quasi-property rights that enable it to influence the board's decisions, particularly as financial distress aggravates. The board must seek the lender's consent where decisions might be assumed to affect the lender's security interests. Ultimately the lender's influence arising from such rights might enable it to direct the decisions of the board to serve its own (lender's) best interests. This matter will be examined further in the later parts of this chapter.

Shareholder Influence

Formal shareholder meetings, with specific resolutions, may be required to formally endorse the decisions of the board of directors as they attempt to resolve situations of financial distress. The employment of new directors does not require prior approval by shareholders although public disclosure of their employment is mandatory. Shareholder influence and endorsement do become critical when the board adopts other rescue strategies, particularly as major institutional shareholders become involved (Short and Keasey 1999). In general, shareholder meeting and voting is required to approve the sale of substantial assets, or the issue of new shares. Listing rules exempt those public companies that are financially distressed from seeking shareholder approval,[2] although disclosure of information still remains mandatory. Where institutional shareholders negotiate with management "behind the scenes" prior to voting at general meetings, they are likely to seek to influence management decisions in advance of any major decisions, and may seek governance changes, including change of directors. They may also seek support from dispersed shareholders prior to any shareholder meeting. The departure of the Chairman of the First Group plc in 2013 is an example of tough institutional shareholders exerting their influence on the composition of a board.

Creditor Influence

Secured creditors: Financial distress may require company directors to make decisions that affect shareholder interests such as changing the structure of corporate assets and liabilities. Such changes may be implemented through the modification of contracts or new contracts that include the creation of additional security interests. In such circumstances, creditors (specifically lenders) may use new contractual obligations to influence management decisions and ultimately the company's direction, and gain effective control if financial distress worsens. As a specific example, the publication of the initial findings of the Tomlinson Report has highlighted the significant role of such creditors in determining the decisions of the directors of small private companies as they attempt to resolve financial distress. There is no regulatory framework to monitor the behaviour of lenders and their influence may result in company directors sidelining their fiduciary duty to consider the interests of shareholders. This transition in the focus of company directors has major implications for current governance codes.

The nature and extent of influence of secured creditors on each informal rescue option varies. Unlike company directors, lenders do not have any direct or indirect duty to the company or its shareholders. Their actions are focused on the protection of their own interests, irrespective of the consequences for the borrowing company. Lenders may require a representative to be appointed to the board as a condition for continuation or extension of funding (see, for example, the case study of Stylo plc in Chap. 7 where a representative of Barclays—the company's lender—was appointed to the board of directors. There is little or no evidence on how far lenders become involved in detailed business operations, and therefore the extent of their influence on cost reduction is unknown. However, the role of lenders in asset sale is more predictable, and related to the type of security interests they have on assets and the scale of such assets.

A lender with a floating charge may not consent to substantial asset sale because this would increase the level of risk that it is already exposed to, particularly if it has the option of enforcing its power of appointment of administrators to recover its debt. Should a company enter administration, the proceeds of the sale of secured assets subject to a floating charge would be used to meet the expenses of administration. Should the net assets subject to the floating charge exceed a certain value, a percentage of the value of such assets would be allocated to unsecured creditors under the prescribed part. However, if the company entered liquidation, the expenses would be paid from the proceeds of the disposal of assets that are not subject to a floating charge (*Buchler v Talbot*). Secured assets cannot be used in such circumstances without permission from the secured creditor or the court and the liquidator cannot use the proceeds of the sale of secured assets to pay unsecured creditors. Therefore, a lender is likely to attempt to protect his interests during the debtor's financial distress by creating a fixed charge where possible. If such charges are created and registered, the lender may not agree with the substantial sale of assets and therefore the board may conclude that piecemeal sale of unencumbered assets is the only available option because it will not damage the existing lender's security interests. There is no regulatory system to monitor the effect of the lender's influence on asset sale.

Where new debt financing is an option, the quality and consistency of information provided by the company is a factor that influences lenders' assessment of the level of risk and the cost of borrowing (Carlson 1994). The company's financial reports in the public domain may imply low risks and perhaps low costs of borrowing (Sengupta 1998); however, lenders are likely to seek assurance by demanding disclosure of further confidential financial information. The costs of borrowing will reflect the lender's overall perception of potential risks in any investment (Mann 1997). This involves a calculation of "the real rate of return and the costs of inflation" (Carlson 1994). In large public companies, the size of any loan sought by the corporate borrower may be substantial. In such circumstances a lender may reject the application, reduce the amount it is prepared to lend or seek the involvement of other lenders in syndicated lending and share the benefits and risk of the investment (Preece and Mullineaux 1996). Where several secured creditors are involved, further negotiations may take place in the form of workout.

A lender is likely to require regular financial reporting as a contractual obligation during the duration of any secured contract. This disclosure may be in addition to any listing requirements. Regular financial reporting allows the lender to make a systematic assessment of the debtor's financial stability and make timely decisions to intervene in the borrower's business or invoke a formal rescue process should the debtor default. The extent to which such monitoring and intervention is possible will depend on the resources available and the priority which is given to the activity. Nevertheless such explicit monitoring, particularly with large corporate loans, is becoming increasingly evident and the costs of such monitoring are likely to be included as a charge to borrowers in the original loan contract (Preece and Mullineaux 1996). Where such borrowing conditions are in place, this represents a marked change in the degree of control that directors have over the activities of the company, and a marked shift in conventional patterns of governance away from director focus on shareholder priorities. Companies are likely to experience a virtual transition of control of many strategic aspects of the company from the board of directors to lenders.

The lender's control over secured assets depends on the nature of the assets and the type of security interests created. Historically, lenders were able to rely on freedom of contract to obtain security interests on any tangible or intangible assets that the company owned. However, English courts began to make a distinction between fixed charges and floating charges based on the nature of assets. Judicial decisions have defined floating charges as those which can be obtained on "a class of corporate assets" that are "present and future" with the possibility of "change" at the discretion of management during the ordinary course of business (*Re Yorkshire Woolcombers Association*). Assets subject to a floating charge can be used in the ordinary course of business. Unless lenders restrict the debtor's ability to dispose of those assets or create other charges on them, they do not have any claims to specific assets unless there is a breach of contract by the debtor. When the debtor defaults, the floating charge crystallises to a fixed charge and becomes payable.

The ability of the lender to create a charge on the debtor's assets has been modified following the judicial decision in *Re Spectrum Plus*. In that case, the House of Lords reversed the decision of the Court of Appeal and held that a charge created over book debts was a floating charge although it was contractually drafted as a fixed charge. The lender had obtained the charge in the form of a debenture following the provision of an overdraft facility to the debtor's current account. The contract described the charge as "a specific charge on all book debts and other debts now and from time-to-time due or owing to the debtor" which seemed to meet the description of a fixed charge under common law principles. The decision relied on the fact that the chargor had control over the assets subject to charge and could withdraw from the relevant account without requiring permission from the bank.

Security interests are included in different forms in loan contracts. A negative pledge is a common feature of secured transactions.

Negative pledges may be used in various areas. For example, a secured creditor may restrict management's sale of secured assets without its permission. It may also restrict management's plan for further secured borrowing unless specific requirements are met. The lender may introduce such a covenant taking the view that the corporate debtor should have more commitment to its business "if it has a more substantial stake in the business – more to gain and more to lose" (Mann 1997). The existence of negative pledges on future borrowing has considerable implications for company directors since security interests must be registered with Companies House and therefore they are in the public domain.[3] It is unlikely that other lenders will jeopardise their interests by violating such negative pledges. In effect, existing lenders retain control over future debt financing with the potential consequence that the company has to revert to its existing lenders for further borrowing.

It has been suggested that the use of negative pledges for further borrowing may be a less problematic issue for public companies due to the level of examination of the borrowers' affairs, their need to return to the debt market and the likelihood of the loss of credit if these companies breach such negative pledges (Mann 1997). However these issues are very complex where the company is not one single legal entity but part of a corporate group and lending relationships may involve different lenders, the parent company and different subsidiaries.

In some circumstances lenders may strengthen their contractual position by including a clause on default, creating a specified time limit and including an acceleration clause that makes the whole debt immediately due and payable. The secured creditor reserves the right to pursue a remedy by taking legal action against the corporate debtor or immediately collecting the total debt due together with interest and associated costs. It may also reserve the right for the debtor to seek renegotiation.

Taken collectively, the rights that secured borrowing can create for creditors have major implications for the governance of financially distressed companies. These rights have increasing impact when the need for the continuation or extension of borrowing increases. There is currently no formal regulatory framework that regulates this process, with the presumption that companies freely choose to accept constraints on their ability to make commercial decisions as a consequence of entering into agreements with lenders.

Unsecured creditors: The response of unsecured creditors to debtors' payment default is different from that of secured creditors. It is hard to argue that unsecured creditors have any direct influence on board change, asset sale and equity issue. The active role of unsecured creditors in informal rescue depends on their resources and ability to bear risks. If the debtor continues to fail to pay their claims, creditors may individually seek judicial intervention and a winding-up order. However, not every company may be actually wound up provided that it is balance sheet solvent.

Unlike a formal insolvency regime, in situations where companies are financially distressed there is no collective mechanism to protect unsecured creditors. Therefore, each creditor acts individually, based on its own self-interest. In general, a creditor has the option of continuing its contractual relationship with the corporate debtor to avoid disruption of its own business, and may extend further credit to the distressed company, agree an extension to the time limit for repayment of debt or attempt to renegotiate the interest rate on the amount owing to compensate for costs. The use of these options depends on the individual creditor's resources, the commercial importance of its relationship with the debtor, and the debtor's willingness to agree to such changes.

Creditors with less resources, such as small independent contractors, may reject these alternatives. Whilst they may be faced with a difficult decision to lose an important contract, they may ultimately terminate their contractual relationship with the company and attempt to find a solution for the payment of outstanding claims. Creditors with greater resources may show greater flexibility and a willingness to take risks depending on the continuing creditworthiness of the debtor company. If the company ultimately loses its credit rating, such creditors may refuse to continue a business relationship.

Quasi-security interests such as the retention of title allow suppliers as creditors to retain their ownership of goods until they are paid for, and request their return should the debtor go into a formal insolvency procedure. However, these creditors will face a moratorium if administration is invoked, and have difficulty in recovering their assets if they have changed in nature or cannot be tracked.

Large suppliers may use credit insurance to safeguard their position when they sell their products to particular clients. When insurers decline or refuse to continue cover, such companies are likely to terminate contracts as soon as they find that their interests will not be protected. The unilateral suspension or termination of such supplier contracts is likely to present significant problems, worsening cash flow and ultimately the company's ability to continue as a going concern. It is beyond the scope of this book to consider how credit insurance ratings ultimately limit the freedom of action of directors in financially distressed companies, but there is clearly a potential for major influence. When unsecured creditors choose to discontinue their relationship with a financially distressed company, their withdrawal of support may lead rapidly to the failure of informal rescue and the initiation of a formal insolvency regime.

Director Liabilities During Financial Distress and Insolvency

In solvent companies, individual directors do not owe any fiduciary duty to creditors. In general, creditors are "voluntary participants" who enter the life cycle of a company after mutual "negotiations" and contractual agreement with management (Easterbrook and Fischel 1991). The nature of any agreement between such participants and the company is formalised in contracts that set out the obligations and interests of the respective parties. Such core contracts play a significant role in the life of large public companies that rely upon the supply of finance, goods and services from many different and varied sources. Easterbrook and Fischel also include contracts made by representatives, that is, contracts made by banks on behalf of investors and contracts with equity trustees on behalf of bondholders. Contracts vary in terms, time limit and mutual obligations between the parties.

In theory, all contractual parties ultimately have equal rights to seek an independent judgment from the courts for the recovery of financial losses as creditors. In practice, contracts may not provide an ideal protective mechanism for creditors partly because the power of a litigating creditor to fully recover its interests depends on the terms of the contract and the creditor's standing. For example, should the company enter a formal insolvency regime, unsecured creditors would have the least priority in terms of recovery of their interests compared to other creditors, that is, secured creditors or preferential creditors.

UK common law does not consider any fiduciary relationship between directors and creditors during financial distress. Historically creditors have been regarded as parties with certain statutory rights that may be invoked against a company and its members under a formal insolvency procedure. However, UK statutory law and the courts have not given much consideration or importance to the matter, which might have influenced directors' continued commitment to shareholder interests rather than a shift to creditor interests. This is illustrated in *Multinational Gas & Petrochemical Co v Multinational Gas & Petrochemical Services Ltd.*, where Lord Justice Dillon stated:

> "A company ... owes no duty of care to future creditors. The directors indeed stand in a fiduciary duty to the company, as they are appointed to manage the affairs of the company and they owe fiduciary duties to the company not to the creditors, present or future or to individual shareholders."

A more consistent approach was developed by UK courts in determining directors' personal liabilities in insolvent companies, leading to the imposition of fines and other civil penalties. This was applied where legal actions were brought by liquidators or administrators under different statutory provisions, to impose financial liabilities on former company directors of insolvent companies if they had little or nothing available to pay unsecured creditors. These liabilities were imposed only if one or more directors were held to be liable for acts of misfeasance, wrongful trading or fraudulent trading.

In *West Mercia Safetywear Ltd. v Dodd,* Dillon J stated that "when a company is insolvent, the interests of creditors should override those of shareholders since they are the actual owners of the company's assets". In *Winkworth v Edward Baron Development Co Ltd.*, the House of Lords upheld the decision of the Court of Appeal that a husband and wife who were the sole directors of a company were held to be in breach of their duties to the company and its creditors by using bank borrowings for their own personal needs. In *Facia Footwear Ltd. v Hinchcliffe* it was held that if the Group and its subsidiary were in a "dangerous financial position, the directors owed a duty to take account of the interests of creditors". In a more recent judgment (*Re Pantone 485 Ltd., Miller v Bain*) it was held that general creditors "form the human equivalent of the company for the purpose of the directors' fiduciary duties". Other case law has also supported the existence of such duties when directors have been found liable for their breach.

UK common law has recognised director duties to creditors when the company is not hopelessly insolvent. In *Colin Gwyer & Associates Ltd. v London Wharf (Limehouse) Ltd.*, the Chancery Division stated that,

> "Where a company was insolvent or of doubtful solvency or on the verge of insolvency and its was the creditors' money which was at risk, the directors when carrying out their duty to the company must consider the interests of the creditors as paramount and take those into account when exercising their discretion."

However, in this case, the court did not provide any definition of "doubtful solvency" or "on the verge of insolvency". This might imply that insolvency practitioners should consider a wider timeframe before the company becomes insolvent in order to challenge the fulfilment of director duties.

Transition of director focus from shareholder interests to creditor interests has been associated with the loss of shareholder interests and creditor vulnerability to directors' excessively risky decisions. According to Mokal (2000), directors retain their discretion to manage corporate wealth and carry out their statutory duties but creditors rather than shareholders are more likely to benefit from their shift in focus. The extent of this shift of duty and its precise timing is not clear and the legislation has also remained silent on the matter. Davies (2006) has suggested that it might be possible to see some company directors taking on "projects with a negative present value" as the company's solvency worsens, since the burden of such risks will be imposed on unsecured creditors whose interests are unprotected.

In public companies there are typically mechanisms in place to assist shareholders and creditors to protect their interests (Hu and Westbrook 2007). For example, the Companies Act 2006 mandates the company directors of medium and large companies to provide an annual review of the company's business performance. The mandatory disclosure of cash flow and balance sheet information is designed to provide a summary statement of the company's position at a specific point in time. However, this information might not be of great help to shareholders or creditors since it may not be regularly updated, especially when the company is financially distressed. Neither is there a requirement to provide detailed information on individual contracts that the company has with different creditors. Public companies are also mandated to comment publicly on how the company's business over the year ahead is likely to be influenced by external and internal risks, and provide a prospective strategy for managing relationships with stakeholders such as employees, environment and the community. Directors retain considerable discretion in modifying such strategies. They may also limit the disclosure of information in areas such as potential redundancy, and disposal of the business in part or as a whole. In financially distressed companies, the board may delay the release of the annual report to maintain shareholder confidence.

English law provides limited means for individual creditors to enforce their own interests. Their remedy exists in the protective mechanisms that the law of contract or security provides (albeit at a cost) if the company is solvent and outside a formal insolvency procedure. Any potential claims are made ex post, that is, retrospectively and collectively, if the company is deemed insolvent and unable to maintain its status as a going concern. Unlike shareholders, creditors do not have an individual right to challenge directors for breach of duty when the company is placed into a formal insolvency procedure although they replace shareholders as the "residual" claimants. It is left to the liquidator or insolvency practitioner to bring such an action against former company directors.

In financially distressed companies, company directors can be held personally liable for any harm caused to general creditors only if the company continues to trade and becomes balance sheet insolvent with the prospect of insolvent liquidation. Section 214 of the Insolvency Act 1986 identifies wrongful trading by a former director of an insolvent company as a civil wrong that potentially obliges that director to contribute to the assets of the company from his own personal wealth. This provision is effectively an exception to *Salomon v Salomon* since it does not make any distinction between corporate assets and those of directors. The pursuit of directors for wrongful trading can only be exercised by a liquidator who has been appointed to deal with the debtor's assets who may seek remedy for the losses suffered by creditors. However, this action is subject to sufficient funding being available to support the costs of litigation. Furthermore, any financial remedy that is obtained belongs to the company and is distributed amongst unsecured and preferential creditors, and so charge holders do not get paid first from proceeds of assets sales.

Under section 214(2)(b) of the Insolvency Act 1986, directors may face personal liability due to wrongful trading if they "knew or ought to have concluded that there was no reasonable prospect that the company would avoid going into insolvent liquidation". The court may order directors to pay an amount to the pool of assets to compensate the company and creditors if it is not satisfied that the director "took every step with a view to minimising the potential loss to the company's creditors". Courts have taken the view that neither financial distress on its own nor the company's decision to continue to trade in a balance sheet insolvent company establishes grounds for a director's personal liability per se (e.g. *Re Purpoint Ltd*). Neither case is a reason for the mandatory closure of a business. The courts have acknowledged the double-edged sword that directors face in dealing with financially distressed companies. In *Re Continental Assurance Co of London plc (in liquidation) (No 4)*, Park J pointed out the difficulty that directors have in determining the continuation of a financially distressed business and the civil liability that they may be subjected to. His justice stated:

> *"An overall point which needs to be kept in mind throughout is that, whenever a company is in financial trouble and the directors have a difficult decision to make whether to close down and go into liquidation, or whether instead to trade on and hope to turn the corner, they can be in a real and unenviable dilemma. On the one hand, if they decide to trade on but things do not work out and the company, later rather sooner, goes into liquidation, they may find themselves in the situation of the respondents in this case – being sued for wrongful trading. On the other hand, if the directors decide to close down immediately and cause the company to go into early liquidation although they are not at risk of being sued for wrongful trading, they are at risk of being criticised on other grounds."*

Common law has taken into account directors' knowledge and their attempt to foresee and avoid the company's insolvent liquidation, as a crucial factor in determining their liability. This was addressed by Lewison J in *Re Hawkes Hill Publishing Co Ltd. (in liquidation)* where he stated that directors are not "clairvoyant" and may make mistakes as to their "rational expectations" of the company's potential future. However, directors' lack of actual knowledge of whether the company may or may not avoid insolvent liquidation needs be taken into account to determine their liability. In *Singla v Hedman*, the sole director and shareholder of a small company did not make any effort to familiarise himself with the financial information of the company. He had no personal stake in the business and had ignored the difficulties that potential insolvency would create for creditors. The court found him liable for wrongful trading as he "was quite prepared to chance his arm". He had a "forlorn hope" as he "gambled" everything with the belief that something "miraculously" would happen.

Directors' production of detailed and correct financial records is evidence of their attention to the company's solvency. In *Re Purpoint*, company directors failed to grasp the degree of the company's insolvency since they had no proper financial records relating to the company's "cash flow forecasts or calculations of the company's net worth". Its bank statements, a wages book and a cash book were the only "exiguous accounting records" to determine the company's financial health. The directors failed to improve revenue and reached a stage where creditors had to resort to county court judgments or debt collection agencies to recover their debt. Similarly, in *Roberts v Frohlich* two directors were held liable for wrongful trading. Despite regular losses, a frequent need for cash injection through director loans, the high costs of employing inefficient staff and hard-to-sell products, no full financial records were maintained by directors.

Courts have shown a reluctance to hold company directors liable if they can demonstrate that they took "a wholly responsible and conscientious attitude" in their management of the company's financial distress and insolvency. Directors' overall conduct in dealing with the company's debt and its distressed situation rather than individual decisions has been taken into account. Courts have adopted an objective approach in examining directors' liability, examining the decisions they made and implemented that might be deemed to have sought to benefit the company, irrespective of whether such decisions may have ultimately been unsuccessful.

In *Re Continental Assurance*, the court dismissed claims for directors' personal liability since there was clear evidence that they approached the company's financial problem in a "direct, close, and frequent" manner. The company directors regularly attended board meetings and sought financial information in a conscious and deliberate attempt to ensure that the company avoided insolvent trading. Similarly, in *Re Langreen Ltd.*, the directors' approach to the company was described as "practical and pragmatic" as they changed the company's unworkable business plan and took personal risks by investing in the company to improve the business after they failed to find external sources of financing. They also engaged actively with creditors to manage the company's debt. A similar approach was adopted by the court in *Re Hawkes Hill Publishing*. In that case, a court declined to hold a company director and the secretary of a small publishing company liable for wrongful trading where there was evidence that they withdrew no salaries for themselves, reduced the workforce to minimise costs and tried to find investors for the business. Their decision followed the advice of their chartered accountant who suggested that the company had "a promising future" and they should either sell it or find sources of cash injection.

Directors' joint and several liability prevents them from leaving their responsibilities to others as an excuse or credible argument for a lack of knowledge of insolvency. A hands-off approach to distress is unacceptable, as is irresponsible delegation of director duties. In *Re Brian Pierson (Contractors) Ltd.*, a wife who despite her directorship had little practical involvement in the company's business was held to be jointly responsible for insolvent trading on the basis that she must have felt obliged to giving "some consideration to the company's affairs", rather than taking the role of "a sleeping director". Similarly, in *Re Kudos Business Solutions Limited,* the sole shareholder and director of a small business who was the sole signatory of the company's bank account and an expert in the business the company was running left all his responsibilities to a member of staff without "putting in place any safeguards" for company creditors. When the company was distressed, the shareholding director took no action to ensure the company had financial reports and accounts. He also failed to "supervise" or "regulate" his decisions over the going concern of the company. Neither did he make any arrangement to provide services to creditors who had paid for such services under contracts.

The judicial approach to determine wrongful trading has taken into account the difference in the roles of non-executive and executive directors and has viewed the conduct of non-executive directors with a degree of leniency. Non-executive directors are perceived to have a monitoring function that cannot extend to "overrule" or replace the role of executive directors. Therefore, the courts may consider their liability to be different from that of executive directors. In *Langreen*, an honest and reliable couple who—as non-executive directors—actively supported the business with continued investment in a private company, actively managed debts, negotiated with creditors, attended regular board meetings and had taken steps to improve cash flow and reduce outgoings, were not regarded as being in the same position as the executive director who had expertise in the business area, developed and adopted the business strategy, and was involved in the day-to-day business of the company.

Wrongful trading by directors does not appear to be as common in large public companies. This might perhaps be due to the considerable requirements of disclosure of information in such companies under statutory law and listing rules. Since it is likely that these companies also use secured borrowing when the company enters financial distress, it is likely that lenders exercise a high degree of influence and control over board decisions, making unlawful trading extremely unlikely. The recent case of *Farepak* is an example of such influence. Chapters 7 to 11 also demonstrate such influence in each of the five case studies.

Wrongful trading requires the liquidator to submit sufficient factual evidence on the directors' failure to minimise the losses to creditors. S/he must be able to indicate the exact date or dates and events, leading to the company entering insolvent liquidation. A liquidator may find it difficult to establish how breach of duty by company directors caused the company to enter insolvent liquidation. A liquidator's decision to challenge former directors or his success in holding them personally accountable depends on the quality and the content of information documented during the days or months before the company is subject to investigation under insolvency law. S/he may also find it difficult to establish the exact value of financial losses that the company has incurred resulting in harm to creditors' interests. Insolvency and the adoption of hindsight to the review of directors' conduct do not in themselves establish sufficient proof of wrongful trading.

Concluding Remarks

This chapter has taken a detailed look at the roles of key parties in situations of informal rescue. Throughout the chapter there are references to the limitations of conventional governance models, which appear to have been developed for situations of business continuity rather than resolving financial distress. In particular it is evident that the role of directors as the agents of the company, empowered to make decisions in the interests of shareholders, is increasingly eroded by a worsening financial position. Each of the informal rescue options brings new influences on the strategy and direction of the company, with secured creditors (lenders) increasingly dominant in influencing the decisions of the board.

Some attention has been paid to the potential of large institutional shareholders to become involved in the decisions of the company, through the appointment of their own nominees. However, the majority of shareholders appear to adopt a relatively passive approach to activities such as director change, asset sale and equity issue. Unsecured creditors, particularly suppliers of goods and services, also appear to take a passive approach, perhaps because they rely on the goodwill of the debtor company and are reluctant to damage this goodwill by withholding supply, which would also damage their own cash flow.

Notes

1. IA 1986, s 248(b). A security interest created by mortgage requires the "transfer of ownership" whilst a charge may be created on the "proceeds of debtor's property for satisfaction of debt due". Lien allows a secured creditor to maintain the retention of possession until full payment of debt. A mortgage requires transfer of ownership.
2. Under rule 10.8 of the *Financial Conduct Authority Handbook*, a financially distressed company may obtain a waiver with regard to seeking shareholder approval when asset sale is initiated.
3. See CA 2006, s 741 relating to registration of debentures and part 25 relating to charges and their registration.

Bibliography

Asquith, Paul and David W. Mullins. 1986. "Equity Issues and Offering Dilution." *Journal of Financial Economics* 15(1–2): 61–89.

Barclay, Michael, Clifford G. Holderness, and Dennis P. Sheehan. 2007. "Private Placements and Managerial Entrenchment." *Journal of Corporate Finance.* 13(4): 461–484.

Burton, Bruce, Christine Helliar, and David Power. 2005. "Practitioner Perspective on the Seasoned Equity Offering Process in the UK." *British Accounting Review* 37(2): 153–175.

Carlson, David Gray. 1994. "On the Efficiency of Secured Lending." *Virginia Law Review* 80(8): 2179–2213.
Chynoweth, Carly. 2013. "Insolvent? Don't Do a Runner: Non-executive Directors Face Huge Challenges When a Company Hits Trouble, but Quitting Is the Wrong Option, Reports Carly Chynoweth." *Sunday Times*, April 28.
Davies, Paul. 2006. "Directors' Creditor-Regarding Duties in Respect of Trading Decisions Taken in the Vicinity of Insolvency." *European Business Organization Law Review* 7(1): 301–337.
Dierkens, Nathalie. 1991. Information Asymmetry and Equity Issues. *Journal of Financial and Quantitative Analysis* 26(2): 181–199. https://doi.org/10.2307/2331264
Dittmar, Amy and Anjan Thakor. 2007. "Why Do Firms Issue Equity?" *The Journal of Finance* 62(1): 1–54.
Easterbrook, Frank H. and Daniel R. Fischel. 1990. "The Corporate Contract." in *Corporate Law and Economic Analysis*, edited by Lucian Arye Bebchuk. New York: Cambridge University Press.
Elloumi, Fathi and Jean-Pierre Gueyie. 2001. "Financial Distress and Corporate Governance: An Empirical Analysis." *Corporate Governance: The international journal of business in society* 1(1): 15–23.
Ferran, Ellis. 1988. "Floating Charges – The Nature of the Security." *Cambridge Law Journal* 47(2): 213–237.
Gilson, Stuart C. 1989. "Management Turnover and Financial Distress." *Journal of Financial Economics* 25(2): 241–262. https://doi.org/10.1016/0304-405X(89)90083-4
Goode, Royston Miles. 1988. *Legal Problems of Credit and Security*. 2nd ed. London: Sweet & Maxwell.
Harpum, Charles, Stuart Bridge, and Martin J. Dixon. 2012. *Megarry & Wade: The Law of Real Property*. 8th ed. London: Sweet & Maxwell.
Hu, Henry T. C. and Jay Lawrence Westbrook. 2007. "Abolition of the Corporate Duty to Creditors." *Columbia Law Review* 107(6): 1321–1403.
Kim, E. Han and Amiyatosh K. Purnanandam. 2006. "Why Do Investors React Negatively to Seasoned Equity Offerings?." *Ross School of Business Working Series* No. 1043, 31. http://deepblue.lib.umich.edu/bitstream/handle/2027.42/48733/1043-EHanKim.pdf?sequence=1. Accessed December 23, 2013.
Langevoort, Donald C. 2004. "Resetting the Corporate Thermostat: Lessons from the Recent Financial Scandals About Self-Deception, Deceiving Others

and the Design of Internal Controls." *Georgetown Law Journal* 93(1): 285–317.
Mann, Ronald J. 1997. "Explaining the Pattern of Secured Credit." *Harvard Law Review.* 110(3): 625–683.
Mattioli, Dana, Joann S. Lublin, and Rachel Emma Silverman. 2011. "Corporate News: Bad Call: How Not to Fire a Worker – In the Wake of Bartz's Departure from Yahoo, Common Practices Get a New Look." *Wall Street Journal*, September 9.
McCormack, Gerard. 2004. *Secured Credit under English and American Law.* Cambridge: Cambridge University Press.
McCormack, Gerard. 2009. *Registration of Company Charges.* 3rd ed. Bristol: Jordan Publishing Limited.
Milman, David. 2013. *Governance of Distressed Firms.* Cheltenham: Edward Elgar Publishing.
Modigliani, Franco and Merton H. Miller. 1963. "Corporate Income Taxes and the Cost of Capital: A Correction." *American Economic Review* 53(3): 433–443.
Mokal, Rizwaan J. 2000. "An Agency Cost Analysis of the Wrongful Trading Provisions: Redistribution, Perverse Incentives and the Creditors' Bargain." *Cambridge Law Journal* 59(2): 335–369.
Neate, Rupert and Jill Treanor. 2013. "Chief Executive of Hovis Owner Premier Foods Quits after 18 Months." *Guardian*, January 28. http://www.theguardian.com/business/2013/jan/28/premier-foods-new-chief-executive
Pearce, John A. and Keith Robbins. 1993. "Towards Improved Theory and Research on Business Turnaround." *Journal of Management* 19(3): 613–636.
Preece, Dianna and Donald J. Mullineaux. 1996. "Monitoring, Loan Renegotiability, and Firm Value: The Role of Lending Syndicates." *Journal of Banking & Finance* 20(3): 577–593.
Rigby, Elizabeth and Kiran Stacey. 2008. "Last of Credit Insurers Pulls Out of Woolies." *Financial Times*, October 8. 23.
Sengupta, Partha. 1998. "Corporate Disclosure Quality and the Cost of Debt." *Accounting Review* 73(4): 459–474.
Short, Helen and Kevin Keasey. 1999. "Managerial Ownership and the Performance of Firms: Evidence from the UK." *Journal of Corporate Finance* 5(1): 79–101.
Stoll, John D. and Sharon Terlep. 2008. "Corporate News: GM Board's Support of CEO Continues; Wagoner Gets Backing Despite Recent Losses; Delivering on Promises." *Wall Street Journal*, August 6. B.3

Thomas, Nathalie. 2013. "Troubled FirstGroup Announces Rights Issue as Chairman Martin Gilbert Steps Down." *Telegraph*, May 20.
Tomlinson, Lawrence. 2013. "Banks' Lending Practices: Treatment of Businesses in Distress." *Tomlinson Report*. Accessed November 15, 2017. http://www.tomlinsonreport.com/docs/tomlinsonReport.pdf
Wilke, John R., 1994. "Striving to Adapt: At Digital Equipment, A Resignation Reveals Key Problem: Selling -Moving Goods but Making Scant Profit, Firm Ousts Head of Its Sales Force—Board Puts Pressure on CEO." *Wall Street Journal*, April 26. A1
Worthington, Sarah. 2006. "Floating Charges: The Use and Abuse of Doctrinal Analysis." In *Company Charges: Spectrum and Beyond*, edited by Joshua Getzler and Jennifer Payne. Oxford: Oxford University Press.
Wruck, Karen Hopper. 1989. "Equity Ownership Concentration and Firm Value: Evidence from Private Equity Financings." *Journal of Financial Economics* 23(1): 3–28.
Wruck, Karen H. and Yilin Wu. 2009. "Relationships, Corporate Governance, and Performance: Evidence from Private Placements of Common Stock." *Journal of Corporate Finance* 15(1): 30–47.

Cases

Brian Pierson (Contractors) Ltd, Re [2001] 1 BCLC 275.
Brightlife Ltd, Re [1987] Ch 200.
Buchler v Talbot [2004] UKHL 9.
Clydebank Football Club Ltd v Steedman 2002 SLT 109.
Colin Gwyer & Associates Ltd v London Wharf (Limehouse) Ltd [2003] 2 BCLC 153.
Continental Assurance Co of London plc (in liquidation) (No 4), Re; Singer v Beckett [2007] 2 BCLC 287.
Cubelock, Re [2001] BCC 523.
Facia Footwear Ltd (in administration) v Hinchcliffe [1998] 1 BCLC 218.
Hawkes Hill Publishing Co Ltd (in liquidation), Re [2007] BCC 937 [45].
Illingworth v Houldsworth [1904] AC 355.
Kudos Business Solutions Ltd, Re [2012] 2 BCLC 65.
Langreen Ltd (in liquidation), Re (October 21, 2011, unreported).
Multinational Gas & Petrochemical Co v Multinational Gas & Petrochemical Services Ltd [1983] Ch 258.
Pantone 485 Ltd, Re [2002] 1 BCLC 266.

Produce Marketing Consortium Ltd (No 2), Re [1989] BCLC 520.
Purpoint Ltd, Re [1991] BCLC 49.
Roberts v Frohlich [2011] 2BCLC 625.
Salomon v Salomon & Co Ltd [1897] AC 22.
Singla v Hedman [2010] 2 BCLC.
Spectrum Plus Ltd, Re [2005] UKHL 41 [95] (Lord Scott).
West Mercia Safetywear Ltd v Dodd [1988] BCLC 250.
Winkworth v Edward Baron Development Co Ltd [1987] BCLC 193.
Yorkshire Woolcombers Association, Re [1903] 2 Ch 284 at 295.

5

Corporate Governance in Insolvency

Overview

This chapter examines the impact of the commencement of formal insolvency procedures on corporate governance. The discussion begins with an examination of the fundamental nature of a CVA and the influence of secured and unsecured creditors and shareholders on the process. Whilst directors may retain general control of the operations of the company during a CVA, an increasing level of influence passes to secured creditors. By virtue of their security interests and contractual position, lenders are able to exert control over any strategic decisions. The second part of the chapter then focuses on administration, where the control of the company is transferred to an insolvency practitioner, who is ultimately responsible for ensuring that the claims of creditors are met, within existing contractual relationships, determining the long-run financial viability of the company and the reality of closure when the financial position is no longer sustainable.

As a company enters a CVA or administration, existing frameworks of governance are challenged by new circumstances, and the review identifies several significant areas where there are as yet no regulatory mechanisms in place to safeguard the interests of the different parties. The influence of creditors—specifically lenders—potentially increases when the company enters administration and insolvency practitioners replace directors in the company. The review also seeks to analyse how far other elements such as post-administration financing limit or enhance the degree of governance that can be exercised by secured creditors.

Company Voluntary Arrangement (CVA)

Board of directors' role: Chapter 3 introduced the CVA as a formal rescue process involving insolvency practitioners, company directors, unsecured creditors and shareholders. These parties are connected through individual contracts with the company which may include specific covenants that are unique to each party. Unsecured creditor approval as well as shareholder approval must be sought and obtained before any proposed CVA can be implemented. In addition secured creditors may have a significant and influential role in the process, both in endorsing any proposed arrangements and in providing interim finance whilst any CVA is implemented. Such influence is implicit and indirect.

When a company is managed outside a formal insolvency regime, company directors retain exclusive power to propose and initiate a CVA. This feature makes a CVA similar to Chapter 11 of the US Bankruptcy Code where companies continue to be run by incumbent managers. It also allows shareholders to maintain their residual position as they retain their right to vote because the company continues as a going concern. However, in a formally insolvent company, the power to propose a CVA lies exclusively in the hands of a liquidator or administrator. Unlike administration, there is no parallel statutory power for creditors to invoke a CVA. Nor is there such a power for shareholders.

As Chap. 3 discussed, company directors are likely to be involved in different stages of a CVA including the appointment of an insolvency practitioner, the formulation of a CVA rescue plan, arranging separate creditor and shareholder meetings and implementing any final creditor-approved CVA. Self-serving company directors may prefer a

CVA to administration because a CVA allows them to retain their control over the company and they can get more involved in the decisions that help "reach a composition of debt" with the company's creditors whilst the company continues as a going concern (Tribe 2009). Before a CVA rescue proposal is formally presented to creditors for approval, company directors need to ensure that their plan is "the best option for the company". Since the plan requires formal support from the insolvency practitioner nominated to take over its implementation, it is reasonable to expect considerable interaction and co-ordination between company directors and the nominated practitioner. However, whilst the statutory provisions prescribe the individual roles of company directors and insolvency practitioners in such circumstances, the exact pattern of interaction and co-ordination remains unclear.

During the implementation of the CVA, company directors retain their control over the overall management of the company and may also pursue an informal rescue process such as asset sale or share issue. The case study of JJB Sports' first CVA presented in Chap. 8, demonstrates this situation. However, a CVA may not ultimately preserve the going concern nature of a company as it does not provide a moratorium for medium- or large-sized companies.

A CVA facilitates the gradual repayment of debt through a creditors' fund, managed and supervised by an insolvency practitioner of the directors' choice and approved by creditors. The insolvency practitioner should ensure that the CVA fund receives either regular payments to meet the claims of unsecured creditors or a specific one-off settlement. The insolvency practitioner is obliged to file information on the commencement and completion of the CVA. However, there is no statutory obligation to file periodic progress reports and therefore creditors may lack comprehensive and useful information about the progress of a CVA including any potential problems that may have arisen, creating a lack of transparency. Company directors have no statutory obligation to publicly report on the implementation of a CVA.

Creditor Influence

Secured creditors: A CVA proposal differs from an administrator's rescue plan, since it excludes the interests of secured and preferential creditors. The claims of such creditors must be protected before unsecured creditor claims can be considered through any proposed CVA. The influence of preferential creditors is not within the scope of this book. The implicit priority given to the claims of secured creditors ahead of any proposals for a CVA shows the privileged status of such creditors. This is not a problem if the company does not have any secured creditors. However, when the company has borrowed on a secured basis, lenders may influence the implementation of a CVA in various ways. Lack of any moratorium for large public companies makes such companies vulnerable to the threat of secured creditors enforcing their security rights unless company directors seek their prior agreement on any proposals.

There is no regulatory mechanism to govern lenders' response to any proposed CVA and lenders may pursue their own interests through objections or proposed modifications. Any response can be given additional weight where the board is dependent on further lender funding to support the implementation of the proposed CVA. Lenders may make the implementation of a CVA a condition for the continuation of financial support. The company may also be required by lenders to complete other informal rescue options in parallel with the proposed CVA. Secured creditors may also act in a self-interested way, perceiving any CVA to be a way of shifting potential losses to unsecured creditors. Lenders may seek opportunities to continue to provide financing if the company has strong balance sheet solvency, provided that they can monitor the implementation of any CVA.

Those lenders that are concerned about the depreciating value of their assets may enforce their security interests as soon as they find out about the company's plans to adopt a CVA, particularly if the company is not large (McCormack 2009). If the company defaults in payment of its secured debt and no further agreement is reached, the lenders may protect their interests by invoking their powers to appoint an administrator resulting in termination of the CVA. Termination of a CVA will incur unrecoverable losses for unsecured creditors especially if payment of their claims is conditional on the completion of the CVA.

Unsecured creditors: The CVA has been viewed as a "statutory contract" that follows unsecured creditors' "consensual agreement" and binds all such creditors (Ho 2008). In a financially distressed company that is cash flow insolvent, the implementation of a CVA proposal creates a new obligation for the company to those unsecured creditors whose contractual rights have been breached. Unlike contracts that require the consent of the individual parties, a CVA replaces all previous contracts with a new collective contract that is binding on unsecured creditors in general, whether or not they have voted in favour or abstained from voting.

Unlike administration, a CVA does not mandate the classification of creditors for voting purposes and therefore the type of claim does not have any impact on the weight of votes each unsecured creditor has. However, unsecured creditor votes are weighted by the amount of debt that each creditor is owed. The rescue proposal itself may also classify creditor claims to provide different terms for payment of different classes amongst unsecured creditors. Examples of such classifications may include overdue rent owed to landlords, debt owed to suppliers of goods or payments to HMRC.

In large public companies, intercompany debt related to transactions between companies may be included in a CVA with the effect that the subsidiaries to which debt is owed are entitled to take part in the voting process. In such a situation the insolvency practitioner may exercise a right to hold separate creditors' meetings for the parent company and each subsidiary. The rescue proposal may also include a condition that the CVA will be effective only if the rescue proposal receives majority support in every creditors' meeting in all subsidiary companies. Ultimately, creditors may be warned that should the CVA fail, there will be no other option than liquidation (or administration). Such an arrangement may result in the failure of any proposed CVA as the creditors of subsidiary companies are likely to vote in a self-interested way on any rescue proposal and it may be hard to get the majority of creditors in each subsidiary to vote in support.

As Chap. 3 discussed there is a mandatory requirement to hold a meeting before any CVA can be implemented at which unsecured creditors must be given the right to vote on any proposals. Any proposal is legally enforceable only when it is approved by a majority of unsecured creditors, and therefore directors' freedom to use this course of action to resolve financial distress is ultimately subject to creditor approval. Whilst company directors may have negotiated with creditors with substantial claims or special classes of claim during the formulation of the CVA proposal, they may not have sought the views of general creditors with smaller claims. A formal creditors' meeting provides the only forum for all creditors to seek more information and express their opposition or support in a formal vote on any proposed plan.

Creditors who object to the CVA proposals may challenge the authority of the insolvency practitioner to make specific proposals such as preferential treatment of some creditors within one class, for example landlords, at the expense of other creditors. Every creditor has the right to initiate a formal legal action against the decisions of the insolvency practitioner. In such circumstances a CVA cannot be enforced until the legal dispute is finalised. Given the cost of legal action, it is unlikely that a creditor with a relatively small stake in the company would challenge the decisions of the insolvency practitioner and therefore proposals for a CVA which have the support of major unsecured creditors are likely to succeed.

Shareholder Influence

Approval of a CVA ultimately depends on shareholders showing their support formally by voting on any proposal. Shareholder votes in favour need to be over 50% of the total votes of all shares represented at the designated meeting, regardless of shareholders voting in person or by proxy. As Chap. 2 discussed, dispersed individual shareholders may frequently be passive in such situations, although institutional shareholders may play a more active role. Shareholders are unlikely to challenge a CVA since it is a cost-effective way of increasing the company's chance of survival.

Administration

Directors' involvement theoretically ceases when they are discharged from their role as soon as the administrator is appointed, although they continue to contribute to the process by providing information and assistance. Where they are involved in pre-packaged administration they effectively become buyers of the going concern and may be expected to exercise more influence on the process.

Administrator's Role

An administrator is the agent of the company and must act in the best interests of creditors regardless of the interests of his appointors. In performing his duties, an administrator is legally recognised as operating as "the officer of the court". This recognition provides the power to act independently. The formal recognition of the administrator is facilitated by accrediting organisations that provide training and support for insolvency practitioners. Typically, such practitioners come from accountancy backgrounds although lawyers may also develop specific expertise in insolvency.

The Cork Report (1982) defined the role of the insolvency practitioner during administration as a "receiver and manager of the whole property and undertaking of a company" which reflects the leading role that accountants have tended to play during administration. Focus on financial issues such as the rescue of the company as a going concern, the payment of different financial claims and the ultimate disposition of the debtor's assets tend to dominate the agenda, placing stress on the importance of a financial background for administrators (Flood and Skordaki 1995). The legal implications of the procedure and the administrator's personal liability to creditors for their decisions make them potentially dependent on professional legal advice.

Competition between insolvency practitioners is not regulated, and there is no regulatory mechanism that determines the choice of insolvency practitioners as administrators. This is treated as a business matter for those making the appointment. Since the appointment of insolvency practitioners is regulated by professional accreditation and the skills and expertise required are frequently specialised, this may result in multiple appointments for a single insolvency practice, where such a practice has a good track record. For example, Deloitte were retained to manage the administration of Stylo plc, Waterford Wedgewood plc and Woolworths Group plc in the case studies featured in Chaps. 7, 9 and 10 respectively.

Evidence on the number of appointments held by one practitioner is anecdotal; however in one example, the retirement of one insolvency practitioner in one practice led to the replacement of the insolvency practitioner in more than 120 cases. Multiple appointments can potentially divide the time and focus of the administrator and potentially jeopardise the effectiveness of the rescue process. The Insolvency Act 1986 resolves the problem of multiple appointments by allowing the appointment of more than one administrator in a single insolvency case; however, it does not provide any guidance on circumstances where joint appointments should be made. Neither are there any guidelines on the maximum number of appointments that may be made in one case, leaving this to the discretion of those who have the power of appointment. Sections 101–103 of Schedule B1 of the Act allow joint appointments of insolvency practitioners with joint and several liability. The process of appointment of administrators and the relationships that develop between them and the board of the company remain comparatively unexplored in the academic literature, and there is very little literature on the dynamics of this relationship. Most of the comments that follow are restricted to the statutory duties of the administrator as prescribed by legislation.

Collaboration between joint administrators in a single corporate insolvency case is likely to expedite any potential rescue process and compensate for the negative effect that multiple appointments may have on each case. Administrators' fees are deducted from the proceeds of sale of corporate assets subject to qualifying floating charges. Due to the costs involved, joint appointments may be more likely to be considered in large companies where the large volume of assets and claims may require such appointments to achieve efficiency. In these companies, subsidiaries require separate appointments due to their separate legal entity status and potentially complex balance sheets.

The appointment of joint administrators may bring more focus to the rescue process. Their number may be increased or decreased by their appointors based on the level of work required. Lack of any mandatory requirement to appoint the same administrators of the parent company as administrators of subsidiaries may lead to confusion and delay in the resolution of the debt problem if different administrators are appointed for each company. This problem has been addressed in large companies by the appointment of joint administrators across the subsidiaries and the parent company. They may also vacate office due to a company's exit from administration, successful litigation by creditors, retirement, illness or death.

Although the appointment of joint administrators may help balance the workload to facilitate a speedy rescue process, it may harm the best interests of the company if administrators are involved in low-level tasks and administrative details. Insolvency law has remained silent as to the level of support that administrators can seek in managing their work. Administrators may exercise discretion in deploying a sufficient number of support staff. However, adding more support staff increases the costs of administration and reduces the proceeds of asset sales that could be distributed amongst creditors; therefore, indirect influence to control costs may be exercised by those creditors who have financial interests in such assets. This issue is identified in the discussion of the case study of Connaught plc in Chap. 11.

Management of the going concern: An administrator's involvement in the management of the business operation is based on three statutory "hierarchical objectives" (Sealy, Milman and Bailey 2018). The administrator must choose one of these objectives and formulate a proposal or a rescue plan. He must detail how he is going to pursue the rescue process and how corporate assets will be deployed or realised to settle creditor claims. Unlike solvent companies, where company directors are required to ensure the survival and growth of the company, the administrator has no obligation to keep the business going and his choice of statutory objectives reflects a commercial judgment influenced by the overall circumstances.

No statutory prescriptions have been set to determine how those objectives should be chosen. The only implicit guidance is that the rescue process should facilitate a practical rescue of the company, leading to better outcomes for company creditors compared with immediate corporate demise or repayment of secured or preferential debt. Alternatively, if the company can be disposed of as a going concern, this is more likely to be of benefit to creditors. Equally, administrators may seek to maintain the business as a going concern on a temporary basis to dispose of specific assets such as stock. In other words, the administrator should ensure the best interests of the company and its creditors by preserving the value of business and assets, rather than moving immediately to actions that lead to closure of the business (if administration is followed by liquidation and dissolution).

Where the administrator believes that the company should continue as a going concern, he may be required to set aside or modify contracts, which may involve negotiation with suppliers (typically unsecured creditors) of goods and services. Such suppliers may be prepared to continue to trade with the company, for the short term at least because of the significance of their vested interests and their concern to minimise their losses. Variations in approach in different situations are evident in the case studies in Chaps. 7 to 11.

Asset sale and recovery: Asset sale is a prerequisite to the payment of creditor claims. It remains the responsibility of the administrator. In an ideal situation, the administrator's primary concern for the company's best interests requires him to seek an independent valuation and marketing of assets through the deployment of specialist advisors. Such advisors are likely to play a significant role in large public companies when the volume of assets is substantial. However, it remains the administrator's responsibility to negotiate and finalise asset sale at the best possible price, subject to the confidential approval of secured creditors (see the case study Waterford Wedgwood Group plc in Chap. 9). The area of asset sale has not been addressed in detail in the literature. Chapters 7 to 11 review the approaches to asset sale adopted by the companies in each of the case studies, drawing out similarities and differences.

In those companies where asset sale is agreed prior to administration but finalised during administration, the company may be assumed to have been subject to a pre-packaged administration where the administrator facilitates the continuation of the business through sale to company directors or their nominees. The role of the administrator seems to be limited in such circumstances to ensuring that the transfer of assets and employees is completed. Typically the details of contractual arrangements between administrators, former company directors and secured creditors remain undisclosed in such circumstances. The existing rules on the administrator's powers during a pre-packaged administration do not seem to require further disclosure during the sales process.

The administrator's right to initiate asset sale is comparable to that of directors during financial distress. Asset valuation is time-consuming and assets may be varied and substantial in large complex businesses. If such assets are not rapidly sold their value may depreciate. To avoid such a problem, the administrators might prioritise asset sale, ahead of preparing a full rescue plan for creditor approval within the statutory time limit. Therefore no prior approval is sought from a creditors' meeting and it becomes a matter of disclosure of information. In cases where valuation and preliminary marketing have already taken place during financial distress, an administrator may expedite the sales process by seeking the temporary involvement of company directors, drawing on their expertise and experience. In a company where assets have insufficient value, further valuation and marketing may not be appropriate and the administrator has no other option other than to move to liquidation or dissolution. This might also happen where substantial assets have already been sold and the remaining assets do not have substantial value.

An administrator may also be involved in asset recovery where transaction at an undervalue becomes a matter of concern. This book does not examine this aspect of asset recovery. Asset recovery may also relate to the discovery of unknown assets at the time of administration. The case study Connaught plc in Chap. 11 provides an example of this situation, highlighting the problems that decisions made by company directors might create in this area in a large public company.

Distribution of proceeds to creditors: Settlement of creditor claims is a statutory responsibility for the administrator and of equal importance to his other obligations. A statutory priority ranking determines the order in which claims should be met. With the exception of qualifying floating charge holders (QFCHs), all secured creditors preserve their protected pre-administration position. Administration expenses also have a quasi-secured position, ranked ahead of preferential creditors and QFCHs. Unsecured creditors and shareholders have a residual position, and are paid after all other creditors. Payment of their claims may not be dealt with during administration and deferred to when the insolvent company enters liquidation.

An administrator has limited discretion in the payment of secured creditor claims and is not likely to be able to resist their demands. Payment to secured creditors is typically done by mutual agreement between administrators and secured creditors—the process can be viewed as a governance issue that has not been prescribed by law. A similar position does not exist for unsecured creditors. Depending on the agreement with administrators, secured creditors may be paid in cash, by acquisition of part of the business or secured assets. The case studies of Stylo plc and Connaught plc in Chaps. 7 and 11, respectively, give examples of these different types of payments.

The administrator is also able to pay his own remuneration and other expenses incurred during the process. Administrator remuneration is payable as either a percentage of the total asset value subject to administration or the number of hours spent on resolving the debt problem. Determining the level of administrators' fees can become a complex issue where more than one insolvency practitioner is involved and a different range of skills are deployed. Further, during administration, an administrator is also entitled to pay other expenses of administration that relate to deployment of the professional services obtained externally to facilitate the rescue process and any other costs. Administrators maintain the discretion to incur expenses that are essential in achieving a speedy rescue process. This was highlighted in *Powdrill v Watson* where Dillon LJ remarked:

> "It is well understood that administrators will, in the ordinary way, pay expenses of administration including the salaries and other payments to employees as they arise during the continuance of the administration. There is no need to wait until the end, and it would be impossible as a practical matter to do that."

In general, the expenses of administration are usually substantial and paid from the assets subject to floating charge. The scale of these expenses may trigger a monitoring role for QFCHs during administration, especially where the rate of recovery is low. The case study of Connaught plc in Chap. 11 is an example of the influence on administration expenses exerted by such creditors.

Unsecured creditors are able to approve administrators' fees and expenses in certain circumstances. An administrator should obtain their approval for proposed fee rates. Any potential dispute, although rare, may be resolved through judicial intervention. It appears that administration expenses is an area that is influenced primarily by secured creditors and unsecured creditors are unlikely to seek to play a substantial role. This is mainly due to the difficulties that unsecured creditors potentially face in exercising their voting rights.

An administrator may pay unsecured creditor claims on a collective basis (pari passu) after all claims are paid. However, this is rare. Under section 176A of the Insolvency Act 1986, he may pay creditors some dividends under the prescribed part depending on the total realisation of assets subject to QFC. However, the substantial costs of distribution may prevent such payments. In such cases, judicial intervention is required to ensure that such treatment of unsecured creditors interests is not in breach of the administrator's duties. It could be argued that administrators are less concerned about unsecured creditors even though their claims may be substantial compared with those of secured creditors. Unlike secured creditors, they are dispersed claimants, have no power of appointment and therefore are unlikely to play an active role.

Management of administration: As soon as administration commences, an administrator is mandated to carry out certain administrative tasks that ensure regular disclosure of information to creditors in general. Formulation and submission of an administration rescue plan allows the administrator to inform creditors of proposed rescue plans. Six-monthly progress reports are required to inform creditors of the progress of administration including asset sale, management of the going concern, payment of creditors' claims, any investigation into the conduct of company directors and the expenses of administration. There is typically no detailed public information in such reports on the nature of transactions and agreements between secured creditors and administrators and third parties. In effect, unsecured creditors remain relatively uninformed about the process.

Investigation into former director conduct: Insolvency law empowers the insolvency practitioner to initiate enquiries about the conduct of company directors and other connected parties who may have played a role in the management of the company prior to its insolvency. Such powers may be used to prepare an investigative report that may be used in out-of-court settlements or ultimately court proceedings against company directors. Section 234 of the Insolvency Act 1986 allows insolvency practitioners to seek a court order to recover "any property, books, papers or records".

Section 235 of the Act enhances the investigatory powers of the insolvency practitioner by imposing a statutory "duty to co-operate" on former and current company directors, employees and those who hold information about the company (e.g. lawyers, auditors or accountants), which in effect makes judicial intervention unnecessary. Both provisions may assist insolvency practitioners to gather information on the conduct of company directors with the potential of holding them personally liable under other statutory provisions.

English case law shows that the exercise of powers under sections 234–235 may sometimes be challenged as excessive, despite the possibility of a fine for failing to co-operate with the administrator. For example, in *GE Capital Commercial Finance Ltd. v Sutton* the insolvency practitioner's intent was to pass on confidential legal documents to a secured creditor, rather than statutory reporting, and in *Re London Iron & Steel Co Ltd.* the assets were subject to dispute and the insolvency practitioner wanted to use investigatory powers to recover those assets.

Under section 236 of the Act, administrators may seek judicial authorisation to "compel" the release of information relating to the conduct of former company directors. This provision enhances the investigative powers of insolvency practitioners to identify sensitive information relating to "the promotion, formation, business, dealings, affairs or property of the company". This information may form part of a confidential statutory report, to be submitted to the Insolvency Service, to consider further insolvency proceedings or procedures such as director disqualification.

A body of case law has developed around section 236 demonstrating that the application is not procedural and the outcome of any application depends on the grounds of enquiry set out by the insolvency practitioner as part of his written statement. The court maintains a wide discretion to consider a range of factors before it exercises its discretion to allow such an enquiry (Sealy, Milman and Bailey 2018). For instance, whilst the administrator's role as an officer of the court may be given "great weight", the court should also balance the need for such an enquiry with the "degree of oppression" that the respondent may go through. Setting an appropriate balance is a matter of judgment since the former company director or any other person subject to the court order is not notified of such an application. The courts have frowned on ex parte hearings in recent times. Even where a court order is obtained, the third party who is asked for such information may refuse to provide it if it has been given "in confidence".

Commencement of administration shifts control powers to the administrator with the effect that company directors are automatically discharged from their exclusive control of the company, its business management and debt resolution. Statute does not stipulate what company directors should do after they are discharged from their responsibilities. Common law also remains silent on this matter. Since executive directors no longer have any authority in the company they should be expected to resign following entry into administration. A similar rationale should apply to non-executive directors. Focus on creditor interests rather than shareholders marks the end of governance as typically defined for solvent companies. Therefore, administration should be followed by the immediate resignation of both executive and non-executive directors. However, this may not always be the case. Examples are given in each of the case studies in Chaps. 7 to 11.

Company directors typically possess confidential and sensitive information about the operations of the company. If the administrator aims to achieve a quick and efficient recovery for company creditors, then directors' familiarity with the business may have considerable value. Finch (2005) describes the incumbent management as "the major reservoir of relevant information" upon whom administrators depend. In this respect executive directors may be of more value than non-executive directors. However, their input to administration is limited to the provision of a statement of affairs and a statement of concurrence. This seems to be a formality, simply giving a summary of the company's assets and liabilities at book value and estimating the current expected realisable value. The statement of affairs is prepared and signed by at least one director. A separate statement of concurrence signed by the other company directors indicates their agreement with the information. In large public companies where administrators are involved this information is not likely to be detailed, and provides only basic financial information.

No research has been done to indicate how long directors tend to stay with the company and why some leave earlier than others. There is no published information on the extent to which directors leave the company before the company exits administration. The individual interests of company directors are preserved as their salaries will be considered as part of the expenses of administration generally having priority over creditor claims. Director salaries may also be modified by agreement with the administrator. Any director remuneration in such circumstances would in theory be measured against the value of any specialist advice or knowledge that he or she could give to the administrator.

Secured Creditor Influence

Appointment of administrators: The role of secured creditors in appointing administrators is conditional on the type of security interest and its timing. Secured creditors whose relationship with the company was created before September 15, 2003, including holders of fixed charges and mortgages are entitled to use receivership. Secured creditors whose lending relationship was based on a floating charge created after that date are expected to appoint administrators should the corporate debtor default. The powers of qualifying floating charge holders (QFCHs) may be invoked only if the corporate debtor breaches the debt covenants and defaults on its financial commitments.

The appointment of an administrator by a QFCH has priority over the appointment of an administrator by company directors and the former can challenge the company directors' choice of administrator. There is no parallel power for company directors to challenge the appointment of an administrator by a QFCH (*Closegate Hotel Development v McLean* [2013]). However QFCHs appear to rarely exercise their power of appointment. The company's entry into administration threatens the financial standing and reputation of company directors and the QFCH may use the power of appointment as a threat to compel company directors to appoint the administrator that it prefers, if company directors are reluctant to do so.

Whilst a QFCH may remain silent when they are happy with the appointment of the insolvency practitioner, they may challenge an appointment that is not from "a reputable firm". It has been suggested that the QFCH may prefer company directors to formally appoint the administrator to avoid any negative reputational impact on the charge holder, although they (QFCHs) make the actual nomination. According to Webb (1991), banks do not wish to be seen as "the party forcing the company into insolvency".

In large public companies, QFCHs may have a limited choice in terms of administrator appointment. The complexity of the rescue process in such companies has led to the development of a small number of insolvency practitioners who have developed sufficient expertise to deal with such companies.

A report by the Office of Fair Trading (OFT) shows that banks and other financial institutions that hold floating charges are "repeat players of insolvency cases" who base their choice of insolvency practitioners on the value of the secured debt. If QFCHs have operated as a syndicate represented by one leading bank, the same leading bank is likely to make decisions about the choice of insolvency practitioners. According to the report, holders of floating charges have a very limited choice of practitioner with the appropriate level of expertise once secured debt exceeds £2 m. In 52% of such insolvency cases examined, the appointment of insolvency practitioners is likely to be made from one of four large firms (known commonly as "the Big Four"), that is, Deloitte, Ernst & Young, KPMG and PricewaterhouseCoopers LLP (PWC). The case studies in Chaps. 7 to 11 confirm this since three appointments were from Deloitte and two were from KPMG.

The appointment of an administrator does not create any direct control over the affairs of a business for secured creditors. Insolvency legislation provides for an automatic moratorium that suspends the enforcement of creditors' contractual rights and security interests. Secured creditors maintain their right to continue contractual obligations with the insolvent debtor by providing further finance. Alternatively, they might choose to suspend or terminate their financial support which may eventually result in frustration of the going concern of the company and its access to funds (McCormack 2007).

Financing administration: Unlike Chapter 11 of the US Bankruptcy Code, UK legislation does not consider post-insolvency financing for administration. If a company does not have sufficient funds to implement administration, this may not be an option without secured creditor support. Financing the rescue process allows secured creditors to influence the administrator's decisions, the quality and outcomes of administration and its timeframe. This is often the case in large public companies where secured creditors are likely to agree to provide financing in advance of the rescue process to avoid any delay. Continued financial support may be needed to achieve the sale of assets and resolve the business interests of the company, particularly across a parent company and diverse group of subsidiaries.

Secured creditors' decisions to continue financing may be influenced by the administrators' rescue plan, particularly if this appears to benefit secured creditors at the expense of unsecured creditors. Secured creditors may also propose a plan for staged financing that links the continuation of financing to the completion of certain targets during administration. Lack of any monitoring mechanism to regulate secured creditors' behaviour gives them considerable scope to influence the process, especially as unsecured creditors generally appear to show little interest in monitoring the rescue process, even where a creditors' committee has been formed. The case study of Connaught plc in Chap. 11 illustrates such a situation.

The role of secured creditors in determining the duration of administration is partly addressed in the Insolvency Act 1986. Under paras 76 and 78 of Schedule B1 of the Act, the period of administration can be extended provided that the insolvency practitioner either applies to the court and obtains a relevant court order or seeks the individual consent of secured creditors regardless of the amount of their claims. There is no legislative guidance on the circumstances where such consent should be given, leaving this to the discretion of secured creditors. The extension of the period of administration adds to the expenses of this procedure and secured creditors are likely to push for speedy completion unless they can see a clear benefit.

Management of going concern and asset sale: Management of the going concern and the realisation of the debtor's assets is another area of potential influence for secured creditors. Insolvency law gives high priority to the rescue of the company as a going concern. It mandates full focus on secured creditor interests, where assets are not sufficient to pay other creditors. The existence of a moratorium preventing the enforcement of security interests does not imply that such interests should be abandoned. Insolvency legislation has implicitly encouraged the controlled involvement of secured creditors in the administration process, allowing them the option to "redeem [their] security" through the purchase of secured assets at a price that reflects the post-insolvency "valuation of secured assets". Secured creditors should also expect that the price "sets off" the value of their secured debt. A secured creditor may also seek to introduce new investors to opportunities to acquire secured assets although the ultimate decision over the sale is formally left to the administrator. The sale of Waterford Wedgwood to an investor facilitated by one of its lenders, the Bank of America, is such an example detailed in Chap. 9.

In large public companies, secured creditors are likely to have spread their security over all the assets of the parent company and its subsidiaries. Since assets in those companies vary in quality, the leading secured creditor is unlikely to redeem its security interests without considering their relative worth. The commercial judgment of the leading creditor and its access to private equity investors who work closely with it may result in the adoption of a cherry-picking approach that chooses the potentially most profitable assets. Such assets may include any going concern elements of the company. Examples include the approach adopted by the Bank of America to the sale of Waterford Wedgwood, as well as the lenders' approach to the acquisition of Connaught Environmental, a subsidiary of Connaught plc, detailed in the cases presented in Chaps. 9 and 11, respectively.

A QFCH may also wish to influence the amount that unsecured creditors are entitled to receive under the "prescribed part". Under section 176(1) of the Insolvency Act 1986, a percentage of the assets subject to floating charge should be used to meet the claims of unsecured creditors. This does not apply to fixed charges. Since a QFCH has better bargaining powers where new debt financing or debt negotiation is an option, it may decide to create a combination of fixed and floating charge as well as mortgages on the same assets to avoid such liability prior to the company's insolvency. It is also possible to change floating charges to fixed charges as the company becomes dangerously distressed.

Setting administrators' fees: Insolvency legislation provides secured creditors with an exclusive statutory right to fix the basis of the administrator's remuneration if no creditor meeting is held or no employees have been retained during the administration. In large public companies, secured creditors typically act in a co-ordinated manner represented by a single trustee. Lenders may be more involved in fixing administrator's remuneration and the general expense of administration if the rate of recovery of their claims is low. The higher the rate of recovery, the less their focus is likely to be on minimising the costs of administration. The Connaught plc case study in Chap. 11 gives an example of creditors' renegotiation of the expenses of administration in a situation where the recovery rate was substantially lower than might have been expected.

Unsecured Creditor Influence

The role of unsecured creditors during administration is substantially different from that of secured creditors. The start of administration results in a temporary suspension of all unsecured claims. Individual actions to recover claims are frustrated since insolvency law requires collective decision-making on rescue proposals.

Potential creditors' meetings form part of the process of administration for unsecured creditors. Unlike the position of shareholders the creditors' right to meet and vote on issues affecting them is not absolute. The decision on whether this takes place is left to the administrator who should determine whether the anticipated rate of recovery and guidelines within statutory objective 3(1)(b) support an initial meeting. A meeting may not be convened where all creditors may recover their claims in full, or where unsecured creditors would not be able to recover any dividends other than the amount included in the prescribed part.

A meeting for unsecured creditors who wish to challenge the decisions of the administrator is available only if their collective or individual debt is more than 10% of total unsecured debt, and they reimburse the costs of the meeting. In effect, only those well-informed, well-resourced creditors who have a substantial stake in the company and can afford such costs can seek a creditors' meeting as a statutory right. In such circumstances individual unsecured creditors with small claims who would fail to meet the minimum requirement of a 10% debt threshold might benefit from the collective efforts of other creditors with greater resources.

The meeting of unsecured creditors is the final opportunity for such creditors to approve the administrator's proposed rescue plan, including the choice of statutory objective of the administration, the realisation of assets, administrators' fees and the payment of secured creditors, preferential creditors and unsecured creditors. There is no statutory provision to facilitate unsecured creditors' collective involvement in formulating the administrator's proposed rescue plan before the creditor meeting is held. There is also no mechanism to ensure full disclosure of information on the degree of insolvency of the company prior to the meeting.

Creditor influence on the outcome of proposals is dependent on the nominal value of their accepted claims. Creditors whose claims have been rejected are excluded from the voting process. Unlike shareholder voting where every shareholder maintains an exclusive right to vote based on the total value of his shares, a creditor's right to vote may be modified in part or rejected by the administrator prior to voting. Again judicial intervention is the only route for dissatisfied creditors, making it impossible for them to challenge the administrator's discretion without significant resources.

The collective decision-making power of unsecured creditors allows them to challenge the administrator's proposals in any proposed rescue plan, seek its partial modification or dismiss it in its entirety, resulting in judicial intervention. However, a favourable court order in such circumstances is rare as judges tend to respect the commercial decisions of administrators. In this sense, unsecured creditors may be compared with dispersed shareholders in terms of their passivity during the formal rescue process.

When creditors approve the administrators' rescue proposal, they may support the administrator by forming a creditors' committee consisting of the creditors with the five largest unsecured claims to monitor the administration's progress and expenses. They can also seek to hold administrators accountable for harm to their interests. However, these rights are conditional on certain requirements being met. If the company continues as a going concern and the administrator makes a new agreement on the payment of debt owed to the five largest creditors, a creditors' committee may not have a real incentive to pursue the interests of other creditors.

If unsecured creditors are not going to receive any share of proceeds from asset sale, they have no incentive to seek a creditors' meeting unless it is for ethical or policy-making issues. The Enterprise Act 2002 has tried to improve the power of unsecured creditors by abolishing the preferential status of Her Majesty's Revenue and Customs (HMRC) and adding it to the category of unsecured creditors. HMRC has shown that it is prepared to challenge the views of the administrator at creditors' meetings and through exchange of correspondence. This is more likely to be the case in small companies and the number of such insolvency cases that HMRC is involved in may deter it from playing an active role in all corporate insolvency cases, except where there are major policy issues involved and a precedent is required. Any monitoring role by HMRC becomes ineffective if excessive overpayments have been made and effectively it becomes a debtor of the insolvent company.

Concluding Remarks

Once a company enters administration the authority of directors is rapidly eroded or terminated. The locus of control of the company changes dramatically and shareholders no longer have priority treatment when decisions are made that affect the future of the company. At this point existing governance models give no further guidance or prescription for the responsibilities, rights and behaviour of directors and shareholders. In contrast, the role of the administrator or insolvency practitioner at this stage is partly prescribed in various provisions of the Insolvency Act 1986—an Act which seems to focus on the interests of creditors rather than the continuation of the business as going concern. Any influence by unsecured creditors is diminished because of the way their claims are treated. Secured creditors retain their influence although the scope of their influence is not specified. There are no explicit comparable guidelines for informal discussions between directors, insolvency practitioners and secured and unsecured creditors, nor is there a clearly defined effective role for shareholders as residual claimants.

Bibliography

Finch, Vanessa. 2005. "Control and Co-ordination in Corporate Rescue." *Legal Studies* 25(3): 374–403.
Flood, John and Eleni Skordaki. 1995. *Insolvency Practitioners and Big Corporate Insolvencies*. London: Published for the Chartered Association of Certified Accountants by Certified Accountants Educational Trust.
Goode, Roystone Mile. 2011. *Principles of Corporate Insolvency Law*. 4th ed, London: Sweet & Maxwell.
Ho, Look Chan. 2008. "Judicial Variation of CVA." *Corporate Rescue and Insolvency* 1(5): 156–158.
McCormack, Gerard. 2007. "Super-Priority New Financing and Corporate Rescue." *Journal of Business Law* 701–732.
McCormack, Gerard. 2009. "Rescuing Small Businesses; Designing an "Efficient" Legal Regime." *Journal of Business Law* 4: 299–330.
Sealy, Len, David Milman and Peter Bailey. 2018. *Sealy & Milman: Annotated Guide to the Insolvency Legislation*. 21st ed. 2 vols. London: Sweet & Maxwell.
Tribe, John. 2009. "Company Voluntary Arrangements and Rescue: A New Hope and a Tudor Orthodoxy." *Journal of Business Law* 5: 454–487.
United Kingdom: Cork Review Committee. 1982. *Insolvency Law and Practice: Report of the Review Committee*. Cmnd 8558. London: HMSO.
United Kingdom. Office of Fair Trading. 2010. *The Market for Corporate Insolvency Practitioners: A Market Study*. OFT 1245. London: Crown.
Wallace, Ian. 2012. "CVAs: Easy as ABC?." *Corporate Rescue and Insolvency* 5(5): 163–165.
Webb, David C. 1991. "An Economic Evaluation of Insolvency Procedures in the United Kingdom: Does the 1986 Insolvency Act Satisfy the Creditors' Bargain?" *Oxford Economic Papers* 43(1): 139–157.

Legislation

Insolvency Act (IA) 1986, ss1–2, s 4(3), s 6, s 176A, 176A(3), s 176A(3), s 176 A (5), s 234(2), s 235(5), s 236(2)(c).
Insolvency Act (IA) 1986, Schedule A1, para 3.
Insolvency Act (IA) 1986, Schedule B1, para 3(1), (2), para 5, para 14, para 25, para 36, para 42, para 49, para 50; para 52 (1), para 52(2), para 54, 55,

paras 57, para 65, para 69, paras 70 & 72, para 78, para 90, para 99, para 99(3), para 103.
Insolvency Rules (IR) 1986 (UK), r 1.19(3), r 1.20, r. 1.26, r 2.47, r 2.106, r 9.2(1), rr 2.34–2.48, rr 2.50–2.63, r 2.67, r 2.85, 2.90, 2.92, 2.106, r 2.106(5A).
Statement of Insolvency Practice 9 (SIP 9).

Cases

Closegate Hotel Development (Durham ltd) v McLean [2013] EWHC 3237 (Ch).
Exeter City Council v Bairstow [2007] BCC 236.
Galileo Group Ltd, Re [1999] Ch 100.
GE Capital Commercial Finance Ltd v Sutton [2004] 2 BCLC 662.
Hydroserve Ltd, Re [2008] BCC 175.
Leisure (Norwich) II Ltd and others v Luminar Lava Ignite Ltd (in administration) and others [2013] 2 BCLC 115.
London Iron & Steel Co Ltd, Re [1990] BCLC 372.
MK Airlines Ltd, Re [2013] 1 BCLC 9.
Polly Peck International plc, Re [1994] BCC 15.
Powdrill v Watson [1994] BCC 172.
Transbus International Ltd (in Liquidation), Re [2004] 2 BCLC 550.

Part II

6

Corporate Governance Research: An Empirical Approach

Overview

Research in the area of financial distress and corporate governance is gradually moving towards an increasing interest in empirical studies to complement the traditional doctrinal analysis of specific cases and judgments based on common law principles and legislative provisions. For example, Lopucki and Whitford (1992) studied 43 large American public companies that had resorted to Chapter 11 of the US Bankruptcy Code during a ten-year period to determine whether directors were more likely to represent shareholder or creditor interests. Frisby (2007) has also reported quantitative research in corporate insolvency, particularly in relation to administration. In one of the relatively few reported UK studies, Armour et al. (2008) carried out empirical research into creditor control in corporate rescue in 284 receiverships and administrations. This is consistent with an emerging view that an empirical approach can help to resolve "theoretical arguments and/or throw a surprising light on legal questions", analyse an ongoing process and test for particular developing patterns. As Lawless et al. (2010) indicate, "the legal academy is changing" by gradually moving beyond the constraints of the current law and reaching more disciplines for the purpose of researching legal topics.

To date empirical research in the area of governance, financial distress and insolvency has largely taken the form of quantitative surveys at a corporate level. Studies have measured aggregate statistics such as the number of executive and non-executive directors, or the dispersion/concentration of share ownership and creditors. The following chapters of this book are based on the premise that an alternative (complementary) understanding can be generated by creating a series of case studies that analyse the transition of a company from solvent trading, through financial distress and ultimately into insolvency as a process taking place over time with antecedents and consequences to decisions at each stage. Such an analysis would identify and analyse the decisions of the key participants (directors, shareholders, creditors and administrators) using available data to create a rich interpretation (case study) of influences on governance. This would be consistent with the American analytical perspective of "path dependence" that takes into account the effects of social, political, cultural and economic environments on accountability and corporate ownership. Chapters 7 to 11 present five case studies of governance in financial distress which have been developed using these principles.

This chapter contains a detailed discussion of the methodology that was used to develop the case studies, detailing how five large public companies have responded to situations of financial distress and insolvency. It includes the justification of the research method, the sources of information that were used to compile each case and the limitations of the data. The cases were developed using a mixture of information compiled from a wide range of publicly accessible sources. The chapter also discusses the rationale for the choice of specific cases.

The Case Study Approach

The use of case studies in research is widely documented in a range of different disciplines. Applications include law, business and management, sociology and education. One of the earliest references to their use in law dates back to 1870 when Christopher Langdell, then Dean of

Harvard Law School (HLS), encouraged the use of cases in teaching law as a "scientific" endeavour. Law students were taught to improve their research skills by learning how to extract legal principles from cases relating to the American Courts of Appeal. The cases were written to demonstrate specific aspects of the law and students were encouraged to identify and analyse judicial opinions, a practice that continues extensively today in some law schools. Case study in this setting was, however, limited to the study of judicial decisions in a specific case.

Case study analysis has been used recently by the HLS in a different way. The School has developed a new initiative called "the Case Development Initiative". The initiative does not focus on case law as developed in court; rather it considers theories, the facts of a particular case, the interests of parties involved, their parties' ethics and their relationships with others. The HLS initiative uses various "interviews, dates, and research to develop written and video summaries of strategies and organisational issues that law and other professional service firms face". The School defends its approach stating that "its case studies help readers take into account multiple perspectives of each case and reconcile the interests of different groups or individuals". This approach does not focus exclusively on judicial opinion. Examples of the case studies carried out under this initiative include "Strategy and Positioning in Professional Service Firms", "Slater & Gordon" and "A Tale of Three Asset Management Teams". Each of these case studies focuses mainly on the management of law firms and professional services.

The research discussed in this book adopts a similar approach to that adopted by the HLS. Case study as a process in this context does not refer to the analysis of specific judicial opinions related to "cases" heard in the UK's higher courts. In this book, "case study" refers to empirical legal research, based on a detailed narrative analysis of processes taking place over a period of time in specific companies in situations of financial distress, with multiple issues and participants. The output, also a "case study", is similar to that described above at the HLS. This research draws from the broader range of research techniques that are used in other areas of social science, particularly in the collection and analysis of secondary data sources.

Yin has defined a case study as "a rich empirical description of particular instances of a phenomenon that is typically based on a variety of resources" (Yin 1984). This book uses this definition and that of Bennett (2004), which describes it as "the investigation of a well-defined aspect of a historical happening that the investigator selects for analysis, rather than the historical happening itself". Case studies have also been defined as "a research strategy which focuses on understanding the dynamics present within single settings". This research creates five case studies, all focused on the same issues of governance and insolvency. The effect of studying a number of cases all focused on the same issue should be to create more detailed "analytic power" and lead to "more robust" conclusions, particularly as the diversity of the cases increases.

This book focuses on UK public companies that have entered administration or CVA following financial distress. An alternative to the case study approach could have been survey research based on structured interviews with a sample of insolvency practitioners, creditors and company directors who have been directly involved in informal and formal rescue processes. Interviews with other parties who have been indirectly involved, for example, debt collectors, and in-house lawyers could also have been extremely helpful. This survey-based alternative was set aside due to the difficulty that potentially existed in identifying and contacting former company directors, who had retired, died or could be assumed to be cautious about describing their apparent failure to manage a distressed company. Such issues would have potentially created considerable issues of validity and reliability in interpreting the findings.

Corporate insolvency is culturally regarded as a failure of management in the UK and there is some evidence that management failure in general is notoriously difficult to research, as reflected in the relative lack of reported case studies analysing business failure compared to the number of cases describing business success. A company's entry into administration also marks the exit of company directors from their positions and perhaps entry into another role. It is unlikely that such company directors would be willing to discuss their experience if they knew that their views might be publicly known and they would be criticised by the public for their failure to pursue shareholder interests. Whilst they and their companies could remain anonymous, this would seriously compromise the reporting of the case studies in this research. There is also the issue of potential ambiguity in interpreting the self-reported behaviour of management and the danger of post-hoc rationalisation of decisions that were made.

Therefore at an early stage in the design of the research a decision was taken to develop a series of case studies that would be based on secondary data that was generally available and in the public domain. Initial analysis of the potential of using such data sources suggested that the approach was viable and indicated that there would be sufficient richness of data to analyse the key issues identified in earlier sections of this book. Moreover, since these sources are generally available to all researchers and are produced to meet certain statutory requirements, it was felt that there should be consistency in the data available that would increase the potential reliability of the information used—a feature that would not necessarily be present in a survey-based approach. The issue of inclusion and interpretation still remains, since different researchers might choose to include some data and exclude other items. The interpretation of the data may also differ from researcher to researcher. However, the same data set is available to any researcher interested in exploring this area and validating any conclusions. A detailed listing of the sources of data used is presented in later sections of this chapter.

Case Selection

The focus of this book is on financially distressed and insolvent companies that go through a formal rescue procedure. The original aim of the book was to compare and contrast UK and US theory and practice. However, it rapidly became clear that a comparison was not going to be possible, certainly within the resources and timescale available to this researcher. This was due to several issues. Most critically, resources did not provide the necessary level of detailed access to US cases. Additionally those cases that were accessible were more relevant to an analysis of judicial authority than governance issues. There was also no single database that could provide detailed information about large Chapter 11 bankruptcies, including motions by unsecured creditor groups. Such information was only available through specific commercial sites at high cost on a case-by-case basis. Information on such cases was also extremely diffuse, and scattered information was only available through attorney websites representing one party, the debtor or the creditors' committee. There was little certainty that any documents were complete and comprehensive in content and number.

The highly litigious nature of Chapter 11 bankruptcies allows a large number of motions to be filed with the court for large companies. In one case identified for potential inclusion (*In re Tousa, Inc.*), the number of motions exceeded 1000. Each motion was detailed and would have required careful examination before the relevant governance issues could be identified and extracted. This was particularly noticeable in cases where more than one group of creditors opposed the reorganisation plan. In *Tousa*, the existence of fraud had led to suspension of Chapter 11 and judicial consideration of the reorganisation plan, and made further analysis of the case impossible. It became clear that a focus on governance issues in real-life US cases would be outside the scope of this book and would need to be reserved for future research. Moreover, as the researcher began to analyse the UK cases, it became clear that there was sufficient richness in these cases to explore the issues of governance in insolvency in the terms identified in earlier chapters.

The empirical research is also focused on large UK public companies rather than privately owned or small- and medium-sized companies. This focus on large public companies increased the complexity of the informal and formal rescue process under investigation, but the secondary data available was considerably greater and more varied due to the reporting requirements imposed on such companies, and the accompanying publicity created by formal announcements and resultant media coverage. Unlike small private companies, large public companies operate typically as a group of companies with a parent company and several subsidiaries, which increased the complexity of the overall case. Subsidiaries may also be public or private companies, based inside or outside of the UK.

The choice of large public companies rather than private or smaller companies was based initially on the assumption that there would be a large volume of accessible information on board decisions and actions during the informal rescue process. This proved to be a valid assumption. The potential reliability and validity of the information were also increased because such information has to be made public and filed to comply with the listing requirement under the Companies Act 2006. This meant that substantial governance issues would be likely to be reported as they occurred. Public companies are obliged to file a detailed Annual Report and Accounts and report all matters approved by shareholders in general meetings. They are also required to publicly disclose and register a range of management decisions, including the appointment of new directors and the re-appointment or termination of employment of existing members of the board. Further, they are required to disclose information on the allotment of equity securities, the disposal of fixed assets and secured debt financing. This information relates directly to strategic decisions analysed in this book including cost reduction, changes to the composition of the board, the sale of corporate assets, the use of equity/share issue and new debt financing/debt renegotiation to increase cash flow. When a company enters a formal rescue process such as administration, the scale of assets involved and the number of creditors, particularly across a parent company with several subsidiaries, create a complex picture that typically requires the involvement of more than one administrator. Upon entry into a CVA, mandatory disclosure continues for company directors, and a CVA supervisor is obliged to file his own report with Companies House under the Insolvency Rules 1986. Once a company enters administration and joint administrators are appointed, it becomes the joint administrators' responsibility to file statutory information relating to proposals, progress reports and any extension of administration report. The administrator is also obliged to disclose information as the company exits administration following the achievement of the objective and enters a formal non-rescue procedure such as creditors' voluntary liquidation or dissolution.

All of these mandatory filings are publicly available through Companies House and provide a very rich source of secondary data, which is used in this book to describe and analyse financial distress and insolvency. In addition, interviews and commentaries were also available online from a range of sources. At the pre-insolvency stage, companies produced a wide range of information to brief shareholders, investment institutions and creditors. This information was a useful, if potentially biased, source of further information on company decisions during financial distress that enriched the information provided by statutory filings and provided further insight into the governance issues that members of the board and creditors in each company had to deal with.

The researcher was unable to identify any definition of large insolvency cases that had already been adopted by the UK judicial system. Therefore, a US definition of what are known as "mega-bankruptcy cases" was adopted and modified to fit the UK formal insolvency context. The use of the US definition of mega-bankruptcy cases was influenced by the adoption of Chapter 11 of the US Bankruptcy Code as a potential model for the UK formal rescue process, initially considered by the Cork Report. The US court recognises a case to be a mega-bankruptcy case if it is "an extremely large case with: (1) at least 1,000 creditors; (2) $100 million or more in assets; (3) a great amount of court activity as evidenced by a large number of docket entries; (4) a large number of attorneys who have made an appearance of record; and (5) regional and/or national media attention" (Bartell and Gibson 2009).

This definition was modified to reflect the UK context. A definition of small-to-medium parent company size was taken from section 466 of the Companies Act 2006 that defines such companies as those which can meet two or more of the following requirements: balance sheet (less than £15.5 m gross), turnover (less than £31.1 m gross) and number of employees (less than 250). In this study, a mega-insolvency case was identified if a company's last annual report showed that the company was at least four times larger, based on two or more of these variables, to create comparability with the definition of a US mega-bankruptcy case. Therefore, a UK insolvency was defined as a mega-insolvency case with (1) at least 1000 employees at the start of the informal rescue process, (2) £62 m or more in total assets at the start of the informal rescue process, (3) £124.4 m turnover in the year preceding the informal rescue process,

(4) the joint appointment of at least three insolvency practitioners (two for the CVAs) and (5) regional and/or national media attention. The most striking difference between UK and US corporate rescue processes is the comparative absence of litigation through the court in the UK, which is a reason for the absence of reference to court activity and attorney involvement in the UK definition of mega-insolvency.

The selection of cases was made from large public companies that have been subject to a formal rescue process, namely CVA or administration. A list of large public companies which had filed statutory documents with Companies House in the UK was identified. Since media attention was one of the requirements and the only cost-effective way to find this information was to use online sources, this research focused on those companies that had entered administration since 2008, attracting media and regulatory attention. The sample is best described as a convenience sample, collected for a specific purpose to provide illustrative value. It does not claim to be representative of all companies in all insolvency situations. Emphasis was given to those companies that had already exited a formal rescue process or had at least experienced two years of administration. Five cases were selected from an initial wider list of alternatives, in retailing, consumer goods and construction services. The final sample consisted of Stylo plc, JJB Sports plc, Waterford Wedgwood plc, Woolworths Group plc and Connaught plc. JJB Sports plc was the only company that had used a CVA twice as a business rescue option. The other companies had used administration.

Whilst the earlier chapters of this book have taken a descriptive and doctrinal perspective on distress and insolvency, the approach in Chaps. 7 to 11 is deliberately descriptive and interpretive, seeking to identify patterns of behaviour from available data on events and decisions. It uses a comparative approach across the five case studies. The purpose of this approach is to develop more confidence in the overall results. As Yin (2012) states, "Multiple-case studies should follow a replication, not sampling logic. This means that two or more cases should be included within the same study precisely because the investigator (researcher) predicts that similar results (replications) will be found. If such replications are indeed found for several cases, you can have more confidence in the overall results. The development of consistent findings, over multiple cases and even multiple studies, can then be considered a very robust finding."

Given the complexity of the issues, and the time and resources available to complete this book, the researcher determined that five case studies would be the maximum number that could be included in this research. Review of the richness of the data from the cases that were produced suggests that this number was sufficient to guide the interpretive analysis, and is consistent with the guidelines proposed by Yin.

Data Collection

Each case provides an overview of the company and its business and financial decisions related to informal rescue during the year before the involvement of insolvency practitioners. The informal rescue process has been limited to one year, as an arbitrary definition of the pre-rescue stage. A one-year time frame was adopted because there is no statutory provision or regulatory instruction to suggest how long the informal rescue process might continue before a company enters a formal rescue process, if it actually does so. UK case law on wrongful trading has also not specified any specific time frame for liquidators or judges to consider before a company enters liquidation. The board of directors needs time to assess the scale of financial distress and develop appropriate rescue options. Whilst it would have been possible to investigate the actions of directors for several years prior to entry into a formal rescue process, this would have taken a disproportionately long time to implement, beyond the limits of this book. Consequently, a decision was taken to limit the analysis to one year on the assumption that the year immediately prior to entry would provide sufficiently rich data for the nature of this research. The extent and detail of the data presented in the case studies serves to validate this decision.

This research also assumes that the company enters a formal rescue process after all the informal rescue options and strategies to keep the company as a going concern have been tried, and failed. It is assumed that the board of directors should have known during the final year at least that the company was operating as an insolvent entity and taken every effort to minimise the losses. With such a perspective, each case presents information on board changes, cost reduction, equity/share issue, asset sale and new debt financing/debt renegotiation. A separate analysis of governance issues follows the discussion of each informal rescue option.

The focus then shifts to the role of insolvency practitioners at the commencement of the formal rescue process and the potential influence of creditors and judicial intervention. If a CVA is adopted as a formal rescue process, then the decisions of the board during the implementation of the CVA are considered and detailed. During administration, attention is also given to joint administrator powers in asset sale (realisation) and the distribution of proceeds of sale among secured and unsecured creditors. Administrator's decisions in facilitating creditor meetings and creditor committees are also considered. Employee interests are excluded from the scope of this research. A separate analysis of corporate governance issues follows the discussion of the formal rescue processes.

Data Sources

This research used multiple sources of information in an attempt to triangulate and enrich the overall picture. Prior to the commencement of administration, the sources of data were varied and the volume of information available was substantial. However, as soon as the company entered administration, the sources of data were mainly reduced to administrator reports which remained accessible at Companies House.

The first source of archived data was mandatory information that public companies are required to disclose under listing rules. This information is available through the Regulatory News Service (RNS), associated with the London Stock Exchange (LSE), and covers a range of issues, including the major topics of this research, namely interim or final trading results, board change, asset sale, equity/share issue and debt financing. This information is available online to the public at no cost. As soon as a company becomes insolvent and is delisted from the LSE, it no longer makes announcements and news releases are not available directly from the company. However an archive of previous news is available online. The researcher accessed RNS-channelled company announcements through the website "FE Investegate" that provides a chronological record of all company announcements online. In the UK the online archival data retrieval facility is run by Financial Express.

The second major source of information is mandatory information that companies are obliged to disclose under the Companies Act 1985 and 2006. This mandatory information reflects specific activity taking place in the company that must be formally registered. The information includes, but is not restricted to director appointments, re-appointment and termination of director appointments.

As soon as a company enters a formal rescue process, the insolvency practitioner becomes responsible for preparation and mandatory filing of specific information, including details of administrator appointments, administrator proposals, statement of affairs, administrator six-monthly progress reports, automatic end of administration, extension of administration, moving from administration to creditors' voluntary liquidation or dissolution. This information is all filed with Companies House and available to public access at no cost.

The third source of information is specific news releases relating to the company itself or its directors from regulatory bodies, including the Serious Fraud Office (SFO) and the Office of Fair Trading (OFT). This information is available to the public through the RNS or directly through the websites of the SFO and OFT.

The last source of information includes a wide range of online comments from commercial and financial media such as *The Financial Times*, *The Guardian*, *Business Insider*, *Accountancy Age*, *Retail Week* and *The Independent*. This information was available through two databases: Nexis and Proquest.

This book has used a combination of mandatory filings at Companies House and subject-specific company announcements under listing rules to obtain information on the rescue options considered and adopted during the informal rescue process. It has used archived information at Companies House as the major source of information on governance issues relating to administration or CVA. The following section details the selection and combination of data for each option. This data is organised into two main categories: data that relates to specific rescue decisions by management during the informal rescue process and data that relates to decisions of insolvency practitioners during the formal rescue process.

Data Collection Prior to Informal Rescue Process

- *Corporate governance*: Detailed information relating to each company, and its corporate governance (including the composition of the board and ownership structure of the company), was extracted from the Company's Annual Report and Accounts—the only source of data that provides accurate information about corporate governance in detail at the end of each financial year.
- *Debt structure*: The Company's Annual Report and Accounts was used to obtain information relating to secured debt, lenders and the type of security interests granted prior to the informal rescue process. This information was supplemented by an analysis of the information filed with Companies House relating to security interests such as existing fixed and floating charges. Information was also obtained from the UK media.
- *Financial distress and associated causes*: Detail on total assets, turnover and debt structure during the informal rescue period was obtained from the Company's Annual Report and Accounts and company announcements.

Data Collection Related to Informal Rescue Process

The data relating to the use of informal rescue processes was taken from subject-specific forms in the RNS-LSE channelled Company Announcements and in filings with Companies House. Online data was also used to supplement the two sources of information where possible. These sources of data were cross-referenced to obtain details of the board's role in the adoption and implementation of rescue mechanisms and their outcomes. Specific sources for each of the different mechanisms were as follows:

– *Board change*: Information relating to board changes was obtained from company announcements that featured the phrase "Board Appointment", "Directorate Change", "Director Declaration", "Non-Executive Director Appointment" or "Management Change". This was used to identify the date of appointments and resignations and the reasons for change where these were given. Company announcements were preferred as the primary source of data due to the detailed and sometimes unique information that they provided, including reasons for a specific director's appointment or termination, a shift between non-executive and executive roles or the temporary appointment of existing directors to dual positions. In cases where the reason for a board change was not clearly specified, comments in the media were analysed in an attempt to explain changes.

Further information was available from company filings with Companies House. Information relating to director appointments was taken from form 288a "Appointment of director or secretary". Information relating to a company secretary or director's resignation or retirement was obtained from form 288b "Terminating appointment as director or secretary" or form TM01 "Termination of appointment of director". Information about a company secretary or director's re-appointment was extracted from form 288c "Change of particulars for director or company secretary". Date of resignation or appointment was used to identify the time and frequency of board changes.

Analysis of company announcements and company filings showed some differences in information between the two sources. These differences related mainly to the date of appointment and resignation of directors. The variation may be attributed to the type of service contract between directors and the company. The second problem related to the lack of relevant company filings in some circumstances when a new CEO was appointed to the company during the informal rescue process. This may be explained where the contract involved the appointment of a director through a third party, that is, an independent company. A third problem emerged when filings did not show the exit of a newly appointed CEO when one company entered the formal rescue process.

- *Equity/share issue*: Primary information relating to the company's intention to use an equity issue to raise share capital was initially obtained from company announcements. Announcements typically included phrases such as "Equity Issue", "Cash Placing", "Proposed Firm Placing and Placing", "Price Monitoring Extension", "Results of Firm Placing and Placing and Open Offer", "Completion of Capital Raising", "Second Price Monitoring Extension" and "Result of Open Offer". Information relating to a move from Main Market to Alternative Investment Market (AIM) and cancellation of stocks was taken from company announcements entitled "Admission of Shares", "Admission of Shares to AIM", "Statement re De-listing" and "Statement re Suspension".

Further information about equity issue was extracted from filings made with Companies House, including the Company's Annual Report and Accounts. Approved resolutions relating to equity issue during shareholder meetings were obtained from the filings to identify such issues as shareholder approval for share issues to increase capital, the "disapplication of pre-emption rights", the purchase of shares other than from capital, the authorised allotment of shares and debentures, the variance in share rights and names, the consolidation of share capital and any alterations to the company's articles of association. Further information was obtained from company announcements under such headings as "Results of the AGM", "AGM Statement" and "Trading Shares Suspension".

- *Cost reduction*: Information relating to management of the going concern was obtained from company announcements containing phrases such as "interim results", "final results" and "trading update". This information was analysed in chronological order to profile the deterioration of the business during the informal rescue process and identify major cost reduction strategies where these were declared.
- *Asset sale*: Company announcements about the sale of assets were also analysed. Titles such as "commencement of formal sale process" related to the sale of the company as a whole, whilst titles such as "asset disposal" and "potential disposals" referred to the sale of specific assets rather than the whole company. Titles such as "assignment of leases" or "store disposal" were transaction or asset specific.

This information was supplemented by the Company's Annual Report and Accounts that typically provided an overview of major asset sales during the year in question. Further information was obtained from announcements from regulatory bodies such as the OFT.

- *New debt financing/debt renegotiation*: Company announcements were the primary source of information on the company's debt financing. Company announcements such as "banking facilities", "financial update", "statement re investment", "extension of standstill" and media commentaries proved helpful. Since the information in company announcements did not include detailed information about the lender and type of security created, further information was obtained from mandatory company filings, including form 395 or MG01 entitled "particulars of a mortgage or charge", which gave short particulars of security interests, and form MG02 entitled "Declaration of satisfaction in full or in part of mortgage or charge".

Further information about debt financing was obtained from media investigation of the company, including interviews with former CEOs and chairmen. The administrator's websites and information provided by marketing and sale agencies were also examined to enrich the data relating to the sale and marketing of the insolvent debtor's assets after the company exited administration.

- *Shareholder influence*: Information relating to shareholder governance was obtained from the Company's Annual Report and Accounts. Information relating to shareholders' approval relating to "equity securities" and other ordinary or special resolutions was obtained from company filings with Companies House. Further information about shareholder conduct at the Annual General Meeting (AGM) and any Extraordinary General Meeting (EGM) was obtained from company announcements.
- *Creditor influence*: Information from announcements in the public domain on debt financing and management of the going concern was used to analyse secured creditors' influence. There was a lack of information about the influence of unsecured creditors. This information was available to a very limited extent in company announcements and online media reports.

Data Collection Relating to Formal Rescue Process

- *Company Voluntary Arrangement (CVA)*: Company announcements were used as the primary source of information relating to any CVA proposal and the influence of lenders. Announcements included "press speculation re CVA proposals", "proposed Company Voluntary Arrangement", "CVA results of creditors' meetings", "CVA result of members' meetings", "results of creditors and shareholder meetings", "CVA first effective date" and "CVA: expiry of statutory challenge period". This information was supplemented by mandatory documents, including form 1.1 "Notice to Registrar of Companies of Voluntary Arrangement taking effect", form 1.4 "Notice of completion of Voluntary Arrangement" and form 1.3 "Voluntary Arrangement's supervisor's abstracts of receipts and payment".
- *Administration*: Information relating to the date of administration and details of appointment of administrators was obtained from company announcements. This information was supplemented by the information included in form 2.12B "Notice of administrator's appointment". Information relating to the total amount of secured debt and unsecured debt was obtained from attachment to form 2.16B "Notice of statement of affairs", whilst attached reports to form 2.17B "Statement of administrator's proposals" provided detailed information regarding the objective of administration, the sale of assets and any secured creditors' plan to enforce their security interests. Form F2.18 "Notice of deemed approval of proposals" related to creditors' approval of the administrator's proposal and the formal recognition of this approval is given by form 2.23B "Notice of result of meeting of creditors".

Information relating to management of the going concern and asset sale during the early days of administration was obtained from attached reports to form 2.17B, whilst attachments to form 2.24B "Administrators' progress report" provided further information on subsequent developments. Form 2.17 was used to obtain information on asset sale. It also provided information on the involvement of professional commercial organisations at various stages of asset sale, including marketing, valuation and compliance with relevant laws. Form 2.17 also provided some information on the administrator's proposed share of assets among creditors. The information relating to administrator's distribution of the proceeds of sales, administrator's fees and administration expenses was taken from attachments to form 2.24B. The same report was used to find information relating to the lender's advanced payment of administration fees, lender's enforcement of their property rights, the rate of debt recovery and payment to unsecured creditors.

Information relating to secured creditors' influence was obtained from the administrator's proposals and progress reports. Information relating to the priority ranking of secured creditors was extracted from form 403A "Declaration of satisfaction in full or in part of mortgage or charge". Information relating to the duration of the administration was obtained from form 2.31B "Notice of extension of period of administration". In cases where the insolvent company had exited administration followed by commencement of a formal non-rescue procedure, further information was obtained from mandatory filings, including form 2.34B "Notice of move from administration to creditors' voluntary liquidation", form 2.35B "Notice of move from administration to dissolution", form 2.39B "Notice of vacation of office", form 4.68 "Liquidator's statement of receipts and payments", and form GAZ2 "Final Gazette".

Limitations of the Data

The multiplicity of data created some problems. Company announcements and filings with Companies House were purposefully presented to meet the minimum legal standards of transparency and disclosure expected from public companies. The data did not include commercially confidential information about the company. Therefore, there was little or no accessible information relating to the interaction between the board and lenders prior to a company's entry into a formal insolvency regime. In those cases that involved the creation of security in debt financing, this research used the information that was filed with Companies House to find out more about the parties to the security interests and the type of security.

The extent and variety of data substantially reduce when the company enters administration. Once the company is delisted, company announcements are no longer available. News and independent commentaries are increasingly limited due to a loss of public interest. Confidential information prevents administrators from disclosing detailed information about the recovery of assets or asset sale and the lender's influence over the process. The administrator is not obliged to provide public disclosure of such information.

Organisation of Case Studies

The presentation of each case in Chaps. 7 to 11 follows the same pattern beginning with an overview of the case, company background, corporate governance and debt structure. The case then describes the financial distress facing the company and its potential causes. The case examines informal rescue attempts initiated by the board, reviewing shareholders' and creditors' influence. The company's use of formal rescue processes, that is, CVA or administration, is then explored. Depending on the type of the rescue process adopted, each case also discusses the role of the insolvency practitioner and creditor and shareholder influences on decisions. Each case summarises the outcome of the formal rescue process and the key issues identified in the case study. Collectively, these case studies present a detailed picture of the "path" through distress to insolvency and the influence of financial distress and insolvency on corporate governance. This detailed picture is analysed in Chap. 12.

Bibliography

Armour, John, Audrey Hsu, and Adrian Walters. 2008. "Corporate Insolvency in the United Kingdom: The Impact of the Enterprise Act 2002." *European Company and Financial Law Review* 5(2): 148–171.

Bartell, Laura B. and S. Elizabeth Gibson. 2009. *A Guide to the Judicial Management of Bankruptcy Mega-Cases*. 2nd ed. Washington, DC: Federal Judicial Center.

Barton, Benjamine H. 2007. "A Tale of Two Case Methods." *Tennessee Law Review* 75(3): 233–250.

Bennett, Andrew. 2004. "Case Study Methods: Design, Use, and Comparative Advantages." in *Models, Numbers, and Cases: Methods for Studying International Relations*, edited by Detlef F. Sprinz and Yael Wolinsky-Nahmias. 19–55. Michigan: University of Michigan Press.

Bryman, Alan. 2012. *Social Research Methods*. 4th ed. New York. Oxford University Press.

Cowton, Christopher J. 1998. "The Use of Secondary Data in Business Ethics Research." *Journal of Business Ethics* 17(4): 423–434.

Eisenhardt, Kathleen M. 1989. "Building Theories from Case Study Research." *Academy of Management Review* 14(4): 532–550.

Eisenhardt, Kathleen M. and Melissa E. Graebner. 2007. "Theory Building from Cases: Opportunities and Challenges." *Academy of Management Journal* 50(1): 25–32.

Fleming, Austin and Bryan C. Hathorn. 2010. "Tragedy on the Descent: The Ascent and Fall of Eddie Bauer." Chapter 11 Bankruptcy Case Studies. Accessed January 14, 2018. http://trace.tennessee.edu/utk_studlawbankruptcy/1/

Frisby, Sandra. 2007. *Report to The Asscoiation of Business Recovery Professionals: A Preliminary Analysis of Pre-packaged Administrations*. London: R3: The Association of Business Recovery Professionals.

Gov.uk. 2014. "Companies House Forms for Limited Companies." Last Modified July 12, 2016. https://www.gov.uk/government/collections/companies-house-forms-for-limited-companies

Gov.uk. 2014. "Companies House Forms for Insolvency (1986)." Last Modified November 17, 2017. https://www.gov.uk/government/collections/companies-house-forms-for-insolvency

Harris, Howard. 2001. "Content Analysis of Secondary Data: A Study of Courage in Managerial Decision Making." *Journal of Business Ethics* 34(3–4): 191–208.

Harvard Law School. "The Case Development Initiative." Accessed January 14, 2018. http://casestudies.law.harvard.edu/the-case-developmentinitiative/

Harvard Law Today. "Singer on Teaching Students to Solve Problems." Accessed January 14, 2018. https://today.law.harvard.edu/singer-on-teaching-students-to-solve-problems/

Killen, Roy. 2007. "Singer on Teaching Students to Solve Problems." 4th ed. Victoria: Thomson Social Science Press.
Lawless, Robert M, Jennifer K. Robbennolt, and Thomas S. Ulen. 2010. *Empirical Methods in Law*. New York: Aspen Publishers.
Lopucki, Lynn M. and William C Whitford. 1992. "Corporate Governance in the Bankruptcy Reorganization of Large, Publicly Held Companies." *University of Pennsylvania Law Review* 141(3): 669–800.
McArdle, Elaine. 2010. "Beyond the Case Method." *Harvard Law Bulletin Summer 2010*. Accessed January 14, 2018. https://today.law.harvard.edu/bulletin/issue/summer-2010/
McCormack, Gerard. 2008. *Corporate Rescue Law – An Anglo-American Perspective*. Cheltenham: Edward Elgar Publishing Limited.
McCormack, Gerard. 2011. "Football Creditors – A Game of Two Halves?" *Insolvency Intelligence* 24(7): 105–108.
Parkinson, Marjan Marandi. 2016. "Corporate Governance During Financial Distress – An Empirical Analysis." *International Journal of Law and Management* 58(5): 486–506.
Robertson, Diana, C. 1993. "Empiricism in Business Ethics: Suggested Research Directions." *Journal of Business Ethics* 12(8): 585–599.
United Kingdom: Cork Review Committee. 1982. Insolvency Law and Practice: Report of the Review Committee. Cmnd 8558. London: HMSO.
Weaver, Russell L. 1991. "Langdell's Legacy: Living with the Case Method." *Villanova Law Review* 36(2): 517–596.
Yin, Robert K. 1984. *Case Study Research: Design and Methods*. London: SAGE Publications
Yin, Robert K. 2012. *Applications of Case Study Research*. 3rd ed. California: SAGE Publications.

Legislation

Companies Act 2006, s 21, ss 162–167, s 41, ss 441–443, s 447, s 743, s 554, ss 560–579, ss 598–604, ss 707–708, s 741, ss 743–748, s 841, ss 860–887.
Insolvency Rules 1986, r 2.19, r 2.20, r 2.21, r 2.24, rr 2.38–2.44, r 2.47(4), rr 2.47–2.53.
Insolvency Act 1986, Sch B1 para 49, para 78(5), para 80, paras 83–84.

7

Case Study 1: Stylo plc

Overview

Stylo plc is an example of corporate governance in a large public company that entered pre-packaged administration following rejection of a CVA proposal. The main cause of its financial distress was increasing costs, linked to a decline in consumer demand for its major products and a failure to innovate quickly enough to keep up with competition. The main governance issue is the directors' control over the informal and formal rescue process. The pre-rescue corporate governance style in Stylo plc is strongly determined by the company's history of concentrated ownership. Like one of the other cases analysed in this book (Waterford Wedgwood plc), shareholding is concentrated in a limited number of family members who were also members of the board of directors. This pattern of ownership and control clearly influenced the scope of the informal rescue options attempted by the board of directors and may account for the board's attempts to maintain the company as a going concern without selling off assets. The company made limited use of informal rescue processes. The board's decision to enter administration and buy back the company through a relatively quick pre-packaged agreement highlights governance issues relating to the informed role of directors who are also major shareholders with concentrated share ownership, something that does not occur frequently in large UK public companies.

The case study covers the informal rescue process between February 17, 2008, and February 16, 2009. It also covers the formal rescue process that covered three years from February 17, 2009, until January 6, 2012, when the parent company exited administration and was subsequently dissolved.

Background: Stylo plc was a large public company established in 1936. The company, with its headquarters in West Yorkshire was initially a family-owned shoe retail business. It converted its corporate classification from private to public company in July 1981 and joined the Alternative Investment Market (AIM) as Stylo plc. The company's two major shareholders were members of the same family, holding executive and non-executive roles on the board of directors of the parent company. Stylo plc operated in two different industries: retailing and property investment. The parent company did not operate any trading activities itself. It had five subsidiaries. Stylo Barratt Shoes Limited and Apper Limited (formerly Shelly's Shoes Limited) sold shoes through 383 stores and 166 concession stores in the UK. Stylo Barratt Properties Limited operated as a property development and management company. The other two subsidiaries were Barratts Shoes Properties Limited and Priceless Shoes Properties Limited. In 2007, the parent company had pursued an informal rescue process including the sale of non-core unprofitable stores. As part of its management of the going concern, the company had focused on substantial investment to modernise its online shopping system and identify new and cheaper suppliers.

At the start of the informal rescue process in February 2008, the parent company had approximately 5,400 employees. Group assets totalled £126 m with a turnover of £223 m for the financial year ending February 2. Therefore, it qualified under the definition of a large public company set out in Chap. 6 of this book.

Corporate governance: Stylo plc was a member of the AIM and therefore was not obliged to comply with the Code; however, the company recognised that "the board is collectively responsible for the success of the company and implicit in achieving this is a commitment to a high standard of corporate governance and risk control". Its board consisted of nine directors including five executive directors and four non-executive directors. The executive directors included the CEO, the Group Director of Finance, the Managing Director of the subsidiary Priceless Shoes limited, the Managing Director of the Barratts Division and one other executive director. The Chief Executive held the role of Chairman of the board and was a major shareholder in the company. The Chief Executive/Chairman and one non-executive director were brothers. The largest shareholders in the company were the CEO with 25% of total ordinary shares and three family members who collectively owned over 30% of total ordinary shares, and acted as trustees of two funds—the Employee Benefit Trust and Stylo 2002 Employee Benefit Trust. Effectively therefore, 55% of the company's shares were owned or controlled by family members.

Debt structure: At the beginning of the informal rescue process, the company's main lenders included Lloyds TSB, Barclays Bank and the Prudential Assurance Company Limited (Prudential). The company's secured debt included bank loans and overdrafts, first mortgage debenture stock, short-term loans, restricted cash deposits, cash borrowings and financial leases. The company's long-term borrowing was to mature in 2014. Its banking facilities were due to be reviewed in autumn 2008 and the board of directors was confident of the lender's support of the company. It also took advantage of derivative transactions that allowed it to manage currency risks resulting from subsidiary operations. Its unsecured creditors included trade creditors whose claims did not bear interest. They were also supportive of the company during the year (2008–2009). The Group's total secured debt was £46 m.

Financial Distress and Associated Causes

Financial distress: The parent company as a going concern was adversely effected by a £12.5 m decrease in revenue (before tax) at the end of financial year 2007, leading to £12 m loss before tax, falling share price and no dividends for shareholders. The company, with total assets of £126 m against total liabilities of £91 m was balance sheet solvent. However, it was cash flow insolvent as its total current assets (£41 m) were less than its total current liabilities (£48 m). The company was in need of some form of informal rescue.

Internal causes: Prior to February 2008, sales were affected by closure of some concessionary stores run by Dorothy Perkins, in a setting of exceptional competition between companies in the retail shoe market. The company acquired the stock and the brand of the insolvent company Dolcis in February 2008, resulting in exceptional costs that were written off at the time of acquisition.

External causes: The company blamed a difficult trading position on "increasing costs in the form of rents, business rates, minimum wage and power costs". It also blamed the effect of "unseasonal weather patterns on the fashion business". It was also concerned over the risks that related to borrowing including interest rates, turbulent changes in foreign currency values, credit risk and liquidity risk. The company's properties were also affected by the crash of financial markets, resulting in a substantial reduction in their value.

Informal Rescue Process

Board of Directors' Role

Overview: The company's informal rescue process started on February 17, 2008, and ended on February 17, 2009, when the parent company entered administration following its failure to obtain creditor approval for a proposed CVA (using the definition of the period of informal rescue discussed in Chap. 6). The main feature of the informal rescue process in Stylo plc is a minimal use of informal rescue options including board change, asset sale and debt financing. This maintained the company as a going concern with its assets and debt almost intact. The approach may be influenced by the strong presence of major shareholders on the board and the Group's strong balance sheet, despite the cash flow problem. It seems that the board aimed to resolve the debt problem at minimum cost to the company and its major shareholders.

Board change included the entry of the representative of a lender as a non-executive director. His entry seems designed to protect the lender's interests as the CEO/Chairman maintains his position through the whole process and does not exit the company, which may be due to his major shareholding. The company has used sale of assets as the first option. However, the sale was limited and did not make a major change to the total value of assets owned by the company. Since the company was listed in the AIM, the board's use of equity issue or share issue was constrained. It was owned mainly by members of one family rather than by dispersed shareholders and they may have been reluctant to lose their control over the company.

Board Change

May 2008: The Managing Director of the subsidiary Barratts Division who was absent from the company for a while resigned to "pursue other career opportunities". A non-executive member of the board who was acting in that position replaced him.

July 2008: The company also appointed a new non-executive director who was a Resolution Team Leader at Barclays Corporate. His role was "to ensure risk to the bank was minimised and income was maximised via effective recovery of distressed debt".

During the first six months of the informal rescue process, the board also sought the assistance of two specialist advisors. One was a turn-around advisor and a footwear specialist to assist in pursuing its "strategic recovery plan", and the other focused on improving its "product development and Barratts' re-brand", respectively. These two people did not become members of the board but provided advice on restructuring. The start and end dates of their collaboration are not clear.

February 2009: One non-executive director resigned.

Analysis: Board change seems to be limited in terms of the total number of directors which remained relatively constant. There was a reduction in the number of non-executive directors whilst the number of executive directors remains unchanged. The board of directors immediately prior to administration consisted of eight members including five executive directors and three non-executive directors. The appointment of a representative from Barclays Bank is also an interesting governance issue showing protection of the lender's interests. The board also seems to have maintained control by deploying advisors rather than appointing new members to the board.

Cost Reduction

May 2008: The company announced that it had suffered poor performance due to the difficult retail trading environment. It aimed to source new suppliers, dispose of unprofitable assets and invest in its stores.

October 2008: The company tried to boost its sale by promotional discounts. It had to "manage stock levels and costs" tightly.

January 2009: The company announced that it would continue to manage stock levels and costs tightly and would explore strategic options for the business. It also referred to "the difficult economic environment" that had had a negative impact on the sector.

Analysis: The board seems to have been transparent as to the financial difficulty that the Group had faced. However, it refused to adopt extreme cost reduction strategies such as redundancies and rationalisation of activities and limited its activities to controlling stock levels.

Asset Sale

March 2008: The company reached an agreement to sell the intellectual property relating to its brand "Shellys" to a Hong Kong–based company.

May 2008: The company announced it would sell further assets to inject £594 k into the company. Subsequently, it disposed of its freehold property interests in Ipswich and Chester.

Analysis: The scope of asset sale seems to be limited. There is no detailed information on whether such limited use of the option was driven by shareholders, lenders or the board; however, it seems that the board aimed to maintain the company's existing asset structure as far as possible.

Equity/Share Issue

January 2009: On January 26, 2009, the company suspended share trading on the AIM following the entry into administration of its main subsidiaries. No equity was issued during the year.

Analysis: Equity issue does not seem to be an option that was attractive to the board at least in terms of inviting new investment in the company. This might imply that the board was concerned about maintaining the ownership structure of the company and perhaps the company's financial distress was limited. There may also have been a concern that they could raise money in this way. There is no information about the influence of lenders.

New Debt Financing/Debt Renegotiation

In the first six months of financial year 2008, the company managed to obtain the support of lenders, resulting in the extension and increase of its credit facilities by £1.5 m.

November 2008: The company renewed its debenture stock with its lender Prudential. The company appears to have extended its credit facilities until 2014 by re-mortgaging shares previously secured by its existing lender.

Analysis: The board seems to have received full support from its lenders although there are no details about the terms of the new deal resulting in the renewal of its debenture. The board seems to have relied upon the Group's strong balance sheet solvency to obtain the lender's positive response to its requests for further lending. The financial wealth and personal credibility of the major shareholders who formed the board of directors may also have influenced the lender's decision positively.

Shareholder Influence

May 2008: The company announced that it would not pay any dividends to shareholders for the previous year.

June 2008: During the AGM, the board obtained shareholder approval for a unique special resolution that allowed company directors to sell or purchase shares from the company without being disqualified. It also allowed the board to approve potential conflicts of interest associated with such transactions, allowing one company director to continue his work with the company.

January 2009: The company announced that both the CEO and his brother, who was also a non-executive director, had used their shares to secure personal loans in January 2005.

Analysis: Shareholders gave their full support to the board despite no dividends being approved. They also approved potential transactions between directors and the company without personal liability. This reflects the position of directors as major shareholders with overall ownership of the business.

Creditor Influence

Secured creditors: Lenders seem to have provided the board with full support which may be partly due to the company's strong underlying economic viability.

Unsecured creditors: There is no detail about unsecured creditors' response to the company's financial distress but they do not seem to have suspended or terminated their contracts with the company.

Formal Rescue Process: CVA and Administration

Overview: The parent company entered a formal rescue regime (administration) on February 17, 2009, when it became clear that a proposed CVA had been rejected by the creditors of each subsidiary. The following sections summarise the CVA process in the subsidiaries. This is followed by a discussion of the joint administrators' role in finalising the pre-packaged administration including sale of a substantial part of the business to its former directors, the realisation of residual assets and distribution to creditors. The formal rescue process covers the time period from February 17, 2009, until January 6, 2012 when the joint administrators filed a notice of the Group's move from administration to dissolution. At the time that administration commenced, the parent company had assets of £79 m, owed £31.4 m in secured debt and had no unsecured debt. The governance feature of the pre-packaged administration is the directors' speedy purchase of the business and the transfer of trading assets to a new company owned by majority members of the board who were also major shareholders in the "old" company.

Company Voluntary Arrangement (CVA)

January 2009: On January 26, the company made the first public step towards the adoption of a formal rescue process with the appointment of three joint administrators from Deloitte LLP covering the five main subsidiaries[1], to handle proposed CVAs. There is no information on the role of lenders in advance of administration but the company's proposed plan implies the support of majority shareholders to provide "substantial further funds to the Group". The focus of the CVA proposal was on landlords and their "high rent obligations" which seems to have become a major cost for the company. A series of informal negotiations appear to have taken place with landlords prior to this appointment, and it seems they had expressed their general support for a proposed CVA. Existing levels of rent appear to have been guaranteed for six months during which landlords were able to find new tenants.

February 2009: The board and its administrators continued negotiations with landlords ahead of a creditors' meeting. Stylo plc publicly declared its intention to enter a pre-packaged administration if the CVA proposal did not receive the approval of individual creditor meetings held for unsecured creditors in each company. However, creditors' meetings rejected the CVA proposal. There is no information about why creditors rejected the CVA proposal. This might be due to the fact that the administrators required the approval of creditor meetings in every subsidiary. The administrators later commented that "given the interlocking nature of the trading and financing of the companies, it was necessary for creditors of all the companies to vote in favour of the CVA to be successful". Due to the rejection of the CVA, there was no formal filing that could help to clarify the exercise of powers by the Chairman during the meeting. Additionally there is no information on total claims, disqualified claims or the specific classification of claims.

Administration

Administrator's Role

On February 17, the Group entered administration following the appointment of three joint administrators of subsidiaries to the parent company Stylo plc by the directors. At the time of administration, the Group owed approximately £31.4 m secured by mortgage debenture stock, fixed and floating charge, letter of credit, bonds, guarantees and indemnities to its lenders Prudential (as security trustee), Lloyds and Barclays Bank. It also had £76 m intercompany creditor loans. The statement of affairs did not include any unsecured debt.

The joint administrators determined that the statutory objective of administration under para 3(1)(b) of Schedule B1 of the Insolvency Act 1986 could be achieved through an "immediate insolvent liquidation". They reasoned that the sale of the business as a going concern would not allow the parent company to be rescued. Their interpretation of the statutory objective is at variance with the business rescue that was ultimately achieved through pre-packaged administration.

Management of the Going Concern

Upon their appointment, the joint administrators continued all of the main subsidiaries as going concerns. Completion of the sale of a significant part of the business (see below) within two days of their appointment (pre-packaged administration) resulted in early transfer of control powers to a new company owned by the former company directors. Sufficient funds were provided by one of the subsidiaries to support the continued business activities of the other companies in the Group. There is no information on the source of fund or its amount; however, the purchase of the business by company directors suggests that they may have provided the funds required.

Asset Sale and Recovery

February 2009: Two days after their appointment, the joint administrators completed the pre-packaged sale of 160 stores and 165 outlet concessions and all intellectual property including brands to a new company, Barratts Priceless Limited, owned by six directors previously employed by Stylo plc. The joint administrators also agreed that the buyers could purchase stock at a valuation of £2.3 m and pay in instalments as the stock was sold.

Prior to the sale, the joint administrators had used Deloitte Corporate Finance to manage a parallel process to broker the sale of the business. The joint administrators used the UK branch of CBRE Group, a commercial real estate services firm and a Fortune 500 company, to "undertake inventories and valuation of stock, plant and equipment, fixtures and fittings and other chattle assets". Within two days of their formal appointment the joint administrators stated that they chose the offer from the existing company directors as it was the best possible offer made by five prospective buyers and allowed the sale of the business as a whole rather than the piecemeal sale of assets.

February 2009–August 2009: The first progress report on the sale of the balance of assets left in the company following the pre-packaged administration indicated that the joint administrators had recovered £1.7 m which related to the company's foreign currency deposits. There was no other major asset sale during this period.

February 2010–August 2010: The joint administrators also asked CBRE to continue to act as their agent for letting and sale of the freehold and long leasehold properties. In the meantime, they also sought professional legal advice from two law firms in relation to the assignment and surrender of leasehold stores. They sold the freehold properties and assigned the leasehold properties to Newco owned by former company directors. The remaining stores were closed. The joint administrators also dealt with issues such as tax, corporate finance and real estate, drawing on Deloitte's specialist expertise. Sale of properties was facilitated through the Drivers Jonas—Deloitte real estate agency; however, there is no detailed information on its role in the administrator's progress report.

The final progress report to creditors in January 2012 indicates that the remaining stores had been closed. The joint administrators disclosed that the freehold properties had been sold for £41 m; however, no information was given about the purchaser as the sale transaction was subject to commercial confidentiality.

Analysis: The pre-packaged sale of the business by the company directors seems to have created a smooth and speedy business transition. The directors' insider position may have put them in the best position to make a bid for the company. The joint administrators do not seem to have addressed the disposal of other non-trading and non-profitable assets. Unlike the speedy sale of the core business that took place within the early days of administration, the sale of other outstanding assets seems to have taken much longer to finalise.

Distribution of Proceeds to Secured Creditors

February 2009: At the time of administration, the company's secured creditors included Barclays, Prudential and Lloyds TSB each with different amounts of claims. Their debt was guaranteed by assets including properties held by different subsidiaries. Although directors had stated that the total secured debt would be £31.4 m, the joint administrators estimated it at £43 m. It seems that a mutual agreement outside administration was made between company directors and lenders over operational secured assets since they were transferred to the new company as part of its operating business. Based on the administrators' proposal, only £1.7 m unrealised assets were left in the parent company and were subject to security interest. However, since the debt was cross-guaranteed by subsidiaries, the joint administrators were able to sell 21 freehold properties and distribute their proceeds amongst secured creditors to discharge the debt.

August 2009–February 2010: As the joint administrators' second progress report shows, lenders received a total of £550 k from the proceeds of a £600 k cash bond previously provided to the Prudential. This payment seems to be made to Lloyds TSB under a letter of set-off, guarantee and debenture in full.

February 2010–August 2010: Secured creditors were paid £29 m realised from the sale of the assets of the subsidiaries.

August 2010–February 2011: £1 m was distributed amongst secured creditors.

August 2011: Lenders were paid £35 m from the sale of freehold properties and other assets belonging to subsidiaries.

Analysis: The joint administrators appear to have repaid more than £36 m of debt to lenders. This recovery rate seems to be substantial compared with the £43 m original claim. Part of the lenders' claims seem to have been transferred to the new company as part of the pre-packaged sale, suggesting that they may have ultimately been fully paid.

Distribution of Proceeds to Unsecured Creditors

At the start of administration, it was believed that there were no unsecured claims. This might have been due to the creditors delaying invoicing the company. Further, the directors' statement of affairs did not indicate the existence of any unsecured debt. However, the first progress report shows that the administrators received invoices that totalled £29 k. The joint administrators dismissed any prospect of payment to unsecured creditors under the prescribed part as the floating charges were created pre-September 2003. They also expressed doubt over the possible payment of dividends to unsecured creditors. By the end of August 2010, unsecured claims had reached £32 k.

It seems that the company had either paid its unsecured debt prior to administration or reached an agreement with unsecured creditors over the transfer of debt to the new company; however, there is no information on the agreements made between administrators and suppliers over pre-sale payments.

Investigation into Directors' Conduct

September 2009: The administrators completed their enquiry into the conduct of company directors and submitted their findings to the Department for Business, Enterprise and Regulatory Reform (DBERR). Although there is no information about the content of the administrators' report on directors' conduct, the administrators' agreement with the directors' acquisition of the company indicates that no significant issues were identified. Therefore, it seems that the company directors had performed their duties appropriately and made informed decisions. Shareholder approval pre-authorised the actions of individual members of the board during the informal rescue process including potential conflicts of interest. The number of directors remaining with the company during administration also appears to have ensured a smooth transition of assets.

Creditor Influence

Secured creditors: It appears that the joint administrators initially proposed to secured creditors that they approve joint administrators' fees. The fourth progress report suggests that lenders approved administrators' withdrawal of fees. There is no detailed information about lenders' influence in the sale of freehold properties.

Unsecured creditors: As mentioned earlier, it seemed that the parent company did not have any unsecured creditors. None were identified in the directors' statement of affairs. The joint administrators proposed that no creditors' meeting should be held for the parent company and no dividend for unsecured creditors was proposed under prescribed parts due to the costs. The progress reports do not indicate any challenge by unsecured creditors of the administrators' proposals.

Administration outcome: Stylo plc exited administration on January 6, 2012, after the joint administrators filed for dissolution, and it was dissolved in April 2012. The administration resulted in the closure of 143 stores and the redundancy of employees working in those stores. As the last progress report shows, administration costs amounted to a total of £260 k, including £150 k administrators' fees for the administration of the parent company. There is no information as to the actual amount of secured debt transferred to the new company as part of its pre-packaged administration; however, it seems that lenders received more than 80% of their claims whilst the relatively small number of unsecured creditors of the parent company did not receive any dividends. The majority of company directors became the shareholders in the new company.

Summary

The pre-packaged administration by the board of directors of Stylo plc demonstrates significant influence by the board of directors and lenders to protect the interests of the company. Although there is no information on the nature of their agreement prior to administration, the company could maintain a going concern through incorporation of a new company. However, the outcome did not protect the interests of those unsecured creditors whose interests were terminated following administration. They may have been successful in recovering their claims through other channels, for example, insurance; however, lack of any hard evidence makes it difficult to make such a judgment. The pre-packaged administration also allowed company directors to influence the procedure to some extent as the majority stayed with the company during administration and it seems that they continued their collaboration with the joint administrators.

Note

1. Stylo Barratt Shoes limited, Stylo Barratt Properties limited, Priceless Shoes Properties Limited and Comfort Shoes Limited.

Bibliography

Apperley Realisations No.2, Limited. Form 2.24B. Registered August 22, 2011. https://beta.companieshouse.gov.uk/company/00657595/filinghistory

Apperley Realisations No.5, Limited. Form 2.35B. Registered January 10, 2012. https://beta.companieshouse.gov.uk/company/03153359/filinghistory

Stylo, plc. CERT7. Registered July 28, 1981. https://beta.companieshouse.gov.uk/company/00314740/filing-history?page=11

Stylo, plc. *Annual Report and Accounts Year to 03 February 2007*. https://beta.companieshouse.gov.uk/company/00314740/filing-history?page=2

Stylo, plc. Final Results. RNS No. 2338V Dated May 27, 2008a.

Stylo, plc. *Annual Report and Accounts 2008b*. https://beta.companieshouse.gov.uk/company/00314740/filing-history?page=2

Stylo, plc. Form 395. Registered November 18, 2008c. https://beta.companieshouse.gov.uk/company/00314740/filing-history?page=2

Stylo, plc. Interim Results. RNS No. 1945H Dated October 31, 2008d.

Stylo, plc. Re Directorate. RNS No. 2311V Dated May 27, 2008e.

Stylo, plc. Re Directorate. RNS No. 4298Y Dated 7 July 2008f.

Stylo, plc. RESOLUTIONS. Registered July 3, 2008g. https://beta.companieshouse.gov.uk/company/00314740/filing-history?page=2

Stylo, plc. Disposal. March 17, 2008. www.investegate.co.uk. Accessed May 1, 2017.

Stylo, plc. Trading Update. RNS No. 3330J Dated December 2, 2008i.

Stylo, plc. Form 2.24B. Registered September 30, 2009a. https://beta.companieshouse.gov.uk/company/00314740/filing-history?page=1

Stylo, plc. Form 12.B. Registered March 14, 2009b. https://beta.companieshouse.gov.uk/company/00314740/filing-history?page=1

Stylo, plc. Result of Creditor Meetings. RNS No. 2636N Dated February 13, 2009c.

Stylo, plc. Form 2.16B with Forms 2.15B/2.14B. Registered June 10, 2009d. https://beta.companieshouse.gov.uk/company/00314740/filing-history?page=1

Stylo, plc. Trading Update. RNS No. 1298M Dated January 22, 2009e.

Stylo, plc. Form 2.17B. Registered April 2, 2009f. https://beta.companieshouse.gov.uk/company/00314740/filing-history?page=1

Stylo, plc. Director/PDMR Shareholding. RNS No. 1826M Dated 23 January 2009g.

Stylo, plc. Director/PDMR Shareholding. RNS No. 1829 Dated 23 January 2009h.

Stylo, plc. Intention to Appoint Administrators. RNS No. 0919N Dated February 10, 2009i.

Stylo, plc. Form 2.12B. Registered February 26, 2009j. https://beta.companieshouse.gov.uk/company/00314740/filing-history?page=1

Stylo, plc. Form 2.24B. Registered September 30, 2009k. https://beta.companieshouse.gov.uk/company/00314740/filing-history?page=1

Stylo, plc. Form 403a (Charge no. 20). Registered July 30, 2009l. https://beta.companieshouse.gov.uk/company/00314740/filing-history

Stylo, plc. Form 403a (Charge no. 22). Registered July 30, 2009m. https://beta.companieshouse.gov.uk/company/00314740/filing-history

Stylo, plc. Form 403a (Charge no. 23). Registered July 30, 2009n. https://beta.companieshouse.gov.uk/company/00314740/filing-history

Stylo, plc. Form 403a (Charge no. 28). Registered July 30, 2009o. https://beta.companieshouse.gov.uk/company/00314740/filing-history

Stylo, plc. Form 403a (Charge no. 4). Registered July 30, 2009p. https://beta.companieshouse.gov.uk/company/00314740/filing-history

Stylo, plc. Proposed CVAs and Appointment. RNS No. 2428M Dated January 26, 2009q.

Stylo, plc. Form 2.24B. Registered January 23, 2010a. https://beta.companieshouse.gov.uk/company/00314740/filing-history?page=1

Stylo, plc. Form 2.24B. Registered March 16, 2010b. https://beta.companieshouse.gov.uk/company/00314740/filing-history?page=1

Stylo, plc. Form 2.24B. Registered September 23, 2010c. https://beta.companieshouse.gov.uk/company/00314740/filing-history?page=1

Stylo, plc. Form 2.24B. Registered March 22, 2011a. https://beta.companieshouse.gov.uk/company/00314740/filing-history?page=1

Stylo, plc. Form 2.24B. Registered September 20, 2011b. https://beta.companieshouse.gov.uk/company/00314740/filing-history?page=1

Stylo, plc. Form 2.24B. Registered January 23, 2012a. https://beta.companieshouse.gov.uk/company/00314740/filing-history?page=1

Stylo, plc. Form 2.35B. Registered January 10, 2012b. https://beta.companieshouse.gov.uk/company/00314740/filing-history?page=1

8

Case Study 2: JJB Sports plc

Overview

JJB Sports plc was a large public company that went through two CVAs with different outcomes. The company was ultimately placed into administration and was dissolved in 2016. This case study focuses on the CVAs. It demonstrates the use of debt financing to resolve cash flow problems and the effect this has on lenders' bargaining power with directors. It also demonstrates how companies can use intercompany debt as an unsecured claim to influence the results of creditor voting in favour of a CVA. The discussion of the informal rescue process covers use of all options including board change, asset sale, share issue and debt financing. The company's entry into administration in 2012 illustrates the implied superior position of secured creditors' interests outside the scope of the CVA.

The case study covers two separate timeframes—April 27, 2008, to April 26, 2009, when the Group was subject to an informal rescue process, and April 27, 2009, to April 26, 2010, when the company was the subject of a successful CVA. This case study also briefly considers the period between March 22, 2011, and October 1, 2012, when a second CVA was in progress but terminated on entry into administration.

Background: JJB Sports plc (est. 1971) was listed on the LSE in October 1994. As the second largest footwear retailer in the UK, JJB Sports plc operated as a parent company with two major trading companies: Blane Leisure Limited and Sports Division (Eireann) Limited. As at January 2008 the company had more than 400 stores and 49 fitness clubs.

Concentrated ownership was a feature of the company. Until 2007, David Whelan, the founder of the company, was a major shareholder. In 2007 he sold 29% of the total shares to a consortium of Icelandic Financial Group Exista and Chris Ronnie. Subsequently Ronnie was appointed to the position of Deputy Chief Executive, later taking on the role of Chief Executive Officer (CEO) in June 2007. The parent company—with a total revenue of £811 m, balance sheet worth of £789 m and 7,600 staff—fitted the definition of a mega insolvency case.

Corporate governance: JJB Sports plc had been listed on the UK stock market for over a decade and had explicitly committed itself to "high standards of corporate governance". The last Company Report and Accounts explicitly stated that the company complied with the Code. In April 2008, the company had a seven-member board of directors including three executive directors and four non-executive directors. Its executive directors included the CEO of JJB Sports plc who also represented the interests of the major shareholder, a property director and a finance director, and its non-executive directors included the chairman, a senior independent non-executive director and two other independent non-executive directors. The company was in compliance with the Code in terms of the balance between executive directors and non-executive directors.

Debt structure: In 1998, the parent company acquired Blane Leisure Limited for £168 m. Instead of using cash reserves, it took out a loan with UBS AG, a Swiss global financial services company. This loan was guaranteed against the cash reserves with loan notes granted to UBS. A relevant security interest was created under a "security deposit agreement" between the parent company and UBS that prevented JJB Sports plc from using the cash reserve without the consent of its guarantor before its maturity date in April 2011.

Financial Distress and Associated Causes

Financial distress: From 2002 onwards the company had experienced a gradual decrease in profitability on a year on year basis. However, the company Report and Financial Statement for 2008 demonstrate that at the start of the informal rescue process the parent company, with total assets of £789 m and total liabilities of £424 m, was balance sheet solvent and therefore economically viable. It was also cash flow solvent as the consolidated current assets were £372 m whilst its current liabilities were £301 m.

Internal causes: The decrease in profitability may have been linked to an aggressive business expansion strategy adopted by a new chief executive/major shareholder who acquired two financially distressed companies, the Original Shoe Company Limited (OSC) and the insolvent Qube Footwear Limited, in early 2008.

External causes: The general loss of consumer confidence following the global financial crisis of 2008 resulted in a marked reduction in turnover and led the company to resort to secured debt to continue to finance the business. The company's core business (sports goods) was also aggressively targeted by a major competitor (Sports Direct International) that moved much more rapidly and effectively into online retailing, serving the same markets, with a wider selection of low-priced merchandise. The management team that was in charge of the company in 2008 failed to respond quickly and effectively to this challenge.

Informal Rescue Process

Board of Directors' Role

Overview: The company undertook its first CVA following creditor approval on April 27, 2009. Based on the definition of the informal rescue process set out in previous chapter, this research assumes that the company was subject to an informal rescue process from April 27, 2008, until the day the CVA was approved. This section takes a chronological approach to the informal rescue process, identifying the main events related to board change, asset sale, equity issue and debt financing.

The main feature of the informal rescue process is the board's use of most rescue options, especially asset sale, equity issue and debt financing. During the informal rescue process, the CEO, also representing a major institutional shareholder, was in charge of the company. The board's success in applying these options may have been due to the company's strong balance sheet solvency which persuaded lenders to finance the going concern of the company. This solvency also attracted new investors. Board changes and asset sale also feature as rescue options.

Board Change

April 2008: The group finance director resigned in advance of his retirement. The commercial director added these roles to his responsibilities, pending a replacement.

May 2008: The commercial director was appointed as the new group finance director.

October 2008: A newly appointed non-executive director who had previously held the position of chairman and CEO of Next plc took on the role of deputy chairman. The new role also allowed him to play a role in the "retail operations of the company". The group property director resigned to "pursue outside property interests". No replacement was made to this position.

January 2009: An executive director for strategic development was appointed with responsibility for restructuring the company. The deputy chairman took over the role of executive chairman and the existing chairman became deputy chairman. In the same month the CEO was suspended from his position and placed under investigation into his business conduct by the company's legal advisors. The CEO's suspension followed his notice that his own private company had sold all his shares in the company to Kaupthing Singer & Friedlander (KSF), an Icelandic Bank and one of the company's lenders (now insolvent). In effect this transferred the rights of a major shareholder with voting rights to KSF.

February 2009: The CEO submitted his resignation "conditional upon reaching agreement on the terms of a settlement", but the board decided not to accept his resignation until the matter was clarified.

March 2009: A new legal and operations director was appointed who also took on the role of company secretary. The CEO was dismissed from the company and the case was referred to the Office of Fair Trading (OFT) for further investigation. The case eventually led to charges of fraud and forgery brought by the Serious Fraud Office against the CEO in 2013.

April 2009: The group finance director resigned following an agreement with the board to "clear the way for a rapid succession". In the meantime, the executive director for restructuring became responsible for overseeing financial matters. The group CEO was dismissed from the company.

Analysis: Board changes were clearly a major feature of corporate governance during this period. The board changes seem to have continued for the whole year causing its instability. Whilst the overall size of the board did not change, the number of non-executive directors on the board reduced due to a shift from non-executive to executive roles.

Cost Reduction

The company adopted a business expansion strategy for the financial year 2008–2009 including the launch of a Training Academy for staff. The strategy might have been expected to increase rather than decrease costs.

May 2008: The company acquired the fashion footwear business Qube Footwear Limited from West Coast Capital for £1. It also announced the completion of a store closure programme that included the assignment or closure of 96 stores. This second measure could be expected to reduce costs as well as raise cash.

September 2008: The company launched its first generation of fitness clubs-superstores in Cardiff. The company also implemented an "extensive stock clearance programme" with the objective of disposing of non-core assets.

Analysis: The board seems to have focused on a mixture of business expansion and cost reduction. Acquisition of a financially distressed company seems to be contrary to the spirit of informal rescue options; however, it may be justified based on the company's strong balance sheet solvency and the low cost of acquisition.

Asset Sale

July 2008: By the end of the month, the company had assigned leases or completed the sale of 96 retail stores.

December 2008: Following a review of its non-core assets, the company engaged Lazard & Co, Limited as joint advisor for sale negotiations of such assets, including fitness clubs. Subsequently, it completed the assignment of the leases of four retail stores to Sports Direct to pay its borrowings.

March 2009: On March 9, the company initiated a series of discussions with its advisors and lenders over the terms of sale of its fitness clubs. Subsequently, the company sold its fitness club business, 53 related stores and stock to David Whelan Sports Ltd., a company owned by the original founder of JJB Sports plc in consideration for a deferred payment. The sale did not require shareholder approval as the company obtained a waiver from the UK Listing Authority as a financially distressed company. The company stated that the proceeds of the sale would be paid to landlords for quarterly rent due in March. At the end of the informal rescue process, the company had 205 remaining stores.

Analysis: Asset sale seems to be spread throughout the year. The board initiated the option by involving professionals to facilitate sale. The acquisition of fitness clubs by the founder and previous major shareholder of JJB Sports plc is significant. The lack of shareholder approval is notable, indicating the ability of the directors of a company to avoid obtaining shareholder consent for decisions taken at a time of financial distress.

Equity/Share Issue

July 2008: The board prepared for a share issue by obtaining shareholder approval for disapplication of pre-emption rights and allotment of shares and debentures.

October 2008: The company issued new ordinary shares and subsequently placed 5% of these shares with its business rival Sports Direct International. The transaction was approved by the OFT.

November 2008: JD Sports Fashion, another business rival, purchased 10% of the shares.

April 2009: The board obtained shareholder approval for a further share issue.

Analysis: Equity issue seems to be a successful means of increasing cash flow. Key parties including shareholders, and the regulatory body, the OFT seem to be supportive of the option. The investment by the company's rivals rather than a private equity firm is interesting, since it demonstrates the keen competitive environment of this particular sector and the desire of competitors to gain any advantage available. It raises the question of whether the board were so committed to raising cash that they were prepared to allow two competitors to gain some element of control over the business.

New Debt Financing/Debt Renegotiation

September 2008: The parent company created guarantees and debentures in favour of Barclays and the Bank of Scotland (BOS) which included fixed and floating charges on all of its assets.

October 2008: The company announced successful negotiations with KSF over a £20 m bridging facility. The company created a similar security interest to the one granted to the other two lenders. Debt negotiations with the BOS and Barclays continued. It also appointed KPMG to "advise on those negotiations".

December 2008: The company had ongoing debt negotiations with its existing lenders. The company appointed Lazard & Co, Limited as its joint financial advisor. On December 10, the company announced that it had obtained a standstill agreement with its lenders that allowed it to defer payment of a £20 m bridging facility to KSF due on December 14, 2008, and instead pay the three banks, £20 m pro rata on that day to reduce the amount of loan outstanding. The standstill agreement allowed JJB Sports to continue to access all bank facilities until the end of January. In return, the interest rate on those facilities was increased and the company agreed to pay £8.3 m in associated fees in February and April 2009.

Subsequently the company registered an account charge in favour of the lenders. The charge reflects the formation of an apparent syndicate between Barclays, the BOS and KSF, led by Barclays. The charge also extended the existing security interests of the parties and required the company to do whatever the security trustee might require or consider expedient at the company's expense. The terms of the charge effectively reduced the discretion of directors to take independent action and arguably compromised directors' duties to shareholders.

February 2009: The standstill agreement was extended, at a cost of £160 K to March 16 provided that the "lenders remain satisfied with the progress of the company's proposed disposal of its fitness clubs".

March 2009: The standstill agreement was further extended until March 24 at no further legal and administrative cost. Soon after, the company reached an agreement with its lenders that the standstill agreement could be extended until a CVA was approved and the deferred payments from the sale of the fitness clubs were received. The company's statements also added that the standstill agreement was dependent on "the lenders remaining satisfied with the progress of the CVA proposal and the trading performance of the Company". The company's statement appears to have shown directors' concern for insolvency as the executive chairman suggested that they were seeking to protect the long-term interests of the company for its stakeholders.

Analysis: Lenders seem to have influenced the informal rescue process between September 2008 and March 2009. The security interests that were created had substantially improved lender's bargaining powers against those of company directors. There is no information on why the company did not approach UBS as the guarantor of the loan notes for a compromise over the use of its £168 m cash reserve, and instead agreed to share control powers with lenders led by the BOS.

Shareholder Influence

July 2008: The board obtained shareholder approval for the re-appointment of two non-executive directors and one executive director at its AGM. Shareholders also approved the board's proposals including director remuneration and shareholder dividends. They approved the board's proposals for those matters that related to equity issue including consolidation of share capital, disapplication of their pre-emption rights, allotment of shares and debentures during the AGM.

Analysis: Shareholders seem to have shown a passive/supportive attitude to the board's behaviour which is a common pattern across the case study companies in this book.

Creditor Influence

Secured creditors: Any influence by secured creditors must have started with their terms and conditions of lending. Lack of access to loan transactions makes it difficult to determine the scope of their security interests. The company's cash flow problem seems to have extended lender's influence. The company acknowledged the "extreme pressure from lenders during its informal rescue process that continued during the CVA which was followed by an increase in fees, and increase in costs".

Unsecured creditors: Between January and October 2008 the company's trade credit insurance risk was downgraded and some of the company's suppliers refused to continue supplying the company under the impression that it was insolvent (Nike and Adidas continued to supply).

October 2008: The company announced that like many other companies in the retail sector, its credit insurance cover had been partly withdrawn but that it was "confident of its trading relationship with key suppliers".

December 2008: An unsecured creditor, Everton Football Club, issued a winding-up petition against the company. Since the company had to pay the creditor to avoid liquidation, it defaulted on its debt obligations leading to further costs payable to KSF and its advisors for a grant of waiver.

The company experienced a 50% reduction in stock availability compared with the previous year and the situation continued until September 2009.

The Annual Report in 2009 shows that the company lost 22% of revenue due to supplier hesitation or refusal to continue to trade.

Analysis: Trade creditors appear to have caused disruption to the company's going concern by their risk-averse approach and as a result the company's financial distress worsened.

Discussion: The company seems to have adopted a comprehensive informal rescue process that initially aimed to increase cash flow. Board change continued throughout the whole rescue process, effectively resulting in a new executive team. Non-executive directors seem to have adopted a hands-on approach featured by the shift of a non-executive director to the role of executive chairman. There was no attempt by the board to appoint a new CEO until December 2009 as the first CVA took effect.

Directors seem to have focused on the payment of secured debt. The significant influence of unsecured creditors in disrupting the business of the company cannot be ignored. Their influence seems to have made the company increasingly dependent on secured debt as a source of finance. The potential influence of lenders can be seen in their contribution to the review of sale offers, their share of proceeds from the share issue and ultimately pressure on the company to use the CVA to resolve cash problems.

Formal Rescue Process: CVA

Overview: The parent company entered a successful CVA (CVA 1) on April 27, 2009, which was in effect until late April 26, 2010. The supervisors paid creditors from the funds until June 16, 2010. A feature of the CVA in JJB Sports plc was supportive creditor voting: the CVA was approved by a majority of creditors; however, a particular feature of creditor voting worth noting is the intercompany debt which allowed the company's subsidiary to have voting rights.

The CVA was preceded by the appointment of two insolvency practitioners from KPMG as administrators for the Original Shoe Company and Qube Footwear Limited who subsequently put 77 stores into a formal rescue process. This move appears to have been agreed with lenders as the company's announcement on February 19 states that this was part of the company's extended standstill arrangement, aimed at preparing creditors for a CVA.

The measures put into place following the first CVA were not successful in restoring the company to a profitable trading situation, and its competitive position worsened during the year following its completion, although the first CVA was successfully completed. A second CVA (CVA 2) was proposed and put into place in 2011, that is, a year later. However, the second CVA was terminated, due to the company's gradual weakening financial position and the company was placed into administration.

Company Voluntary Arrangement (CVA 1)

Process

April 2009: On April 6, 2009, the company submitted its CVA proposal to a nominee from KPMG, all unsecured creditors of the parent company and its subsidiary and shareholders. The CVA proposal focused on the rents owed to the landlords of the premises of 140 closed JJB stores and its subsidiary Blane Leisure Ltd. It modified landlords' overdue claims up to a total of £10 m—the sum to be paid from a fund set up for this purpose and allowed the landlords of the open stores to vary the terms of their leases and to be paid monthly rent rather than quarterly rent on a temporary basis. In brief the proposal aimed to modify the rent and lease or assign unwanted retail stores, leaving open stores to operate normally.

JJB Sports plc seems to have already received the support of secured creditors as the company expected that the CVA would be funded by various amounts and types of loan. The company had proposed to shareholders that they would issue warrants to BOS. The creditor meeting was held on April 27 under the chairmanship of an insolvency practitioner from KPMG ahead of a shareholder meeting on April 29. The documents filed by the chairman show that some creditor claims were disqualified or modified. However no detailed information is provided on the reasons, only the total amount subject to disqualification. Total creditor claims amounted to £263.6 m.

The CVA proposal shows the two largest unsecured creditors were Blane Ltd. (£145.3 m) and Sports Division (Eireann) Limited (£22.2 m), both subsidiaries of JJB Sports. This debt may relate to the costs of acquisition of these two businesses, or internal sales transfers, although there is no information in the CVA documentation. Other creditors include HMRC (£8.9 m), Nike European Operations (£8.6 m) and Adidas (UK) Limited (£8 m). Effectively the parent company was able to get its proposals for the CVA through, because of the large proportion of intercompany debt that voted in favour of the resolution. Only one creditor sought modification; there is no information on creditor objections or challenges prior to creditor voting. Records of the meeting indicate that the CVA proposal received creditor approval with 99.9% of creditor value in favour, perhaps indicating the landlords' reluctant acceptance of the inevitable. Its approval was not challenged within the statutory deadline.

The CVA proposal and other special resolutions obtained majority shareholder approval during the AGM held in April 2009. In the absence of any further challenge to the CVA it was approved. There is no further information in the form of a progress report about the implementation of the CVA in company announcements or in mandatory corporate filings during its implementation, leaving questions about the treatment of creditor claims during the CVA and creditor influence. The CVA was completed within a year. During its implementation, the company paid the landlords of closed stores 10% of the £55 m that was owed.

April 2010: The CVA was completed. According to the report submitted by the supervisors of the CVA fund, the company continued its payments to secured creditors and preferential creditors without further default. Landlords of closed stores received payment of their modified claims in two instalments.

Analysis: The board was successful in obtaining creditors' support for its CVA proposal. The insolvency practitioner seems to have played a key role in drafting the CVA proposal prior to the creditors' meeting. The question remains as to how much landlords individually were owed compared to other classes of unsecured creditors. The chairman's role is limited to accepting or rejecting claims during the creditors' meeting. There is no detailed information as to whether accepted claims were modified.

The main supporters of the CVA were holders of intercompany debt, that is, the company itself. It seems that the approach taken by the chairman towards intercompany debt was different from the approach that is generally taken by administrators. The passivity of HMRC seems justified as the CVA did not have any impact on its claim.

Board Change

May 2009: A new finance director was appointed and a new director of retail and product joined the board. The restructuring director who had served the board as an executive director left the company.

July 2009: The executive chairman moved to a part-time position following disclosure of his personal borrowing from the CEO of the rival business Sports Direct. The senior independent non-executive director resigned. The deputy chairman retired from his position. A senior independent non-executive director joined the board.

December 2009: A new CEO was appointed.

January 2010: Two new non-executive directors were appointed. The executive chairman resigned from his position "for health reasons" but remained as a non-executive director. Subsequently, the senior independent non-executive director moved to the role of acting chairman.

March 2010: The director of retail and product retired after ten months in position. The role does not seem to have been replaced.

Analysis: Change at the board level remains a feature of the company during the implementation of the CVA. The change is not limited to executive directors and extends to non-executive directors. It seems that the company sees external appointments as the way forward, bringing in new blood rather than shifting roles between members of the board. Potential director personal liability can be seen in the resignation of the executive chairman after his personal borrowing from the CEO of Sports Direct International (a major shareholder who had acquired 5% of the newly issued shares) was disclosed. No further enquiry was made by the regulatory body, following the resignation of the executive chairman. However, in December 2014 he was convicted of fraud, sentenced to four years imprisonment and disqualified from being a director of a company for eight years.

Asset Sale

May 2009: The company finalised the sale of its 31 retail stores to Sports Direct International following approval by the Office of Fair Trading.

July 2009: The company sold non-core assets including a helicopter to David Whelan Sports Ltd., JJB's founder. It also sold its shares in the fashion brand Kooga to DJ Sports.

Analysis: The first CVA seems to have facilitated completion of asset sale. The board seems to have used asset sale during the implementation of the CVA to a limited extent. The involvement of the founder of JJB Sports as the purchaser of those assets is significant. It suggests that he believed that there was still potential for the company.

Equity/Share Issue

July 2009: At the AGM, the board obtained shareholder approval for an increase in share capital, the allotment of relevant security interests for cash or shares, the disapplication of pre-emption rights, the buy-back of company shares and the adoption of new Articles of Association. Shareholder approval paved the way for the board to implement these actions.

October 2009: The board announced to investors that the company intended to increase its share capital by £100 m through private placement and a public offering with the intention of paying 25% of the proceeds towards repayment of the debt owed to the BOS, and an extension of the maturity date of credit facilities from September 2010 to September 2012. Further announcements show that the company received a positive response from investors, resulting in an increase in share capital, payment of £30 m to the BOS and extension of the maturity date to September 2012.

Analysis: It seems that the implementation of the CVA did not minimise the board's power to use equity issue on a large scale. Investors' positive response seems to have helped the board achieve the result.

New Debt Financing/Debt Renegotiation

June 2009: The company received £50 m in new credit facilities as part of a financing agreement for its CVA with Barclays and the BOS, and repaid its short-term loan to KSF. According to the agreement that followed implementation of the CVA, the company was obliged to return 50% of the new credit facility to Barclays in August 2009. The maturity date of the loan from the BOS was September 2010. The company was also expected to issue share warrants in favour of the BOS. Loans were secured by a mortgage and fixed charges whilst the company was released from the account charge previously created in favour of the three lenders.

December 2009: The company repaid its debt to Barclays and obtained release from fixed charges previously created.

Analysis: Lender influence seems to have decreased following the company's repayment of its debt although the company still had assets secured with one lender scheduled to mature in September 2011.

Company Voluntary Arrangement (CVA 2)

February 2011: The company provided a final draft of a new CVA proposal and delivered it to the BOS. According to the company, the proposal was based on constructive discussions with landlords.

March 2011: On March 3 company directors sent their CVA proposal to the nominee, shareholders and creditors. The CVA proposed closure of 43 stores by April 2012 and another 46 stores by April 2013. The rents owed were modified to 50% of contractual values. It also proposed to landlords of closed stores a reduction of contractual rent value of 50%. A compromised lease fund was proposed for March 2013, subject to successfully transferring the company's shares to the AIM and the sale of the company. In March 2011, a meeting of creditors and shareholders voted in favour of the new CVA proposal. The proposal was approved without modification. Total claims owed to creditors amounted to £225 m. The proposal received 96% of the votes by nominal value. Twenty two out of 694 creditors voted against the proposal. Amongst creditors, the subsidiary Blane Leisure Limited (£109 m), Sports Division (Eireann) Limited (£33 m), Neon B V (£11 m) and Adidas (£10 m) had the largest claims. Creditors voting against the proposal, with total claims of £9 m, had no chance of success. The chairman dismissed a group of creditors with total claims of £4 m without including any reasons. No challenge was brought by creditors during the statutory deadline and therefore the CVA took effect, under the supervision of two insolvency practitioners from KPMG.

May 2011: Intensive negotiations continued with the bank over the grant of further banking facilities.

May 2012: The supervisors of the CVA fund released their statutory report that revealed that no payment had been made to landlords for pre-CVA arrears of rent.

In October 2012 the parent company entered administration and CVA (2) was terminated. During this period, landlords of open stores received 50% of their rent on a monthly basis. According to the CVA proposal, landlords of the closed stores were not entitled to any dividend, as the fund was not subject to the sale of assets. The failure of the CVA and the Group's entry to administration led to more than 2,000 redundancies. Business rival Sports Direct acquired only 20 stores as part of the business in a pre-packaged purchase.

Summary

The scope of informal rescue options adopted by JJB Sports plc is wide. Delayed sale of parts of the business limited the success of the informal rescue process, leading to increases in secured debt financing and the beginning of enhanced secured creditor influence. The successful formulation and implementation of the CVA enabled a timely payment of debt to lenders at the expense of the disposal of a large volume of potentially profitable assets. The lender's influence throughout the implementation of the CVA is unknown.

The failure of the second CVA in 2011–2012 reflects the company's gradual weakening financial stability. Commencement of administration by the company directors suggests that lenders were ultimately dissatisfied with the way their interests were protected and may indicate balance sheet insolvency. Use of three formal rescue processes within four years suggests that in the long run the company's financial position was unsustainable, and could not be resolved through informal rescue process or CVA.

Bibliography

Competition and Markets Authority Press Release, January 28, 2009. "Sports Direct International plc/JJB Sports plc." https://www.gov.uk/cmacases/sports-direct-international-plc-jjb-sports-plc, Accessed April 15, 2017.

JJB Sports, plc. Form 395. Registered September 16, 1998. https://beta.companieshouse.gov.uk/company/01024895/filing-history?page=12

JJB Sports, plc. 2006. *Annual Report and Financial Statements for the 52 Weeks to 29 January 2006*. Wigan, Lancashire: JJB Sports plc.

JJB Sports plc. 2007. *Annual report and Financial Statements for the 52 Weeks to 28 January 2007*. Wigan, Lancashire: JJB Sports plc.

JJB Sports, plc. Form 395. Registered December 24 2008a. https://beta.companieshouse.gov.uk/company/01024895/filing-history?page=6

JJB Sports plc. 2008a. *Annual Report and Financial Statements for the 52 Weeks to 27 January 2008*. Wigan, Lancashire: JJB Sports plc.

JJB Sports, plc. Assignment of Leases. RNS No. 2518J Dated December 1, 2008c.
JJB Sports, plc. Business Update. RNS No. 5282J Dated December 4, 2008d.
JJB Sports plc. Form 395. Registered December 24, 2008e. https://beta.companieshouse.gov.uk/company/01024895/filing-history?page=6
JJB Sports, plc. Form 395. Registered October 11, 2008f. https://beta.companieshouse.gov.uk/company/01024895/filing-history?page=6
JJB Sports, plc. Acquisition. RNS No.1289V Dated May 22, 2008g.
JJB Sports, plc. Interim Management Statement. RNS No. 8688J Dated December 10, 2008h.
JJB Sports, plc. Interim Results. RNS No. 3877E Dated September 26, 2008i.
JJB Sports, plc. Resolutions. Registered July 29, 2008j. https://beta.companieshouse.gov.uk/company/01024895/filing-history?page=6
JJB Sports, plc. AGM Statement. RNS No. 7689Z Dated July 24, 2008k.
JJB Sports, plc. Business Update and Board Change. RNS No. 9315F Dated October 15, 2008l.
JJB Sports, plc. Cash placing. RNS No. 1817G Dated October 20, 2008m.
JJB Sports, plc. Potential Disposals. RNS No. 7590F Dated October 14, 2008n.
JJB Sports, plc. Form 395. Registered September 29, 2008o. https://beta.companieshouse.gov.uk/company/01024895/filing-history?page=6
JD Sports Fashion. Statement re Holding in JJB Sports. RNS No. 8369I Dated November 25, 2008p.
JJB Sports, plc. AGM Statement. RNS No. 2357W Dated July 24, 2009a.
JJB Sports, plc. Board Change. RNS No. 1167Q Dated April 3, 2009b.
JJB Sports, plc. Annual Financial Report. RNS No. 9308T Dated June 15, 2009c.
JJB Sports, plc. Detailed Results from Creditor Meetings. RNS No. 3158R Dated April 28, 2009d.
JJB Sports, plc. Director Suspension. RNS No. 9591L Dated January 20, 2009e.
JJB Sports, plc. Director Update. RNS No. 9751N Dated February 26, 2009f.
JJB Sports, plc. Director/PDMR Shareholding. RNS No. 5764L Dated January 13, 2009g.
JJB Sports, plc. Directorate Change. RNS No. 0305L Dated January 2, 2009h.
JJB Sports, plc. Extension of Standstill. RNS No. 2726N Dated February 13, 2009i.
JJB Sports, plc. Further Extension of Standstill and Fitness Clubs Disposals. RNS No. 9664O Dated March 17, 2009j.

JJB Sports, plc. Interim Management Statement. RNS No. 2665E Dated December 7, 2009k.

JJB Sports, plc. Interim Management Statement. RNS No. 6259S Dated May 21, 2009l.

JJB Sports, plc. Issue of Equity. RNS No. 6435A Dated October 12, 2009m.

JJB Sports, plc. JJB Sports plc Appoints John Clare as Senior Independent Non-Executive Director. RNS No. 5503W dated July 20, 2009n.

JJB Sports, plc. Results of Creditor Meeting. RNS No. 2177R Dated April 27, 2009o.

JJB Sports, plc. Results of Firm Placing. RNS No. 5246B Dated October 28, 2009p.

JJB Sports, plc. Results of General Meeting. RNS No. 3891R Dated April 29, 2009q.

JJB Sports, plc. Statement re Fitness Club Business & Financing Arrangements. RNS No. 5021P Dated March 26, 2009r.

JJB Sports, plc. Statement re Press Speculation. RNS No. 8717L Dated January 19, 2009s.

JJB Sports, plc. Strengthens Senior Management team. RNS No. 4421S Dated May 18, 2009t.

JJB Sports, plc. Statement re Financing Arrangements. RNS No. 3103T Dated June 3, 2009u.

JJB Sports, plc. Declaration of Satisfaction in Full or in Part of Mortgage of Charge. Charge No. 33 Dated June 24, 2009 registered July 21, 2009v.

JJB Sports, plc. Statement re Fitness Clubs. RNS No. 5021P Dated March 26, 2009w.

JJB Sports, plc. 2009. Statement re Lifestyle Division' RNS No.: 0688N Dated February 10, 2009x.

JJB Sports, plc. Statement re Press Speculation. RNS No. 5243O Dated March 9, 2009y.

JJB Sports, plc. Update re CVA Proposal. RNS No. 2495Q Dated April 7, 2009z.

JJB Sports, plc. Form 1.1. Registered May 11, 2009aa. https://beta.companies-house.gov.uk/company/01024895/filing-history?page=6

JJB Sports, plc. Form 395. Registered June 12, 2009ab. https://beta.companieshouse.gov.uk/company/01024895/filing-history?page=6

JJB Sports, plc. Form 395. Registered June 17, 2009ac. https://beta.companies-house.gov.uk/company/01024895/filing-history?page=5

JJB Sports, plc. Form 288a Registered August 7, 2009ad. https://beta.companieshouse.gov.uk/company/01024895/filing-history?page=5

JJB Sports, plc. Form 288b. Registered August 5, 2009ae. https://beta.companieshouse.gov.uk/company/01024895/filing-history?page=5

JJB Sports, plc. Form 288b. Registered April 7, 2009af. https://beta.companieshouse.gov.uk/company/01024895/filing-history?page=6

JJB Sports, plc. Resolutions. Registered August 98, 2009ag. https://beta.companieshouse.gov.uk/company/01024895/filing-history?page=5

JJB Sports, plc. Resolutions. Registered May 7, 2009ah. https://beta.companieshouse.gov.uk/company/01024895/filing-history?page=6

JJB Sports, plc. 2009ai. *Annual Report and Accounts 2009*. Wigan, Lancashire: JJB Sports plc. www.Investegate.co.uk. Accessed April 15, 2017.

JJB Sports, plc. Form 1.1 Registered May 11, 2009aj. https://beta.companieshouse.gov.uk/company/01024895/filing-history?page=6

JJB Sports, plc. Administration of Lifestyle Division. RNS No. 5705 Dated February 19, 2009ak.

JJB Sports, plc. Directorate Change. RNS No. 1901J Dated March 25, 2010a.

JJB Sports, plc. Trading Update & Board Change. RNS No. 2439G Dated January 28, 2010b.

JJB Sports, plc. Form 1.3 Registered 28 June 2010c. https://beta.companieshouse.gov.uk/company/01024895/filing-history?page=5

JJB Sports, plc. 2010d. *Annual Report and Accounts 2010*. Wigan, Lancashire: JJB Sports plc.

JJB Sports, plc. Final Results. RNS No. 2407H Dated May 25, 2011a.

JJB Sports, plc. Update on CVA Proposal and Transfer to AIM. RNS No. 2365C Dated March 3, 2011b.

JJB Sports, plc. Update re Proposed Company Voluntary Arrangements. RNS No. 8923B Dated February 25, 2011c.

JJB Sports, plc. Form 1.1. Registered April 15, 2011d. https://beta.companieshouse.gov.uk/company/01024895/filing-history?page=6

JJB Sports, plc. Form 1.3. Registered November 15, 2012a. https://beta.companieshouse.gov.uk/company/01024895/filing-history?page=2

JJB Sports, plc. Form 1.3. Registered May 19, 2012b. https://beta.companieshouse.gov.uk/company/01024895/filing-history?page=2

JJB Sports, plc. Form 1.3 Registered May 23, 2012c. https://beta.companieshouse.gov.uk/company/01024895/filing-history?page=2

JJB Sports, plc. JJB Sports plc appoints Keith Jones as Chief Executive. RNS No. 9153D Dated December 10, 2013.

Office of Fair Trading press release. "OFT considers divestments in Sports Direct's acquisition of JJB Stores." May 1, 2009. http://webarchive.nationalarchives.gov.uk/20100402132147/; http://www.oft.gov.uk/news/press/2009/50-09. Accessed April 15, 2017.

Serious Fraud Office (SFO), "JJB Sports (C Ronnie, D Ball, D Barrington)." Modified April 4, 2017. https://www.sfo.gov.uk/cases/jjb-sports-cronnie-d-ball-d-barrington/

Smale, Will. 2012. "What Went Wrong at JJB Sports?" *BBC News*. October 1. http://www.bbc.co.uk/news/business-19635988. Accessed April 15,2017.

9

Case Study 3: Waterford Wedgwood plc

Overview

Waterford Wedgwood plc is a case study of a large public company that was subject to a formal insolvency regime. The company was a parent company with UK and non-UK subsidiaries. All of its non-UK subsidiaries entered receivership but its only UK main subsidiary, Waterford Wedgwood UK plc, entered administration. This case study relates to attempts at informal rescue of the parent company and the three-year rescue process attempt at its UK main subsidiary between January 2008 and April 2011, at which point the UK subsidiary entered creditors' voluntary liquidation. This case study covers a one-year informal rescue process starting on January 5, 2008, and a two-year formal rescue process between January 5, 2009, and April 26, 2011, during which the company was subject to administration.

A particular feature of corporate governance in the Waterford Wedgwood plc case is the continued influential presence of major shareholders in non-executive roles and family members/shareholders in executive roles. The stability of the board and minimal board changes during the informal rescue process distinguish the company from other case studies in this book. A further differentiating factor is a reliance on equity issue and debt financing as the main way to resolve balance sheet problems. The effect of receivership of the parent company on the administration of its main UK subsidiary is also an important factor influencing the level of control that joint administrators may actually exercise.

Background: Waterford Wedgwood plc (est 1986) was an Irish parent company operating as a manufacturer, retailer and supplier of ceramics, crystalware and pottery. It had a main UK subsidiary, Waterford Wedgwood UK plc, that in turn owned a range of private limited companies. The parent company's brands had a global reputation and distribution, especially Waterford Crystal, Royal Doulton, Wedgwood and Rosenthal AG. The parent company was listed on the Irish and UK Stock Exchanges whilst its UK subsidiary was listed on the London Stock Exchange. The parent company with a consolidated balance sheet worth of €519.2 m, total revenues of €671.8 m and more than 8,000 staff qualified under the definition of the mega insolvency cases used in this book.

Corporate Governance: The company's Annual Report and Accounts for 2008 indicate that the board of directors of the parent company had given a commitment to comply with the Code 2006. The board consisted of 14 members including 5 executive directors and 9 non-executive directors. A particular characteristic of the board of the parent company was the presence of a number of shareholding family members with executive or non-executive roles. Its executive directors included the CEO of the parent company, Chief Financial Officer and three CEOs of the subsidiaries: Rosenthal AG, Waterford Crystal Limited and Waterford Wedgwood plc UK.

Non-executive directors included the Chairman, the majority shareholder in the company, a Deputy Chairman (the Chairman's brother-in-law) who was also the second major shareholder, a director of Waterford Wedgewood UK plc, the Chairman of Waterford Crystal Limited, the Chairman of Waterford Institute of Technology, a non-executive director who was also a member of the Chair's family and one senior independent non-executive director. The Chairman was the former Chairman and CEO of Heinz, who had stepped down from the Heinz board in 2000.

The Chair and the Deputy Chair had invested €133 m in 2007 in the company's preference shares. Two executive directors from Lazard Investment LLC (Lazard) had also joined the board as non-executive directors, following an investment by Lazard in preference shares. Major shareholders had key director roles and there was effectively little separation of ownership and control in the company.

Debt Structure: Between 2003 and 2007, the company had borrowed €181 m on a secured basis. It had also issued different numbers of high-yield bonds to a group of investors with different types of security interests. Lender interests were contractually senior to those of the investors. Bank of America (BOA) represented the interests of investors. This investment generated fixed interest payments at over 9% per annum plus expenses, payable in June and December of each year until 2010 when repayment of the original investment of €166 m was due. Any default would allow BOA to invoke an insolvency procedure.

The Group's other major debts included a bank overdraft, short-term and long-term bank borrowings and leases on premises. On January 5, 2007, the parent company granted fixed and floating charges on all of the Group's assets including plant and machinery, shares, bank accounts and receivables to BOA together with substantial rights to scrutiny of financial information.

Financial Distress and Associated Causes

Financial distress: The parent company was balance sheet insolvent since its consolidated total assets (€519.2 m) were much lower than its total liabilities (€839 m). The parent company remained cash flow solvent due to an in-year equity issue successfully completed in the previous year. No dividends had been paid to ordinary shareholders since 2004.

Internal causes: During 2007 the parent company aggressively pursued a business expansion strategy financed by the creation of debentures and the issue of shares. However despite these efforts, analysis of the Group's sales shows that the turnover fell by €100 m at the end of financial year 2007, compared to financial year 2006.

The parent company struggled with manufacturing and distribution of its products in the critical sales period prior to Christmas 2007, partially due to financing difficulties triggered by a delayed payment of €50 m from Lazard, a new subscriber to preference shares. This reduced cash flow, putting pressure on payments to suppliers and potentially creating a lack of confidence amongst such suppliers.

External causes: The Group's sales continued to be hit in 2007 by a fall in consumer confidence with the board blaming "consumer slowdown" in the USA and the UK as one of the major causes of declining revenues.

Informal Rescue Process

Board of Directors' Role

The company entered administration on January 5, 2009. The informal rescue process is defined as beginning one year prior to the company entering into administration, which covers the period between January 5, 2008, and January 4, 2009. The main features of the informal rescue process in Waterford Wedgwood plc include a primary focus on equity issue and debt financing and a minimal effort on asset sale and board change. This might be justified based on the concentrated shareholding structure of the parent company and the Group's balance sheet insolvency.

Board Change

April 2008: The Chief Executive Director of the parent company resigned "to pursue his own business interests" and an executive director of a small subsidiary, Josiah Wedgwood & Sons Limited, with a background of working in Heinz took over the role of interim CEO.

August 2008: The acting CEO of the parent company was confirmed as permanent.

Analysis: Board change seems to be kept to a minimum to maintain its stability; therefore board size does not change, nor does the proportion of executive directors to non-executive directors. The replacement of the CEO of the parent company by an existing non-executive director who shares a working history with the Chair seems to be designed to ensure co-ordination between governance and executive control and rule out any potential conflict in the decisions that the company subsequently makes. Therefore, the decisions of the board remain dominated by major shareholders.

Cost Reduction

February 2008: The company introduced a restructuring plan in its German subsidiary Rosenthal that involved downsizing the production unit in Germany, increased automation and outsourcing employees, leading to 311 staff redundancies.

April 2008: The board continued operations in all companies in 2008. The company also began to develop a three-year restructuring plan that aimed to save costs. This included redundancies at Waterford's Killbarry factory and the German subsidiary Rosenthal AG, and the merger of the two subsidiaries Wedgwood and Doulton.

August 2008: The company closed its loss-making retail units in the UK. No detailed information was provided.

October 2008: 280 staff redundancies were also announced at the UK subsidiary, Waterford Crystal.

Analysis: Cost reduction seems to have focused on staff redundancies and closure of unprofitable units. The board of directors seems to keep the company as a going concern by implementing minimal cost reduction changes focused on the small subsidiaries.

Asset Sale

June 2008: The parent company engaged JP Morgan Cazenove (an institutional financial advisor) to sell its share in its German subsidiary Rosenthal AG. However no sale was realised.

Analysis: The board seems to have considered asset sale as an option on a small scale and no actual outcome was achieved. There is no information to show whether the company received any offers for the purchase of its subsidiary. The state of balance sheet insolvency and the board's need to receive permission from the lenders for asset sale raise the question of whether asset sale was minimal due to lenders opposing the option.

Equity/Share Issue

August 2008: The board announced a plan to raise €120 m by share issue by December 2008. The plan was supported by major shareholders.

September 2008: The company released information on a modified plan to raise €153 m through private placement and open offer. The shares were mainly preference shares. Major shareholders including the Chairman and the Deputy Chairman and investor Lazard committed to subscribe to shares up to a total value of €75 m. The company subsequently acknowledged that the proceeds would be used to support a three-year restructuring plan and repayment of its debt. The board engaged JP Morgan Cazenove, a leading financial advisor, and Lazard, the owner of Corporate Partners II, to find UK and US private investors, whilst also offering shares on the Irish and London Stock Exchanges.

October 2008: The board held an EGM during which it obtained shareholder approval for an increase of share capital from £215 m to £5 bn through the issue of ordinary and income shares.

December 2008: The parent company was still looking for interested investors for a private placement. However, on December 17, the company sought a delisting of shares from the LSE. Subsequently, the board held a last AGM for shareholders and obtained their approval for all proposed resolutions, empowering the board to allot equity securities.

January 2009: The company sought a delisting of its shares from the Irish Stock Exchange which suspended all its share activities.

Analysis: Equity issue seems to be the focus of the board's strategic plan to resolve the Group debt problem. It might also reflect their confidence in the attractiveness of its brands and the company's history. It seems that major shareholders—largely members of the board—were willing to invest more in the company and also allow their shareholding to be diluted in order to protect the company from any potential takeover. Lenders appear to have shown a positive approach to equity issue by extending the company's access to new credit facilities. However, this option was high risk mainly due to the recession and global financial crash of 2008.

New Debt Financing/Debt Renegotiation

April 2008: The board started negotiations with its lenders over its access to a restricted €200 m multi-currency credit facility and sought the bank's agreement over use of proceeds from disposal of its non-core assets. The company sought financial assistance from the Irish government in a form of a three-year state guarantee for a €39 m bank facility for the subsidiary Waterford Crystal. There is no information about the response from the Irish government but the board of directors later on acknowledged that it had "received remarkable support in this effort at the highest levels from the Irish and the UK governments and certain Irish banks".

July 2008: The company obtained lender's approval for access to a €15 m multiple-currency credit facility until September 2008. It also intended to raise more funding through an additional share issue.

August 2008: The company created a rent deposit deed in favour of its landlord, Daejan Investment.

December 2008: The company announced that it had obtained its lenders' agreement to a standstill on repayment until December 5, 2008. It also stated that it had received the support of its banks on non-payment of dividends to preference shareholders since this would result in a breach of debt covenants. The company also acknowledged that it needed the support of lenders to complete the €150 m financing through equity issue, as the search for investors for its private placement continued.

On December 5, the standstill agreement was extended to December 12 with the hope that the company could still complete its private placement. On December 12, senior lenders agreed to extend the agreement until January 2, 2009. In the meantime, lenders sought professional advice from the insolvency firm Deloitte to prepare a financial analysis of the Group and draft a rescue plan.

Analysis: The company could not obtain substantial new loans or credit facilities from its existing lenders. It did not seek any new credit facility from other lenders. There is no information from lenders on why further loans were not extended to the company. It seems that lenders had ultimately lost faith in the company's long-term survival prospects and moved towards recovering their claims when the board's attempts to raise cash through share issue failed and the company became totally dependent on the secured debt financing.

Shareholder Influence

October 2008: During an EGM, shareholders approved the board's proposed increase in share capital from £215 m to £5 bn. They also authorised sub-division, consolidation and re-designation of income shares. They disapplied their pre-emption rights and the board was also empowered to allot securities and equity securities. Directors were authorised to allot and issue 155 bn shares.

December 2008: At the general meeting held on December 19, 2008, ordinary shareholders approved the board proposal on disapplication of their pre-emption rights over unissued shares as part of three special resolutions. They empowered company directors to allot equity security in connection with a rights issue, open offer or any other pre-emptive in favour of ordinary shareholders and holders of equity securities.

Analysis: Shareholders showed their support by exercising their voting rights in favour of the proposals submitted by the company. The focus of resolutions is on equity securities. There is no report of shareholder challenge or a derivative claim. This is perhaps due to the majority ownership of shares by directors, notably the Chair, Deputy Chair and other directors who represented the preference shareholders. There appears to have been strong support from the company's institutional shareholder, Lazard. Shareholders seem to have avoided further investment in the company perhaps partly because of the company's failure to pay dividends for several years and plummeting share prices.

Creditor Influence

Secured creditors: During the informal rescue process, secured creditors were represented by BOA as the security trustee. As part of the agreement between BOA and Wedgwood in 2003, the board did not have the right to sell assets without the prior approval of the Bank. Cash flow was also monitored by the Bank as cash was deposited in bank accounts controlled by secured creditors. The board did not have any power of sale or closure of the business without prior permission of BOA.

Its supportive approach to the company could be seen in its provision of finance ahead of the company's private placement and public offer. The bank also provided the company with a standstill agreement that was extended without any costs. Although there is no further information on the lender's explicit role in preventing the company's attempt to implement a proposed asset sale and debt financing through other lenders, it could be suggested that potential lenders might have been concerned about the high level of risk.

Unsecured creditors: There is no public information on the response of suppliers or trade creditors to the Group's financial distress. Neither is there any information to suggest that the company defaulted on payment of its debt to suppliers, landlords or trade creditors. This might reflect the cash flow solvent position of the company, able to maintain its status as a going concern without impairing the interests of unsecured creditors.

Discussion: The board seems to have attempted all five of the informal rescue options although the outcome was influenced by investors and lenders. In those areas where the board required existing shareholder approval, it received their support; however, it appears that external investors have demonstrated their lack of interest by not buying shares. Lenders have also shown their influence by refusing to provide the additional financing sought by the board or allowing changes to the assets of the company.

The board does not seem to have been successful in the implementation of informal rescue options although it received strong support from shareholders. Both external and internal causes appear to play a significant role in influencing the board's efforts. Lenders and unsecured creditors seem to have been careful in assessing the level of risk that was involved in supporting the informal rescue process. Unlike shareholders, lenders seem to be influenced by the Group's balance sheet insolvency. The board's failure to implement all potential informal rescue options may also be influenced by the board's determination to keep the Group as a going concern and the lender's refusal to consent to asset sale.

Formal Rescue Process: Administration

Overview: The parent company Waterford Wedgwood plc entered receivership as a result of a petition by its lender, BOA, on January 5, 2009, due to its default on payment of 2008 December interest, a year before the security matured. On the same day, four insolvency practitioners from Deloitte LLP were appointed as joint administrators by the lenders over the UK subsidiary Waterford Wedgwood UK plc. At the time of administration, the UK subsidiary's debt totalled £338 m, secured by fixed and floating charges and cross-guarantees, whilst it owed £37 k unsecured debt excluding £437 k VAT contingent liability. The joint administrators determined to adopt the second statutory objective of administration by "pursuing a parallel strategy of continued trading in the stores and concessions whilst seeking a sale of the Group". The substantial business of the Group was sold to an investor, sourced and supported by BOA, and the UK-based main subsidiary company exited administration in April 2011, entering liquidation.

Administrator's Role

Management of the going concern: At the start of the formal rescue process, the joint administrators secured financing from lenders obtaining advanced payment of €2 m and further permission by lenders to access funds from debtors' accounts. The administrators' proposals suggest that their main focus was on maximising the business value of the company by maintaining its status as a going concern. They tried to maintain the goodwill of the supply chain by negotiating with suppliers who had liens or retention of title over stock. They also sought landlords' agreements over rent reductions. They attempted to reduce finished goods inventory in the supply chain from factory to customer.

Asset sale and recovery: The administrators' intention appears to be to sell the company as a going concern within a tight timeframe, without making themselves vulnerable to potential liabilities. As the statement of proposals shows, the joint administrators also drew on the detailed knowledge of former company directors to achieve a sale. They put bidders in touch with company directors to get a comprehensive picture of the company's potential. They also pursued the work that had been initiated by company directors. For instance, they approached Lazard, who had already identified seven potential investors in the Group as part of its marketing process and continued negotiations with them. They also sought additional assistance from JP Morgan Cazenove, which specialised in the marketing of individual subsidiaries.

On January 8, 2009, the administrators agreed to sell the UK business to a private equity firm KPS Capital Partners as part of KPS's bigger plan to purchase the Group. According to the statement of administrator's proposals, KPS had been actively involved in sale negotiations with the former company directors prior to administration and they expected to finalise the sale by March 2009. The sale was followed by the immediate delegation of control of the business to the buyer facilitating a smooth handover of assets and business in compliance with the law. Lambert Smith Hampton and Wyle Hardy and Co Ltd. were deployed to assist in the valuation of commercial properties, and the valuation of plant, machinery and other chattel assets, respectively.

August 2009: The company's first progress reports show that they had sold the majority of the Group's business and assets by the end of March 2009. The sale included substantial UK assets including retail stores and some global business. They also indicated that the joint administrators were in the process of granting licences to the buyers for retail stores. The joint administrators appear to have pursued the realisation of the remaining piecemeal assets through sale after July 2009. During the process, the joint administrators tried to discharge their liabilities by retaining the services of Linklaters, a legal firm with specialised knowledge and capacity in large-scale insolvency situations. An interview with a manager from KPS reveals that the sale was facilitated through BOA which also provided the purchaser with bank facilities. The first progress report shows that the piecemeal sale of assets followed the substantial business sale. The remaining assets included a freehold property and some land. The administrators' second progress report demonstrates that they managed to recover a substantial amount of the money owed to the company by debtors.

August 2010: As the company's third progress report shows, all concession debts were successfully recovered.

Distribution of proceeds to secured creditors: The company's secured creditors seem to have secured their claims by holding fixed and floating charges over all the company's assets. It appears that such lenders with claims of €181 m ranked ahead of holders of preference shares or high-yield bondholders with total claims of €166 m.

July 2009: As the company's first progress report in July 2009 shows, secured creditors were paid €30 m from the UK main subsidiary within the first six months of administration.

January 2010: The second progress report indicated that joint administrators were going to be paid another €25 m from the Group.

July 2010: The third progress report showed that lenders had received another €4 m within the previous six months.

Analysis: There is no information as to the total amount lenders were supposed to receive from the sale of assets. This information appears to have remained confidential due to the scope of administration in the UK main subsidiary.

Distribution of proceeds to unsecured creditors: Joint administrators' proposals did not make it clear whether unsecured creditors should expect any payment from the proceeds of asset sale as the last group of creditors. Neither did they clarify whether they would receive any dividends under the prescribed part.

January 2009–July 2009: The first progress report indicates that joint administrators did not believe there would be any payments to unsecured creditors other than under the prescribed part.

July 2010–January 2011: The joint administrators stated that although they had considered dividends under the prescribed part for unsecured creditors, they were not sure how much each company would pay to its creditors.

Analysis: Joint administrators' focus on lenders' interests seems to distract them from providing any final information as to the dividends unsecured creditors would receive in each company. No payment was made to unsecured creditors during administration.

Investigation into directors' conduct: The administrators prepared a report on directors' conduct and submitted this to the Department for Business, Innovation and Skills. There is no detailed information on results of this investigation.

Analysis: It seems unlikely that directors faced any personal liability for their actions as they were the original investors in the company. They also sought professional advice in all business and informal rescue matters. Their ultimate failure to save the company was partly due to external circumstances, and the lender's potential objection to the sale of assets.

Creditor Influence

Secured creditors: There is no detailed information about lenders' roles during the administration of the UK subsidiary Waterford Wedgwood UK plc. As was indicated earlier, the influential role of secured creditors can be seen in major strategic decisions involving placing the Group into receivership (excluding the UK subsidiary). They also appointed the joint administrators against the wishes of the board of directors, financed the administration process and contributed to the sale of a substantial part of the business. Further influence of the lenders could be seen in their agreement to the business sale to a third party under terms and conditions that remain confidential.

Unsecured creditors: The joint administrators' proposals indicate that the joint administrators considered all unsecured creditors of the parent company and its subsidiaries as one entity and proposed a creditors' meeting for all unsecured creditors in the group although their proposals had not clarified potential payment for unsecured creditors to consider their proposals, their time-based fees and payments. They also proposed a creditor committee for each of the main subsidiaries. Subsequently, unsecured creditors showed their support for the administrators by voting in favour of their proposals and approving the basis of their remuneration without any modification. Only unsecured creditors of the subsidiary Josiah Wedgwood asked for the formation of a creditor committee.

January 2009–July 2009: The creditors' committee successfully organised four meetings during the first six months of administration.

July 2009–January 2010: As the company's second six-monthly progress report shows, no further committee meeting was held.

January 2010–July 2010: The creditors' committee held its last meeting.

Analysis: There is no indication of any challenge or disagreement by unsecured creditors of the joint administrators' proposals which could be interpreted as their passive acceptance of administration. It seems that the creditors' committee was supportive of proposals and fees as there is no detailed information about potential disputes or debates between the creditors' committee and the joint administrators.

Administration outcome: The company entered liquidation in late April 2011 with the three administrators appointed as liquidators. Lenders were expected to receive a total of €55.9 m from realisation of the assets of the UK subsidiary. The final figure may have been smaller or larger than this as the administrators' statutory filings do not provide any detailed information on the Group sale contract including the price paid by KPS. No distribution was made amongst unsecured creditors of the UK main subsidiary although there may have been some individual agreements between administrators and those unsecured creditors who continued business support during administration.

Summary

The board of Waterford Wedgwood plc managed to maintain the company's business for several years due to the high level of support they received from their lenders and the cash flow solvency of the company. The board's failure to rescue the company through an informal rescue process seems to have been negatively affected by its strong balance sheet insolvency. The administration of Waterford Wedgwood UK plc was directly linked to the receivership of the Group companies. There is no detailed information on the lenders' involvement during the formal rescue process. Unsecured creditors appear to have been minimally involved during administration, paralleling the passive response of shareholders to share offerings.

Bibliography

Byrne, John A. 1997. "The CEO and the Board." *Business Week*, September 15. 106-116.
Deutsch, Claudia H. 1988. "Tony O'Reilly Astride Two Worlds; At Heinz, a Bottom-Line Leader." *New York Times*. May 8.
Heinz, H. J. 2000. *Company Annual Report* 2000.
Taylor, James. "Crystal Clear." *Private Equity International*. March 2012.
Waterford Wedgwood, plc. 2008. *Annual Report and Accounts*.
Waterford Wedgwood U.K., plc. Form 2.34B. Registered May 10, 2011. https://beta.companieshouse.gov.uk/company/02058427/filing-history?page=1
Waterford Wedgwood U.K., plc. Form 2.24B. Registered August 5, 2010. https://beta.companieshouse.gov.uk/company/02058427/filing-history?page=1
Waterford Wedgwood U.K., plc. Form 2.24B. Registered August 6, 2009. https://beta.companieshouse.gov.uk/company/02058427/filing-history?page=1
Waterford Wedgwood U.K., plc. Form 2.24B. Registered August 7, 2009. https://beta.companieshouse.gov.uk/company/02058427/filing-history?page=1
Waterford Wedgwood U.K., plc. Form 2.24B. Registered February 10, 2010. https://beta.companieshouse.gov.uk/company/02058427/filinghistory?page=1
Waterford Wedgwood U.K., plc. Form 2.24B. Registered February 2, 2011. https://beta.companieshouse.gov.uk/company/02058427/filinghistory?page=1
Waterford Wedgwood U.K., plc. Form 2.24B. Registered February 23, 2010. https://beta.companieshouse.gov.uk/company/02058427/filinghistory?page=1

Waterford Wedgwood U.K., plc. Form 2.34. Registered May 10, 2011. https://beta.companieshouse.gov.uk/company/02058427/filing-history?page=1

Waterford Wedgwood U.K., plc. Resolutions. Registered January 9, 2009. https://beta.companieshouse.gov.uk/company/02058427/filinghistory?page=2

Waterford Wedgwood U.K., plc. Resolutions. Registered June 11, 2008. https://beta.companieshouse.gov.uk/company/02058427/filing-history?page=2

Waterford Wedgwood U.K., plc. Resolutions. Registered November 5, 2008. https://beta.companieshouse.gov.uk/company/02058427/filinghistory?page=2

Waterford Wedgwood U.K., plc. Resolutions. Registered November 7, 2008. https://beta.companieshouse.gov.uk/company/02058427/filinghistory?page=2

Waterford Wedgwood U.K., plc. Form 2.16B. Registered March 9, 2009. https://beta.companieshouse.gov.uk/company/02058427/filing-history?page=2

Waterford Wedgwood U.K., plc. Form 2.17B. Registered March 12, 2009. https://beta.companieshouse.gov.uk/company/02058427/filing-history?page=2

Waterford Wedgwood U.K., plc. Form 2.23B. Registered April 1, 2009. https://beta.companieshouse.gov.uk/company/02058427/filing-history?page=2

Waterford Wedgwood, plc. Form 395. Registered December 11, 2003. https://beta.companieshouse.gov.uk/company/02058427/filing-history?page=5

Waterford Wedgwood, plc. Form 395. Registered December 17, 2003. https://beta.companieshouse.gov.uk/company/02058427/filing-history?page=5

Waterford Wedgwood, plc. Form 395. Registered December 9, 2003. https://beta.companieshouse.gov.uk/company/02058427/filing-history?page=5. Note Four Different Charges (116, 117, 118 and 119) Have Been Registered with Companies House on This Date.

Waterford Wedgwood, plc. Form 2.23B. Registered April 1, 2009. https://beta.companieshouse.gov.uk/company/02058427/filing-history?page=2

Waterford Wedgwood, plc. Results for The Year Ended 5 April 2008b. RNS No. 4741A Dated August 1, 2008.

Waterford Wedgwood. 2008 Equity Issue – Update. RNS No. 3265F Dated October 8, 2008.

Waterford Wedgwood. Appointment of Chief Executive. RNS No. 4779A Dated August 1, 2008.

Waterford Wedgwood. Directorate Change. Dated April 2, 2008. www.investegate.co.uk. Accessed May 20, 2017.

Waterford Wedgwood. EGM Statement. RNS No. 9423D Dated September 22, 2009.

Waterford Wedgwood. Further re Financing. RNS No. 0972K Dated December 12, 2008.

Waterford Wedgwood. Further re Financing. RNS No. 5724k Dated December 22, 2008.

Waterford Wedgwood. Further re Financing. RNS No. 6081J Dated December 5, 2008.

Waterford Wedgwood. Interim Management Statement. February 15, 2008. www.investegate.co.uk. Accessed May 15, 2017.

Waterford Wedgwood. Interim Management Statement. RNS No. 4753A Dated August 1, 2008.

Waterford Wedgwood. Issue of Equity. RNS No. 5885D Dated September 16, 2008.

Waterford Wedgwood. Result of Annual General Meeting. RNS No. 4884K Dated December 19, 2008.

Waterford Wedgwood. Results for the Year Ended 5 April 2008. RNS No. 4741A Dated August 1, 2008.

Waterford Wedgwood. Results of The Year. RNS No. 4741A Dated August 1, 2008.

Waterford Wedgwood. Statement Re De-listing. RNS No. 2848K Dated December 17, 2008.

Waterford Wedgwood. Statement re Manufacturing Op. RNS No. 9935F Dated October 16, 2008.

Waterford Wedgwood. Statement re Press Comment. Dated April 11, 2008. www.investegate.co.uk. Accessed May 15, 2017.

Waterford Wedgwood. Statement re Suspension. RNS No. 0663L Dated January 5, 2009.

Waterford Wedgwood. Update on Financing. RNS No. 2519J Dated December 1, 2008.

Waterford Wedgwood. Waterford Wedgwood Announcement. RNS No. 2591X Dated June 23, 2008.

10

Case Study 4: Woolworths Group plc

Overview

Woolworths Group plc is a case study of one of the largest retailers in the UK, entering administration as an early victim of the UK financial crisis. The case reflects an informal rescue process characterised by the board's minimal use of rescue options. The main governance issue is the lender's influence over the sale of the business created by the board's use of secured debt financing at the start of the informal rescue process. The role of unsecured creditors in aggravating the company's financial distress through suspending or terminating their supply contracts is also significant.

The commencement of administration at Woolworths Group plc transferred control powers to the joint administrators. However, the administrators' powers were not exercised significantly at Group level due to the limited value of assets owned directly by the parent company. At the retail subsidiary, such powers were substantially exercised in the process of asset sale, and distribution of proceeds amongst secured and unsecured creditors. The administrators' deployment of a wide range of professional advisors during the formal rescue is notable. The lack of a role for unsecured creditors at the parent company and the formation of a creditors' committee at the subsidiary is another feature of governance during administration.

© The Author(s) 2018
M. M. Parkinson, *Corporate Governance in Transition*, Palgrave Studies in Governance, Leadership and Responsibility, https://doi.org/10.1007/978-3-319-77110-6_10

This case study covers the informal rescue adopted by Woolworths Group plc, the parent company. The informal rescue process covers the period between January 27, 2008, and January 26, 2009. The formal rescue process covers the period between January 27, 2009, when the parent company entered administration and February 2010, when it exited administration and entered creditors' voluntary liquidation. The case also covers the period between November 27, 2008, when the retail subsidiary Woolworths plc entered administration and November 12, 2010, when it exited administration and entered compulsory liquidation.

Background: Woolworths Group plc (originally est. 1909) was a large public company listed on the LSE operating as a major retailer and a major entertainment/media distributor, ranked second in turnover after Tesco in the UK. The company was formed following a demerger of the general merchandise business of Kingfisher plc and was listed on the LSE in 2001. Its business operations were managed through three major subsidiaries: Woolworths plc, Entertainment UK Limited and 2Entertain Limited. The Group employed more than 30,000 employees in its 818 stores nationwide. At the start of the informal rescue process, the parent company with a total revenue of £2.9 bn, balance sheet worth of £2.1 bn and 25,000 staff was a mega insolvency case as defined in Chap. 6.

Corporate Governance: The board of directors at the parent company was responsible for "financial and operational strategic decisions of the Group including subsidiaries". It had ten members, including five executive and five non-executive directors. Executive directors included the Chief Executive, Group Finance Director, Director for Retail and Distribution, Managing Director of Entertainment UK and Commercial and Marketing executive director. The equal number of executive and non-executive directors complied with the Code regarding the composition of a board of directors.

The company had a number of large institutional shareholders including Unity Investments, Resolutions Asset Management and Barclays plc, which collectively had a total of 22% of the ordinary shares. According to its Annual Report and Accounts, executive directors had regular meetings with these major shareholders. In these meetings such shareholders could be assumed to have had the opportunity to influence the governance of the company during briefings on the board's strategic plans. Their collective shareholding also meant that they could have a major influence on the results of shareholder voting.

Debt structure: Prior to the commencement of the informal rescue process, Woolworths Group plc had unsecured borrowings of £40 m and no secured debt. It did not have any trading activity; therefore, it did not have any trade creditors. The Group as a whole, including subsidiaries, owed £633.1 m to trade creditors as part of current liabilities at the start of the informal rescue process. Unsecured creditors therefore had a substantial stake in the company and they had a vested interest in the company continuing as a going concern.

Financial Distress and Associated Causes

Financial distress: The Group had previously faced a situation of financial distress in 2007 which it had resolved by pursuing a cost reduction strategy that included sourcing an increasing amount of products from Asian, East European and Middle Eastern suppliers. It had also reduced its stock levels, reduced its delivery costs and changed marketing strategies. The Group had also disposed of some of its retail stores.

At the start of 2008, the parent company's total current assets were £882 m and its total liabilities were £800.6 m. Using the legal cash flow insolvency test, the company was cash flow solvent; however, looking closely at its current assets, a significant proportion of its current assets was in the form of inventory (£390 m), which would be excluded by accountants when using a more rigorous short-term cash flow solvency test. The company's dependency on rapid stock turnover to remain cash flow solvent becomes apparent.

The company was balance sheet solvent since its total assets were £1.3 bn whilst its liabilities were £1 bn. Therefore, it could be said that the company was both cash flow solvent and balance sheet solvent.

Internal causes: The company was not able to compete with other UK retailers. The Group failed to respond quickly enough to the challenge of online shopping. The company's entertainment division continued to focus its efforts on sales through retail outlets and became increasingly uncompetitive against new digital entertainment companies such as

Apple (iTunes) and Amazon who were successfully competing against high street stores through online sales.

External causes: The company was a victim of the financial crisis in 2008. Consumers' loss of confidence and lower spending power was another factor that affected the company. Woolworths had historically pursued a strategy of scrambled merchandising in its retail outlets, with its stores selling a wide range of products from paint and decorating materials, to music and electrical goods, and confectionery. This format had become increasingly outdated, particularly in a period of economic downturn and the company had lost focus in a market where consumers were faced with choices from more specialised retail outlets and online suppliers and were increasingly selecting more carefully targeted "value-based" retail offers.

Informal Rescue Process

Board of Directors' Role

Adopting the criterion used in this book, January 27, 2008 marks the start of the informal rescue process ending on January 27, 2009, when Woolworths Group plc entered administration. The board's reliance on secured debt financing created a major governance issue for the company. It created a position where lenders were able to influence the sale of the retail subsidiary Woolworths plc, leading to the start of administration of the parent company.

Board Change

January 2008: The Managing Director of a subsidiary, Entertainment UK, resigned from the board. The Director for Retail and Distribution took over his role.

February 2008: A new non-executive director with a strong background in the retail sector was appointed to the board.

June 2008: The board announced that the CEO would be standing down from his position within the next three months but would collaborate in finding a successor.

July 2008: The company employed a team of strategy consultants to carry out a review of the Group's businesses.

August 2008: A new CEO was appointed with a background in retail to start work in September.

October 2008: The Group Finance Director resigned from his position. A new Group Finance Director was appointed.

November 2008: One non-executive director died.

Analysis: Board change seems to be a constant governance issue during the informal rescue process. Board change featured the replacement of two key executive directors, that is, CEO and CFO, as well as the deployment of advisors. Non-executive directors remain virtually unchanged with only one new appointment.

Cost Reduction

February 2008: The company continued its strategy of cost control, margin control and cash generation.

July 2008: The company used a stock management strategy that focused on stock clearance at reduced prices in its entertainment and retail sections. Further, the Group improved its quarterly revenues by reducing stocks and focused on finding major clients for its entertainment wholesale business.

August 2008: The Group implemented its plan to reduce prices under its "Price Drop campaign". This problem was more pressing for the retail rather than the entertainment division of the company.

September 2008: The company planned to recruit 5,000 temporary staff in advance of December 2008 sales which would incur temporary extra costs for the company.

Analysis: Cost reduction seems to be limited to reducing stock levels by discounting prices. The board has not used cost reduction strategies such as staff redundancies or downsizing which indicates its intention to retain the business as a going concern and survive without significant change.

Asset Sale

June 2008: The company assigned four leasehold stores to Waitrose subject to the permission of its landlords.

August 2008: The board dismissed a takeover offer by *Iceland* for the acquisition of its retail division on the basis that it "required a complex restructuring … and undervalued the assets of the company … and required the [parent] company to maintain the pension liabilities".

October 2008: The company reached an agreement to dispose of nine stores to Tesco plc. However, no immediate cash payment was made. The company was expected to receive the proceeds in six months and subsequently pay this to lenders. It also started intensive negotiations over the sale of the Woolworths Group to Hilco UK Limited, a specialist in retail turnaround, with the intention of including debt transfer as part of the sale agreement.

November 2008: On November 26, the board confirmed that negotiations over the sale of its retail business and its 40% stake in 2 Entertainment were in place. It stated that any sale agreement would be subject to lenders' approval, indicating uncertainty over the likelihood that such approval would be forthcoming. On November 27, the company announced that it did not see any prospect for maintaining the group as a going concern and therefore applied for administration.

It later became clear that the company had produced a restructuring plan led by its CEO, a new financial director and professional advisors. The restructuring plan would have allowed the company to sell Woolworths plc to Hilco UK Limited as a going concern including the transfer of all its liabilities. The company would have sold its share in the digital media supplier 2Entertain to BBC Worldwide; however, the proposal was dismissed by secured creditors.

Analysis: The board seems to have primarily focused on piecemeal sale of assets rather than the substantial sale of the business. Their approach may be driven by their attachment to the company or the influence of institutional shareholders. Lender's concern to minimise risk could also explain the board's choice of piecemeal asset sale.

Equity/Share Issue

June 2008: The board obtained shareholder approval for resolutions that renewed the board's authority to allot shares, to renew disapplication of pre-emption rights and to purchase its own shares.

November 2008: The board sought suspension of Group shares on the LSE suggesting that there was "no certainty" that the lender had agreed to the sale of the company as a going concern.

Analysis: The board has not used equity issue as an informal rescue option. There is no information to explain why the board did not use equity issue. This might be linked to a share issue in the previous year, which exhausted the potential demand for additional new shares. It might be also justified because of the instability of stock markets in 2008.

New Debt Financing/Debt Renegotiation

January 2008: The company entered a new financial agreement with lenders which changed the basis of its borrowing to a four-year secured loan, providing it with a total loan of £385 m. Three hundred and fifty million pounds of the asset-based loan was facilitated and underwritten by Burdale Financial Limited and the American GMAC Commercial Finance plc. The loan also involved the transfer of control to lenders of the company's 40% shares in 2 Entertainment (jointly owned with the BBC).

The remaining £35 m involved a second loan provided by ADM Maculus Fund III. A debenture provided the lender with fixed and floating charges over group assets. The charge gave security interests to lenders over all assets of the Group including its equipment, accounts, benefits, intellectual property and licences owned by the parent company and its subsidiaries. The charge restricted the ability of the company to dispose of assets or assign them without the prior approval of lenders whilst GMAC reserved its right to convert the floating charge to a fixed charge should the company default on payment of its debt.

The company also agreed to grant security to the Group Pension Fund, for a loan of £63 m which put the Fund in a prime position as the first creditor to receive £50 m of proceeds from disposals.

November 2008: On November 25, the company granted a deed of charge over its credit balances in favour of Barclays Bank plc. The fixed charge included all monies that were deposited in one specific bank account at Barclays. In effect, Woolworths could not use the deposits without the prior written consent of the bank.

Analysis: It seems that the board used debt financing on a large scale as its primary rescue option; however, debt financing seems to have taken away board control over assets. The board did not obtain any standstill agreement or new credit facility from existing lenders which may be assumed to reflect the lenders' perception of the risks involved. The board must have also obtained the consent of existing lenders relating to the new security interest created in favour of Barclays.

Shareholder Influence

June 2008: During the AGM on June 18, shareholders approved the board's plan to disapply their pre-emption rights and authorised the board to allocate equity securities of £18 m. They also approved proposals to buy back up to £18 m shares at market value, and payment of a reduced dividend on the basis that "payment of a dividend at this level represents an appropriate balance between providing a return to shareholders and preserving the financial flexibility necessary to support the plans and ongoing development of the business over both the short and longer term".

June–July 2008: A new individual shareholder made a substantial purchase of ordinary shares, resulting in individual ownership of 10% of shares.

September 2008: The new individual shareholder met Icelandic private equity investor Baugur who had offered to take over the retail subsidiary Woolworths plc. He supported the board's decision to dismiss the offer.

Analysis: Shareholders have traditionally supported board proposals relating to asset sale and debt financing. The new major shareholder continued to support their approach. It appears that financial distress does not seem to have changed the shareholder's supportive approach.

Creditor Influence

September 2008: The company faced withdrawal of credit insurance but made it clear that "a substantial proportion of its suppliers" collaborated with the company without obtaining credit insurance.

October 2008: Following a five-month continuous fall in share price, three big credit insurers including Euler Hermes, Atradius and Coface withdrew their insurance for suppliers to Woolworths, leading to several suppliers ceasing to trade with the company.

November 2008: Two winding-up petitions were served on the parent company. The identity of these creditors could not be identified.

December 2008: The parent company was served with more winding-up petitions. There is no information about who these creditors were.

Analysis: It seems that unsecured creditors continued to trade with the company whilst the board implemented various rescue options. However, they ultimately responded negatively to the withdrawal of trade credit insurance indicating their risk-averse approach when there were no safeguards. Legal actions by some creditors also show their individual lack of tolerance of risk and desire to recover their claims. It also seems that stock markets responded negatively to company announcements relating to the board's adoption of informal rescue options, resulting in a gradual lack of confidence in the chances of the company's survival.

Discussion

The board adopted a range of different informal rescue options on different scales. The board did not use business sale or share issue. Its use of debt financing seems to include a substantial part of group assets. There was no resistance from shareholders to the board's decisions. The influence of institutional shareholders remains unclear. Lenders' self-interest and their reluctance to take further risks seem to have created their implicit disagreement with business sale, which would have maximised the interests of creditors as a whole. Markets disrupted the continuing business operations of the company and the boards' informal rescue plan when insurance cover was withdrawn and trade creditors suspended their business relationships with the company.

Formal Rescue Process: Administration

Overview: The formal rescue of Woolworths Group plc started on January 27, 2009, with the formal appointment of three insolvency practitioners from Deloitte LLP. These insolvency practitioners had been nominated by secured creditors in November 2008 to provide support to the Group board and they were subsequently confirmed as the administrators of the insolvent retail subsidiary Woolworths plc. Their appointment to the parent company was made by the court and joint administrators were appointed on application made by company directors. This was due to the winding-up orders that had already been sought by individual unsecured creditors.

At the start of administration, the parent company had £729.7 m assets (book value), £425.1 m secured debt subject to floating charges, crossguaranteed by subsidiaries and owed £16 m to unsecured creditors. The joint administrators planned to achieve statutory objective 3(1)(b) of Schedule B1 of the Insolvency Act 1986 for the parent company. They reasoned that the parent company was not attractive enough to external investors and was not able to obtain lenders' support to restructure its debts. The parent company exited administration on January 21, 2010, and entered liquidation. This case study examines the activities of the joint administrators in resolving the claims of lenders and those of unsecured creditors in the parent company. It also examines similar issues in the retail subsidiary Woolworths plc.

Administrators' Role

Management of the going concern: The parent company did not have any trading activities. At the commencement of administration, the joint administrators proposed that the parent company should immediately be liquidated and that assets should be realised in an orderly manner. The parent company was closed on their appointment and staff were made redundant.

Retail subsidiary: Substantial assets of the parent company were owned by its insolvent retail subsidiary, Woolworths plc (£708.4 m). The joint administrators decided to maintain the retail subsidiary as a going concern for up to 42 days to maximise stock sale, and made a series of arrangements with relevant creditors to facilitate the process. They entered into "commercial settlements" or new arrangement with 150 suppliers who had retention of title and lien claims against Woolworths plc. They also retained retail staff and supplied stock to stores. The joint administrators also made interim arrangements with landlords and other trade creditors. They sought credit insurance from a new provider called Willis. Subsequently, they assigned the realisation of stock and daily management of Woolworths retail stores to Hilco. These measures meant that prior to the closure of the retail subsidiary on January 6, 2009, the company had generated £172 m in net trading surplus.

Asset sale and recovery: The assets owned by the parent company were not substantial. The joint administrators did not provide any proposals relating to assets owned by the parent company. The joint administrators' first progress report indicated a realisation of funds from a captive insurance policy and deposits totalling approximately £5 m, which seems to have been the whole of the assets owned by the parent company. These funds were realised within the first six months of administration. The parent company was also the proprietor of two brands: Woolworths and Ladybird.

Since most of the assets were owned by the retail subsidiary, the joint administrators focused on their sale. Their statement of proposals for Woolworths plc shows that upon their appointment, they took the first steps towards selling the business by instructing Deloitte's Corporate Finance Advisory—a department of the insolvency firm where the joint administrators worked—to draft a detailed report that included significant information about the company's financial and business status. This was done with the assistance of company directors.

Subsequently, the joint administrators approached potential investors and shortlisted 20 out of 100 investors who declared an interest in the purchase of the company. Following a series of negotiations between potential investors, the joint administrators and some company directors, the joint administrators concluded that no investor was interested in the purchase of the business as a whole, largely because of a poor national economic climate. Therefore, they began to sell assets piecemeal with the view of ultimately liquidating the company.

The joint administrators took the first step towards the sale of 800 retail stores by deploying Deloitte's Real Estate Advisory Team—another division of their insolvency firm—and engaging Hilco Retail Property Services (HRPS). They also involved CBRE, a firm specialising in the valuation and marketing of large leases. Five major law firms including Blake Lapthorn, Crystal, Dechert, Eversheds and Memery Crystal provided legal advice to the joint administrators to avoid any problems with the legal assignment of commercial leases. At the time of release of their statement of proposals, 150 properties had been assigned.

November 2008–May 2009: The joint administrators' first progress report indicates complete assignment of 168 stores. The company's intellectual property in brands including the company name Woolworths was sold, resulting in a change of the company's name to WW Realisations 1 Limited and release of those brands from security interests. The company also recovered 10% of its book debt through Largo. They also sold assets including fixtures and fitting on a piecemeal basis.

June–November 2009: As the joint administrators' second progress report shows, they disposed of 608 leases through assignment or termination. The joint administrators sold a freehold property in Jersey. The company also recovered 9% of the total book debt it was owed after deploying the law firm Largo.

November 2009–May 2010: As the third progress report shows, the sale of freehold property was completed by June 2010. The remaining book debts were also collected.

April–May 2009: The joint administrators seem to have facilitated the sale of the company by releasing it from charges and holding a general meeting to obtain shareholder approval for change of name to WW Realisation 1 Limited and re-registration as a private company.

Distribution of proceeds to secured creditors: As the parent company's second report indicates, secured creditors were paid £3.4 m from asset realisations directly owned by the parent company. The major part of their claims was recovered from asset sale in subsidiaries totalling £324.9 m.

The joint administrators' second report on the retail subsidiary shows that senior lenders were paid £233.7 m from the assets of the retail subsidiary. The third progress report shows that the second charge holders were paid a small proportion of their claim (£3.5 m) whilst no payment was made to the third group of secured creditors between January 2010 and June 2010.

May 2010–November 2010: A proportion of claims owed to second charge holders were paid from the realisation of Group assets (£3.5 m); no further payments were made to secured creditors from the retail subsidiary.

Distribution of proceeds to unsecured creditors: At the parent company, the joint administrators had dismissed the potential of any recovery for unsecured creditor claims in their proposals due to insufficient assets to pay lenders and preferential creditors. They initially proposed that there would be sufficient funds for payment of dividends to unsecured creditors under the prescribed part in the parent company. However, no payment was made during administration and their claims were rolled over to the liquidation stage.

At the retail subsidiary, the joint administrators had initially proposed that there were only sufficient funds under prescribed parts for the unsecured creditors subject to costs.

May 2009–November 2009: The second progress report suggests that the administrator found it "disproportionate" to make a distribution amongst a large number of unsecured creditors due to the costs involved. They also declared their plan to seek direction from the court.

May 2010–November 2010: In July 2010, the joint administrators obtained a court order that allowed them to not make any distribution to unsecured creditors.

Investigation into directors' conduct: In July 2009 the administrators submitted an "interim report" on directors' conduct. They did the same for the subsidiary. No information was available on their views of the directors' conduct and potential liability for wrongful trading.

Creditor Influence

Secured creditors: The role of secured creditors in the parent company can be seen in approving the joint administrators' remuneration together with preferential creditors. Unsecured creditors were subject to statutory exclusion from approving joint administrators' proposals (see the following section). There is no indication that secured creditors approved the joint administrators' fees in the parent company and as the reports show no fees were withdrawn to pay the administrators in Woolworths plc.

Unsecured creditors: At the parent company, no creditors' meeting was proposed due to lack of sufficient funds for unsecured creditors other than the prescribed part. No creditors' committee was recommended. Subsequently, no request was made by creditors for a creditor meetings' or creditors' committee. Therefore, the administrators' proposals were approved with no modification. There is no report of any individual or collective activity by unsecured creditors during administration despite their collective £16 m claim.

At the retail subsidiary, unsecured creditors had a more active role summarised below in chronological order. In February 2009, a creditors' meeting was proposed by the joint administrators of Woolworths plc to consider the formation of a creditors' committee. Subsequently, a creditors' meeting was held during which creditors approved the joint administrators' proposals without modification, including the formation of a creditors' committee. The committee consisted of five representatives from the largest unsecured creditors. Two co-opted members were also appointed. The creditors' committee was responsible for approving administrator fees and ensuring the "action and progress of administration".

November 2008–May 2009: As the first progress report shows two creditors' committee meetings were held in the first six months of administration in the retail subsidiary.

May 2009–November 2009: One more meeting was held in September 2009. The creditors' committee approved the administrators' withdrawal of expenses and their fees and all withdrawals made to the end of 2009.

November 2009–May 2010: The third progress report shows one more creditors' committee meeting was held.

The fifth and the last creditors' committee meeting was held during the last six months of administration.

On September 23, 2010, the joint administrators informed the creditors' committee of their plan for winding up the retail subsidiary

Woolworths plc. Subsequently, they obtained a court order for their petition for placing the company into compulsory liquidation.

Administration Outcome: In January 2010, the joint administrators informed creditors of their plan that the parent company would exit administration through a creditor voluntary liquidation; however, the subsidiary Woolworths plc exited administration and entered creditors' compulsory liquidation. No reason was given as to why the joint administrators did not choose voluntary liquidation for the subsidiary. This may have been due to opposition from the creditors' committee. The subsidiary exited administration and was made subject to a compulsory winding-up order in November 2010.

Summary

During the formal rescue process, control powers transferred from company directors to joint administrators upon their appointment. The role of joint administrators in both parent company and subsidiary was limited to statutory duties including asset sale, and the distribution of proceeds amongst creditors, including secured and unsecured creditors. It appears that different governance patterns emerged. Whilst the joint administrators pursued the same statutory tasks in the parent company and subsidiary, the scope of the exercise of their powers was extensive in the subsidiary due to the complexity and scale of assets involved. The joint administrators seem to have been reliant on the assistance of legal and financial advisors in facilitating asset sale in the retail subsidiary.

The role of lenders in the parent company is limited to approving administrators' remuneration. Such an influence is minimised in the retail subsidiary as a creditors' committee was formed. Lack of information about the lenders' role during administration means that no comments can be made about the extent of their active involvement.

Unsecured creditors did not have any influence on decisions made about the parent company. At the subsidiary company, they supported the administrators' proposals and remuneration. They also formed a creditors' committee to oversee the administrator's conduct. Lack of information about their communication with the administrators leaves it unclear about how they influenced the administrators' decisions. There is no report of any disagreement with the joint administrators. The same applies to unsecured creditors in the retail subsidiary who due to their large number and the costs of distribution were deprived of any dividends under the court order.

Unsecured creditor involvement does not influence their share of any potential remaining assets. Although unsecured creditors in the parent company are entitled to dividends under the prescribed part, they do not receive any dividends during administration. At the retail subsidiary, they are deprived of any dividends due to the costs of distribution. As a result, no dividends are paid during administration.

Bibliography

Braithwaite, Tom. 2008. "Walker Holds Talks over Woolworths." *Financial Times*, September 5.
Britton, Anne and Chris Waterston. 2009. *Financial Accounting*. Essex: Pearson Education Limited.
Stacey, Kiran and Elizabeth Rigby. 2008. "Last of Credit Insurers Pulls Out of Woolies." *Financial Times*, October 7.
"Woolworths Set for Administration." *BBC.com*. http://news.bbc.co.uk/1/hi/7751064.stm. Accessed December 30, 2013.
"Woolworths to Focus on Xmas Despite Slump." *Personnel Today*, September 9, 2008.
Woolworths Group, plc. Directorate Change Dated January 29, 2008. www.investegate.co.uk. Accessed April 17, 2017.
Woolworths Group, plc. 2008. *Annual Report and Accounts*.
Woolworths Group, plc. 2007. *Annual Report and Accounts*. Registered August 22, 2008. https://beta.companieshouse.gov.uk/company/03855289/filing-history?page=2
Woolworths Group, plc. Resolutions. Registered June 23, 2008. https://beta.companieshouse.gov.uk/company/03855289/filing-history?page=2
Woolworths Group, plc. Form 2.17B. Registered March 26, 2009. https://beta.companieshouse.gov.uk/company/03855289/filing-history?page=1
Woolworths Group, plc. Form 2.24B. Registered August 25, 2009. https://beta.companieshouse.gov.uk/company/03855289/filing-history?page=1

Woolworths Group, plc. Form 2.24B. Registered February 3, 2010. https://beta.companieshouse.gov.uk/company/03855289/filing-history?page=1

Woolworths Group, plc. Form 2.34B. Registered February 11, 2010. https://beta.companieshouse.gov.uk/company/03855289/filing-history?page=1

Woolworths Group, plc. Form 2.24B. Registered August 25, 2009. https://beta.companieshouse.gov.uk/company/03855289/filing-history?page=1

Woolworths Group, plc. Form 2.24B. Registered February 3, 2010. https://beta.companieshouse.gov.uk/company/03855289/filing-history?page=1

Woolworths Group, plc. Directorate Change. RNS No. 1206B Dated August 12, 2008.

Woolworths Group, plc. Directorate Change. RNS No. 3862G Dated October 22, 2008.

Woolworths Group, plc. Directorate Change. RNS No. 8034H Dated November 10, 2008.

Woolworths Group, plc. Directorate Change. RNS No. 9533W Dated June 18, 2008.

Woolworths Group, plc. Final Results Dated 2 April 2008. www.investegate.co.uk. Accessed April 17, 2017.

Woolworths Group, plc. Financing Dated 30 January 2008. www.investegate.co.uk. Accessed April 17, 2017.

Woolworths Group, plc. Form 2.12B. Registered February 7, 2009. https://beta.companieshouse.gov.uk/company/03855289/filing-history?page=1

Woolworths Group, plc. Form 395. Registered December 13, 2008. https://beta.companieshouse.gov.uk/company/03855289/filing-history?page=2

Woolworths Group, plc. Form 395. Registered February 8, 2008. https://beta.companieshouse.gov.uk/company/03855289/filing-history?page=2

Woolworths Group, plc. Form 2.16B with Form 2.14B. Registered March 14, 2009. https://beta.companieshouse.gov.uk/company/03855289/filing-history?page=1

Woolworths Group, plc. *Group of Companies' Accounts Made up to 3 February 2008.* https://beta.companieshouse.gov.uk/company/03855289/filing-history?page=2

Woolworths Group, plc. Holding(s) in Company. RNS No. 9019X Dated June 30, 2008.

Woolworths Group, plc. Interim Results. RNS No. 6024D Dated September 17, 2008.

Woolworths Group, plc. Result of AGM. RNS No. 0270X Dated June 18, 2008.

Woolworths Group, plc. Statement re Press Comment. RNS No. 0413J Dated November 27, 2008.

Woolworths Group, plc. Statement re Press Comment. RNS No. 4905B Dated August 17, 2008.
Woolworths Group, plc. Statement re Suspension. RNS No. 9519I Dated November 26, 2008.
Woolworths Group, plc. Statement re. Press Comment. RNS No. 4905B Dated August 17, 2008.
Woolworths Group, plc. Store disposal. RNS No. 5650F Dated October 10, 2008.
Woolworths Group, plc. Store Disposal. RNS No. 9532W Dated June 18, 2008.
Woolworths Group, plc. Trading Statement. RNS No. 0576A Dated July 29, 2008.
Woolworths, plc. Form 2.17B. Registered January 21, 2009. https://beta.companieshouse.gov.uk/company/00104206/filing-history?page=3
Woolworths, plc. Form 2.23B. Registered February 18, 2009. https://beta.companieshouse.gov.uk/company/00104206/filing-history?page=2
Woolworths, plc. Form 2.26B. Registered February 10, 2009. https://beta.companieshouse.gov.uk/company/00104206/filing-history?page=2
Woolworths, plc. CERT11. Registered May 6, 2009. https://beta.companieshouse.gov.uk/company/00104206/filing-history?page=2
Woolworths, plc. Form 2.12B. Registered December 8, 2008. https://beta.companieshouse.gov.uk/company/00104206/filing-history?page=3
Woolworths, plc. Form 2.12B. Registered December 8, 2008. https://beta.companieshouse.gov.uk/company/00104206/filing-history?page=3
Woolworths, plc. Form 2.16B with Form 2.14B. Registered January 28, 2009. https://beta.companieshouse.gov.uk/company/00104206/filing-history?page=3
Woolworths, plc. Form 2.17B. Registered January 21, 2009. https://beta.companieshouse.gov.uk/company/00104206/filing-history?page=3
Woolworths, plc. Form 53. Registered May 6, 2009. https://beta.companieshouse.gov.uk/company/00104206/filing-history?page=2
Woolworths, plc. Form 53. Registered May 6, 2009. https://beta.companieshouse.gov.uk/company/00104206/filing-history?page=2
Woolworths, plc. Resolutions. Registered November 24, 2008. https://beta.companieshouse.gov.uk/company/00104206/filing-history?page=2
WW Realisation 1, limited. Form 2.24B. Registered June 23, 2010. https://beta.companieshouse.gov.uk/company/00104206/filing-history?page=2
WW Realisation 1, limited. Form 2.24B. Registered June 24, 2010. https://beta.companieshouse.gov.uk/company/00104206/filing-history?page=2

WW Realisation 1, limited. Form 2.24B. Registered June 29, 2010. https://beta.companieshouse.gov.uk/company/00104206/filing-history?page=2

WW Realisation 1, limited. Form 2.24B. Registered July 14, 2010. https://beta.companieshouse.gov.uk/company/00104206/filing-history?page=2

WW Realisation 1, limited. Form 2.24B. Registered November 23, 2010. https://beta.companieshouse.gov.uk/company/00104206/filing-history?page=2

WW Realisation 1, limited. Form 2.33B. Registered November 23, 2010. https://beta.companieshouse.gov.uk/company/00104206/filing-history?page=2

WW Realisation 1, limited. Form 2.31B. Registered December 23, 2009. https://beta.companieshouse.gov.uk/company/00104206/filing-history?page=2

WW Realisation 1, limited. Form 2.24B. Registered December 23, 2009. https://beta.companieshouse.gov.uk/company/00104206/filing-history?page=2

WW Realisation 1, limited. Form 2.24B. Registered June 26, 2009. https://beta.companieshouse.gov.uk/company/00104206/filing-history?page=2

WW Realisation 1, limited. Form 2.24B. Registered June 29, 2009. https://beta.companieshouse.gov.uk/company/00104206/filing-history?page=2

11

Case Study 5: Connaught plc

Overview

Connaught plc is an example of corporate governance in a large public company that encountered cash flow insolvency mainly due to unexpected dissipation of its assets (suspension of contracts). The main feature of Connaught plc during the informal rescue process is the board's limited use of informal rescue options. The lenders' preference for some assets over others is a feature of the formal rescue process. The informal rescue process covers the period from September 8, 2009, to September 7, 2010. The case also examines the governance issues arising between September 8, 2010, and February 25, 2014, when the company exited administration.

Background: Connaught plc was established in 1996. In November 1998, the company changed its corporate classification from private to public and was listed on the LSE as Connaught plc. The Group operated as a parent company with three main subsidiaries: Connaught Partnerships Limited, Connaught Compliance Ltd. and Connaught Environmental Limited. The company and its subsidiaries were active in three different industries: the supply of services to public social housing partnerships, physical/regulatory compliance and third-party environmental management.

Connaught plc was the main contractor on behalf of its subsidiaries and provided specific shared services including specialised labour and finance. It also provided after-sales service for the customers of each subsidiary. Connaught Partnerships focused on construction and social housing services; Connaught Environmental Limited focused on environmental issues and Connaught Compliance provided gas, energy and fire protection services. The parent company with a total revenue of £659.6 m, balance sheet of £470.9 m and more than 8,300 employees fitted the definition of mega insolvency case defined in Chap. 6.

Corporate governance: The parent company had a six-member main board including three executive directors and three non-executive directors. Its executive members included the Executive Chairman/Co-Founder, Chief Executive and Group Finance Director. The non-executive team included a Deputy Chairman/senior independent director and two other independent non-executive directors. The composition of the board complied with the Code.

In addition, the Group had a "Group Executive Board" consisting of the executive directors of the three subsidiaries, a Group HR Director and Divisional Chief Executives. A third board called "Divisional Boards" was also active. The contribution of these two boards to the role of the main board of directors is not clear. The focus of this case study is not on the sub-boards; rather, attention is focused on the actions of the main board, which had overall control of the Group.

The parent company had more than 2,400 ordinary shareholders. Large institutional shareholders included Blackrock Inc., Co-operative Asset Management and Parvus Asset Management. Between them they owned 25% of ordinary shares. Executive directors held regular meetings with the institutional shareholders, which implied that these shareholders were able to influence board strategy.

Debt structure: Prior to the start of the informal rescue process, the parent company had granted fixed and floating charges to a syndicate of banks including Barclays Bank plc, National Westminster Bank plc, Wilmington Trust Ltd and the Royal Bank of Scotland, in return for a total of £201 m in credit facilities which was scheduled to mature in 2012.[1] This loan was cross-guaranteed by all of the subsidiaries in the Connaught Group. The company had other debt obligations under finance leases and hire purchase contracts. Furthermore, it had obtained a $91 m loan through private placement at the end of August 2009 which would mature in two parts in 2014 and 2016.

Financial Distress and Associated Causes

Financial distress: At the end of financial year 2009 (August 31) the company was cash flow solvent with £218.7 m current assets and £162.8 m current liabilities. It was also balance sheet solvent as its total assets (£470 m) were substantially higher than its total liabilities (£303.4 m). Therefore, the company seems to have been solvent and not in a financially distressed position. However 50% of its assets were intangible, including goodwill, and the company had underestimated the potential losses from unfulfilled contracts. The company also had a £2.8 bn order book putting it in a strong position in terms of its apparent ability to pay short- and long-term liabilities.

Internal causes: The Group's financial position was highly dependent on continuing to secure service contracts. A termination of these contracts or non-payment for services provided would substantially change the position reflected in its balance sheet and have a direct impact on solvency. Since a high percentage of its costs was direct contracted labour, any economic turndown or fluctuations in business volume would have an immediate impact on cash flow and profitability unless steps were taken quickly to reduce the size of the labour force.

Perhaps recognising this vulnerability, the Group had attempted to diversify its business through acquisition. In 2008 the Group acquired four separate businesses: the Lowe Group Ltd., certain assets of the insolvent company Predator Pest control plc, the loss-making UK Fire International Ltd. and Igrox Ltd. The total amount of investment that the company needed to invest in these companies to restore their financial stability was not accurately determined by the company at the time of acquisition which may have imposed unexpected increased costs on the Group.

The Group seems to have suffered from poor commercial management. A BBC report on the administration process which began in September 2010 suggests that directors opted for large, long-term contracts with various public and private entities frequently making bids that were too low to cover the real costs of providing the service required. It also seems that the parent company used "an aggressive accounting treatment which – without careful reading – appeared to flatter revenues and underplay contract start-up costs" (Bowers 2010). The post-administration analysis also shows that the company had a poor accounting system and inadequate financial records, leaving 50,000 invoices received from creditors for work done unprocessed at the time that the company entered administration.

External causes: One of the major potential causes of financial distress was the global financial meltdown, leading to a reduction in central government spending, which in turn forced UK city councils to temporarily suspend social housing contracts, a major source of business for Connaught. Connaught's board claimed that the real cause of financial distress was "public spending cuts"; however, this view was challenged by rivals and analysts who blamed the problem on mismanagement of contracts.

Another cause might have been related to a sudden change in banks' lending behaviour to large corporate clients during the first three years following the crash of financial markets in 2008. However there is no hard evidence that this external factor had any impact on the Group.

The third and perhaps the most important cause may relate to legal proceedings that were under way relating to the grant of a substantial number of social housing contracts to Connaught. These legal proceedings were brought by a former supplier of these services and did not involve Connaught directly. However, Connaught had underestimated the broader impact that they would have on future business, and failed to react appropriately.

Informal Rescue Process

Board of Directors' Role

Overview

Board changes and cost reduction continued throughout the rescue process whilst debt financing was the final (unsuccessful) attempt to resolve the company's problems. Ultimately the board's decision to put the company into administration was triggered by lenders' refusal to provide further finance to the company.

The company entered administration on September 8, 2010. Adopting the definition adopted in Chap. 6 of this book, the informal rescue period was between September 8, 2009, and September 7, 2010. The main governance feature of this case is the primary focus on board change in an attempt to rescue the business, that is, CEO exit and the appointment of advisors to the board. Less focus was given to cost reduction and debt financing during the final year prior to entering administration. This is perhaps because the board had already borrowed substantially in July and August 2009, in particular in the form of the $91 m loan through private placement. The board's hesitation and delay in the use of informal rescue options may indicate that it had underestimated the impact of drastic problems in the national economy on the company's economic viability. Institutional shareholders' exit from the company and lenders' inflexibility and influence in invoking administration are also notable.

Board Change

January–February 2010: The company announced that the CEO of the parent company had decided to resign at the end of the August 2010 "to seek new challenges elsewhere". However, the board asked him to leave the board with immediate effect "to ensure strategic continuity and clear leadership". On February 1, his appointment as a director was formally terminated, but he remained as an advisor. The Executive Chairman and co-founder took over the Chief Executive role. The company announced that it would create a "new non-executive chairman role" to improve corporate governance. The senior independent director became the acting non-executive chairman for an interim period and the company started to look for a new non-executive chairman.

May 2010: The board appointed a new non-executive chairman who currently held various non-executive roles in other companies and had served as the Chief Executive of Centrica plc, the holding company of British Gas.

July 2010: On July 8, the company announced that the "co-founder-CEO had agreed with the Chairman to relinquish his role but stay in the company to help him find a successor". The newly appointed Chief

Executive Director of the subsidiary Connaught Compliance took over the role of CEO on an interim basis. The company also announced the Group Chief Financial Director's plan to stand down in October 2010.

The company announced on July 26 that the non-executive chairman had appointed four former directors from British Gas to different advisory and operational roles. One advised him on "financial and funding matters", the other chaired "a steering committee responsible for major cost-saving" strategies, the third appointee took over "the full operational role of acting Chief Executive" of the subsidiary Connaught Partnerships Ltd. and the fourth person provided advice on "communication and reviewing management processes".

Analysis: Board changes include resignation, shift of roles and new appointments. The size of the board is reduced from three executive directors to two executive directors and four non-executive directors. New advisors have also been appointed for various operational tasks. Changes seem to follow directors' personal decisions to leave the company.

Cost Reduction

October 2009: The company announced that it had designed an "integrated service model" to meet clients' cost-saving expectation.

June 2010: The company adopted an "emergency budget" following deferment of 31 contracts with a potential £120 m loss of revenue for its social housing subsidiary.

July 2010: The company announced reduced business activities and rationalisation in its major subsidiary—Connaught Compliance—as a result of the existing economic climate.

Analysis: The board seems to have focused more on business development rather than on cost reduction. For example, in September 2009 the parent company purchased the entire shares of the financially distressed Fountain Plc and agreed to pay £13 m as part of a scheme of arrangement. Cost reduction where this has taken place has been in response to suspension and deferment of contracts, and has taken place only at the last stages in the informal rescue process, and arguably too late to have had any effect.

Asset Sale

The company did not report any disposal of its assets or business during the informal rescue process.

Analysis: The company's failure to use asset sale as part of an informal rescue process may reflect the balance sheet position where comparatively few of the assets were tangible fixed assets. The majority were goodwill or service contracts. Those assets that were tangible may also have been largely subject to security interests. This increased the difficulties of obtaining secured credit or refinancing debt.

Equity/Share Issue

December 2009: The board held a deferred AGM and obtained shareholder approval for all ordinary resolutions endorsing its business performance. It also obtained shareholder approval for four special resolutions that related to "allotment of shares in accordance with statutory pre-emption rights", and "purchase of shares otherwise than in accordance with statutory pre-emption rights".

September 2010: On September 7, the company suspended its shares on the LSE with immediate effect.

Analysis: The company does not seem to have used share issue as a means to raise cash during the informal distress period. This was perhaps due to the successful completion of the $91 m private placement in August 2009. The board may have regarded a further share issue as a costly and inefficient financing option which would have been unlikely to have succeeded because of the existing poor economic climate and the comparatively recent previous placement.

New Debt Financing/Debt Renegotiation

July 2010: The board announced that the Group net debt was rapidly increasing and they had entered ongoing negotiations with its existing lenders to resolve the cash problem before the Group breached loan covenants. On July 29, 2010, the board obtained its lenders' approval for an additional £15 m short-term overdraft facility, deferral of interest and principal payments (standstill agreement) due on its existing facilities in July and August.

August 2010: Directors' shift of duty to stakeholders started to become apparent in August 2010 when the Chairman suggested that the board's refinancing would be for the benefit of stakeholders. His statement might imply an articulation of their shift of duty to creditors due to company's insolvency.

September 2010: On September 7, the company announced that the board aimed to restructure the Group's financing for the longer term and subsequently would continue its debt negotiations with existing lenders. On the same day, the board called in administrators after its negotiations with the bank failed. The failure came after the Chairman was unable to persuade the Royal Bank of Scotland (RBS) to accept a new business plan requiring a £15 m loan. The company confirmed that existing lenders were not willing to provide further loan or credit facilities to the company. However, the board indicated that it would continue to look for other sources of financing.

Analysis: Debt financing appears to have been adopted as the last informal rescue option by the board of directors. The board seems to have initially been successful in obtaining a standstill agreement and a short-term credit facility. There are no details available about the standstill agreement. It appears to have been aimed at maintaining the business as a going concern by seeking further finance from lenders. It is interesting to note that when the board sought further loans to pay other stakeholders its lenders were no longer willing to take further risks prioritising their own interests over those of the company and other creditors. Arguably the lenders' approach compelled the board to put the company into administration.

Shareholder Influence

Shareholders' support for the company and its directors, nine months prior to the company entering administration, was reflected in their approval of the board's proposals at what was in effect its last AGM. It appears that institutional investors continued to give their full support to the company and the board until June 2010, when the company issued a profit warning and institutional shareholders exited the company. Despite this profit warning, some of the institutional shareholders, including Barclays, increased their shareholding a month before the company was placed into administration.

Analysis: The board seems to have the general support of both institutional and dispersed shareholders, based on their experience of investing in companies in construction and service indutries.

Creditor Influence

The lenders' influence could be seen in their increasing unwillingness to extend further loan facilities, ultimately resulting in the appointment of administrators. The company also seems to have faced increasing pressure from suppliers and sub-contractors to pay their invoices before it entered administration.

Analysis: Lenders appear to be very cautious in response to the board's attempt to secure further borrowing. It seems that the unsecured creditors adopted a tolerant approach towards the company's delay in the repayment of their claims reflected in the large number of unpaid invoices.

Formal Rescue Process: Administration

Overview: On September 7, 2010, the board announced that it would appoint joint administrators from KPMG for Connaught plc and Connaught Partnerships Ltd. whilst the other subsidiaries would continue as going concerns with the support of their funders. On September 8, 2010, three insolvency practitioners were appointed as joint administrators of the parent company Connaught plc. The parent company owed £94.3 m to secured creditors and £39.4 m to unsecured creditors whilst its total assets were £108.8 m. Four insolvency practitioners were appointed as joint administrators of the social housing subsidiary

Connaught Partnerships Ltd. The administrators' involvement in Connaught plc seems to have commenced prior to their appointment evidenced by the "pre-administration costs" that were later claimed as part of their expenses. No further details were provided on the nature of their involvement. Connaught plc did not have any trading activities. It operated as the strategic and controlling part of the Group and processed functions relating to "payroll, finance, treasury, central HR and shared services including IT, fleet and insurances".

Administrator's Role

The joint administrators determined that the best option would be to adopt statutory objective para 3(1)(b) of Schedule B1 of the Insolvency Act 1986 since maintaining the business as a going concern was not possible. They also anticipated that dissolution or liquidation would be alternative exit routes for the company.

Management of the going concern: The joint administrators had to maintain the parent company as a going concern because it operated as the central hub for all client services. The activities and assets of the parent company were intertwined with those of the subsidiary companies. They planned to separate the essential components of the parent company from those of the subsidiaries in order to facilitate an independent valuation, marketing and sale of each company.

Maintaining the parent company as a going concern enabled an "orderly transition" period to maximise the proceeds from the sale of the business and the assets of its subsidiaries. To ensure continuity of the business new agreements were made between the joint administrators and six "key suppliers" for the provision of related goods and services until the end of 2010.

September 2010–March 2011: The administrators' first progress report states that retained staff in the parent company were responsible for paying suppliers and cataloguing the contents of over 10,000 boxes of accounting records that related to various subsidiaries.

Asset sale and recovery: The statement of administrator's proposals also shows that at the start of administration, the joint administrators assumed that secured creditors would take over Connaught Environmental and the profitable parts of Connaught Compliance which had cross-guaranteed repayment of debt owed by the parent company. This sale was subject to an independent valuation by Deloitte.

The statement of administrator's proposals also shows that the assets and business goodwill of the insolvent subsidiary Connaught Partnerships were sold to Lovell Partnerships Limited (part of the Morgan Sindall Group) two days after their appointment. The sale included 89 out of 128 contracts, all work in progress, receivables and debt balances. The assets included all physical assets including any stock, plant and machinery, and fixtures and fittings owned by the subsidiary. The sale of the business resulted in the transfer of more than 50% of staff (2,500 out of 4,400) to the buyer.

Nine out of 29 remaining contracts were sold to Mears on September 10, 2010. In October 2010 (a month after entering administration), the administrators sold the gas and electrical businesses of the subsidiary Connaught Compliance to British Gas. The influence and connections of the previous non-executive chairman and his advisory team, who all came from British Gas, may have facilitated the sale agreement, although there is no direct factual evidence to support this.

The joint administrators appear to have reached an agreement with secured creditors over the purchase of the solvent subsidiary Connaught Environmental and the remaining business goodwill and assets of Connaught Compliance. Lenders planned to transfer the assets and business from those companies to new companies (special purpose vehicles) they had set up as part of the process of handling their claims. Following an independent evaluation by Deloitte and marketing by KPMG LLP Corporate Finance, the administrators put Connaught Compliance into administration, and finalised the sale of the advisory and services business.

The administrators also planned to sell the remaining assets owned by the parent company. During the sale process, they deployed the law firm SNR Denton for professional advice on all matters relating to the sale and transfer of assets to lenders and third parties with the view of discharging personal liability to creditors.

The third progress report shows the identification and sale of a freehold property ultimately owned by Connaught plc. Recovery of a £160 k deposit from a bank account at National Westminster Bank illustrates the diligence of the administrators in recovering assets.

Distribution of proceeds to secured creditors: At the time of administration, a lenders' syndicate led by the RBS and Wilmington operating as the trustees of the noteholders represented secured creditors with claims exceeding £215 m. The Group had granted fixed and floating charges to its lenders that were cross-guaranteed by subsidiaries. According to the statement of administrator's proposals, the administrators did not believe that the Group had enough assets to pay its lenders from the proceeds of sale—they believed that the lenders would suffer a substantial shortfall. The first progress report indicates that lenders recovered almost 20% of their debt by taking over the ownership of Connaught Environmental at its valuation at the time of transfer and 20% of their debt from the realisation of other assets.[2] The third progress report showed another 10% of debt paid to secured creditors arising from the realisation of assets.

The bargaining powers of administrators can be implied from the statement that they sold Connaught Environmental which they had acquired "at a price equivalent to the high-end valuation" in March 2011. The lenders changed their original plan to purchase Connaught Compliance as part redemption of their debt (set-off) as they began to appreciate the loss-making position of the company. Therefore, the administrators sold the assets of the company piecemeal by disposing of its "Advisory and Service divisions".

The first progress report shows a potential disagreement between secured creditors and administrators on the administrator's costs for the first seven months of administration. The administrators' first progress report indicated costs of £6.6 m for work completed between September 2010 and March 2011. However, these costs were challenged by secured creditors. The report states that administrators were in discussion with secured creditors and agreed to give substantial discounts on their fees due to the scale of work involved. The third progress report demonstrates that the administrators were allowed to withdraw some funds from the company to pay fees but were still in negotiation with creditors and needed further permission to draw down fees for the work already carried out. The fees were modified to an interim payment of £2.3 m which was substantially lower than the original invoice.

In Connaught Partnerships Ltd., secured creditors and preferential creditors ultimately fixed the total remuneration of administrators at £4 m excluding investigatory work. This amount was fully drawn down during the administration period.

Distribution of proceeds to unsecured creditors: The administrators' proposals suggest that the parent company had insufficient assets, making it unlikely that dividends would be paid to unsecured creditors and therefore it was unnecessary to hold a creditors' meeting. They also suggested that although unsecured creditors were legally entitled to a payment under the prescribed part, they anticipated that there would not be sufficient realisation of assets after costs to enable such a payment.

The same proposal was adopted for unsecured creditors in the subsidiary Connaught Partnerships with the exception that unsecured creditors were entitled to dividends under the prescribed part. According to the administrators' proposals for both the parent company and its subsidiary, unsecured creditor approval was unnecessary and matters were referred to secured creditors to approve, including hourly fee rates for different categories of staff. The proposals also noted that KPMG would provide professional advice relating to "forensic, tax, health and safety and pensions" and proposed that they would charge for such services based on "time costs at a rate that reflects the complexity of the assignment". They also sought authorisation to draw from the company's proceeds of assets "from time to time".

The total debt identified as owed by the parent company to unsecured creditors at the time of administration was £11 m. However, both Schedule A1 of the Statement of affairs and the first progress report show that Group unsecured debt exceeded £39 m, reflected in the purchase ledger, contingent liabilities and other creditors. This difference in unsecured debt value might be partly due to contingent debt and creditor delays in the submission of proof of their debt. It also seems that administrators were pre-occupied by the secured debt and less concerned about debt owed to unsecured creditors because they did not expect unsecured creditors would receive any dividends after payment of costs and expenses.

The statement of administrators' proposals for the parent company classifies unsecured creditors as trade creditors, HMRC and unsecured employee claims. Amongst those creditors the following had the largest claims: HMRC (£1.3 m), Castlemead Insurance Brokers (£1.1 m), O2 UK (£1.1 m), Azzurri Communications Ltd. (£930 K) and 2e2UK (£711 K). However, it later became clear that the debt owed to HMRC was much more than initially stated. The first progress report for Connaught plc increased the value to £14 m.[3] It does not seem that any request was made to convene a creditors' meeting and, therefore, administrator proposals were approved.

According to the parent company's first progress report, the administrators had to transfer the subsidiary Connaught Environmental tax-free to lenders, which means they had to clear any debt owed to HMRC. They also entered negotiations with HMRC to clarify the tax position of the Group. These discussions continued until December 2011 and the submission of the third progress report.

The administrators' proposal shows that they had reached an agreement with some suppliers (e.g. Azzurri) over the continued delivery of goods and services to maintain the going concern status of the parent company. This might indicate that some kind of agreement had been reached over pre-administration claims. The third progress report reveals that suppliers were owed substantial amounts, on which administrators were able to receive some rebates. There is no information whether any suppliers recovered their debt through insurance or retention of title. Although suppliers were unable to recover their goods through retention of title, due to the difficulty in identifying those goods and their attachment to other fittings and fixtures, they might have been approached by Lovell, the company which acquired the contracts, to continue to supply products or services with the aim of recovering their debt in part.

Unsecured creditors of the subsidiary Connaught Partnerships were treated in a similar fashion to those of the parent company. The total debt owed to unsecured creditors amounted to £159 m, although the statement of proposals initially fixed the overdue unsecured debt at £74 m. Amongst the creditors, HMRC with £21 m, and three other creditors whose names were withheld had the highest claims. As the administrators had determined, unsecured creditors were entitled to less than 1p in the pound; however they indicated that they should apply to the court for the authority to distribute dividends. The amount appears to have been fixed at £600 k, based on the prescribed part obtained from assets subject to charges created post September 15, 2003. The administrators were obliged to seek the approval of "secured creditors and preferential creditors" for their proposals and to agree on their "time costs" and fees. No request for a creditors' meeting was made and ultimately the proposal was approved without modification.

The first progress report shows that the administrators returned all the leasehold properties that did not form part of the sale to Lovell. The fourth progress report relating to the subsidiary shows that the costs of the administrators' investigation and the costs of distribution of the prescribed part continued into the liquidation stage, amounting to an estimated £300 k.

Investigation into directors' conduct: There is no information on the administrators' report on directors' conduct and their liability for wrongful trading. The last progress report indicates that this investigation was completed but there was no indication of wrongful trading.

Creditor Influence

Secured creditors: Secured creditor influence began with their financing of administration costs. The third progress report indicates that the RBS initially provided a £5 m overdraft facility for administration. The interest rate and charges were not specified. At the end of the first year of administration, it agreed to pay £2.5 m to fund administration costs. The first progress report summarises the results of negotiations between administrators and secured creditors. It indicates that secured creditors intended acquiring all shares of the solvent subsidiary Connaught Environmental as part of their claim,[4] and not buying Connaught Compliance—a change in their original plan. A significant influence of lenders can be seen in approving administration fees. According to the first progress report, the administrators claimed £6.6 m for their remuneration and the professional advice offered by KPMG. Drawing down their fees was subject to the lenders' approval of the plan which did not take place until the second progress report was submitted to creditors.

Unsecured creditors: In the absence of any potential dividends for unsecured creditors at the parent company, this category of creditors were unable to influence administration in a collective manner. The same applied to the unsecured creditors of the subsidiary Connaught Environmental. It seems that creditors made individual decisions as to how to deal with the company following administration.

Administration outcome: During administration, unsecured creditors did not receive any collective dividend. Secured creditors received 30% of their total claims excluding the acquisition of Connaught Environmental (valued at £55 m). On March 11, 2013, Connaught Partnerships entered liquidation. Connaught plc, the parent company exited administration and entered liquidation on February 25, 2014.

Summary

Connaught plc appears to have been relatively successful until changes in the business environment challenged its existing business model, leading to increasing financial difficulties. Its decision to acquire new (unprofitable and distressed) businesses indicates a desire to diversify, offering a range of services to private and public customers. The costs of these acquisitions, coupled with a downturn in the business environment, led to a situation where the company was increasingly cash hungry, resulting in a $91 m placement in 2009. Without this injection of capital the company would not have been solvent as it entered the year prior to formal rescue. The pressures of repayment of capital, coupled with a decline in business particularly with public sector clients, led to increasing pressure on the board. These pressures led to the resignation of the founder-CEO and the introduction of a new senior team.

During the year of informal distress the board attempted to reduce costs through rationalisation of business activity, and greater efficiencies through reduction of duplication of centralised tasks such as invoicing and customer management. However, the size and complexity of the task revealed in hindsight by the administrators' report was too great and the company ran out of cash. Secured lenders did not believe that the company would be able to survive as a business in its current shape, and their view was key. The interrelated nature of the parent company and its subsidiaries and the cross-guarantees of debt in place meant that it was difficult, if not impossible, to sell off part of the Group as a separate entity to ease the distress situation.

Notes

1. *See* Charges No 15–18 registered between July 23 and 28, 2009. See also Charge No 19–21 registered between August 25 and 26, 2009.
2. Connaught Environmental was transferred at £55 m which might reflect a discount. Administrators also suggested that lenders received another 20% from realisation of assets. Therefore, it seems that their recovery was more than 45% of total debt.
3. £1.3 m to £14 m.
4. The valuation price was £35–55 m and lenders agreed to take Connaught Environmental at £55 m.

Bibliography

Bawden, Tom. 2010. "Morgan Sindall Fears Connaught Deal Won't Be Worth as Much as Anticipated." *Guardian,* November 9. Accessed 30 December 2015. https://www.theguardian.com/business/2010/nov/09/morgan-sindall-connaught-contracts-in-doubt

BBC News. 2011. "Connaught Administrators Find 50,000 Unpaid Invoices." *BBC. Com.* January 17. Accessed 13 May 2017. http://www.bbc.co.uk/news/mobile/ukengland-12203959

BONDCO 611, Limited. NEWINC. Registered April 11, 1996. https://beta.companieshouse.gov.uk/company/03184319/filing-history?page=15

Bowers, Simon. 2010. "Connaught Social Housing Maintenance Group Warns of 'Material Loss'." *Guardian,* August 6. Accessed 13 May 2017. https://www.theguardian.com/business/2010/aug/06/conaught-social-housing-loss-warning

Bowers, Simon and Ian Griffiths. 2010. "Departing Executives at Ailing Housing Contractor Connaught Sold £16.6m in Shares." *The Guardian,* July 8. Accessed 13 May 2017. http://www.theguardian.com/business/2010/jul/08/construction

Connaught Holdings, Limited. CERTNM. Registered May 28, 1996. https://beta.companieshouse.gov.uk/company/03184319/filing-history?page=15

Connaught Partnerships, Limited. Form 2.12B. Registered January 16, 2012. https://beta.companieshouse.gov.uk/company/01838150/filinghistory?page=3

Connaught Partnerships, Limited. Form 2.24B. Registered January 15, 2013. https://beta.companieshouse.gov.uk/company/01838150/filinghistory?page=3

Connaught Partnerships, Limited. Form 2.24B. Registered July 13, 2012. https://beta.companieshouse.gov.uk/company/01838150/filing-history?page=3

Connaught Partnerships, Limited. Form 2.24B. Registered March 14, 2013. https://beta.companieshouse.gov.uk/company/01838150/filinghistory?page=3

Connaught Partnerships, Limited. Form 2.12B. Registered September 17, 2010. https://beta.companieshouse.gov.uk/company/01838150/filinghistory?page=4

Connaught Partnerships, Limited. Form 2.16B with form 2.14B. Registered November 16, 2010.

Connaught Partnerships, Limited. Form 2.17B. Registered November 8, 2010. https://beta.companieshouse.gov.uk/company/01838150/filinghistory?page=4

Connaught Partnerships, Limited. Form 2.18. Registered November 30, 2010. https://beta.companieshouse.gov.uk/company/01838150/filinghistory?page=4

Connaught Partnerships, Limited. Form 2.24B. Registered March 14, 2013. https://beta.companieshouse.gov.uk/company/01838150/filinghistory?page=3

Connaught Partnerships, Limited. Form 2.24B. Registered April 13, 2011. https://beta.companieshouse.gov.uk/company/01838150/filing-history?page=4

Connaught Partnerships, Limited. Form 2.34B. Registered March 5, 2013. https://beta.companieshouse.gov.uk/company/01838150/filing-history?page=3

Connaught Partnerships, Limited. Form F2.18. Registered November 30, 2010. https://beta.companieshouse.gov.uk/company/01838150/filinghistory?page=4

Case Study 5: Connaught plc 241

Connaught Partnerships, Limited. RESOLUTIONS. Registered September 27, 2010. https://beta.companieshouse.gov.uk/company/01838150/filing-history?page=4

Connaught, plc. Form 2.24. Registered September 5, 2011. https://beta.companieshouse.gov.uk/company/03184319/filing-history?page=2

Connaught, plc. Form 2.16B with Form 2.14B. Registered November 23, 2010. https://beta.companieshouse.gov.uk/company/03184319/filinghistory?page=2

Connaught, plc. Form 2.17B. Registered November 04, 2010. https://beta.companieshouse.gov.uk/company/03184319/filing-history?page=2

Connaught, plc. Form 2.17B. Registered November 9, 2010. https://beta.companieshouse.gov.uk/company/03184319/filing-history?page=2

Connaught, plc. Form 2.18B. Registered November 30, 2010. https://beta.companieshouse.gov.uk/company/03184319/filing-history?page=2

Connaught, plc. Form 2.24B. Registered April 12, 2011. https://beta.companieshouse.gov.uk/company/03184319/filing-history?page=2

Connaught, plc. Form 2.24B. Registered January 12, 2012. https://beta.companieshouse.gov.uk/company/03184319/filing-history?page=2

Connaught, plc. Form 2.24B. Registered September 5, 2011. https://beta.companieshouse.gov.uk/company/03184319/filing-history?page=2

Connaught, plc. Form 2.24B. Registered September 7, 2011. https://beta.companieshouse.gov.uk/company/03184319/filing-history?page=2

Connaught, plc. Form TM01. Registered February 1, 2010. https://beta.companieshouse.gov.uk/company/03184319/filing-history?page=3

Connaught, plc. *Annual Report & Accounts 2009*. Registered February 9, 2010. https://beta.companieshouse.gov.uk/company/03184319/filinghistory?page=3

Connaught, plc. F2.18. Registered November 30, 2010. https://beta.companieshouse.gov.uk/company/03184319/filing-history?page=2

Connaught, plc. Form 2.12B. Registered September 17, 2010. https://beta.companieshouse.gov.uk/company/03184319/filing-history?page=3

Connaught, plc. Form 2.16B. Registered November 23, 2010. https://beta.companieshouse.gov.uk/company/03184319/filing-history?page=2

Connaught, plc. Form 2.16B. Registered November 23, 2010. https://beta.companieshouse.gov.uk/company/03184319/filing-history?page=2

Connaught, plc. Form 2.17B. Registered November 4, 2010. https://beta.companieshouse.gov.uk/company/03184319/filing-history?page=2

Connaught, plc. Form 2.17B. Registered November 9, 2010. https://beta.companieshouse.gov.uk/company/03184319/filing-history?page=2

Connaught, plc. Form 2.24B. Registered January 12, 2012. https://beta.companieshouse.gov.uk/company/03184319/filing-history?page=2
Connaught, plc. Form 2.33B. Registered March 13, 2014. https://beta.companieshouse.gov.uk/company/03184319/filing-history
Connaught, plc. Form 2.24B. Registered March 14, 2014. https://beta.companieshouse.gov.uk/company/03184319/filing-history?page=1
Connaught, plc. Form 2.24B. Registered January 15, 2014. https://beta.companieshouse.gov.uk/company/03184319/filing-history?page=1
Connaught, plc. Form 2.24B. Registered July 16, 2013. https://beta.companieshouse.gov.uk/company/03184319/filing-history?page=1
Connaught, plc. Form 2.24B. Registered July 17, 2013. https://beta.companieshouse.gov.uk/company/03184319/filing-history?page=1
Connaught, plc. Form 2.31B. Registered September 5, 2011. https://beta.companieshouse.gov.uk/company/03184319/filing-history?page=2
Connaught, plc. Form 395 (charge 15). Registered July 25, 2009. https://beta.companieshouse.gov.uk/company/03184319/filing-history?page=4
Connaught, plc. Form 395 (charge 16). Registered July 23, 2009. https://beta.companieshouse.gov.uk/company/03184319/filing-history?page=4
Connaught, plc. Form 395 (charge 17). Registered July 28, 2009. https://beta.companieshouse.gov.uk/company/03184319/filing-history?page=4
Connaught, plc. Form 395 (charge 18). Registered July 23, 2009. https://beta.companieshouse.gov.uk/company/03184319/filing-history?page=4
Connaught, plc. Form 395 (charge 19). Registered August 26, 2009. https://beta.companieshouse.gov.uk/company/03184319/filing-history?page=4
Connaught, plc. Form 395 (charge 20). Registered August 25, 2009. https://beta.companieshouse.gov.uk/company/03184319/filing-history?page=4
Connaught, plc. Form 395 (charge 21). Registered August 25, 2009. https://beta.companieshouse.gov.uk/company/03184319/filing-history?page=4
Connaught, plc. Form 395 (Charge no 22). Registered September 21, 2009. https://beta.companieshouse.gov.uk/company/03184319/filing-history?page=3
Connaught, plc. Form 403a (charge 10). Registered August 10, 2009. https://beta.companieshouse.gov.uk/company/03184319/filing-history?page=4
Connaught, plc. Form MG04 (charge No 11). Registered March 15, 2011. https://beta.companieshouse.gov.uk/company/03184319/filing-history?page=2

Connaught, plc. Form MG04 (charge No 12). Registered March 15, 2011. https://beta.companieshouse.gov.uk/company/03184319/filing-history?page=2

Connaught, plc. Form MG04 (charge No 16). Registered March 15, 2011. https://beta.companieshouse.gov.uk/company/03184319/filing-history?page=2

Connaught, plc. Form MG04 (charge No 18). Registered March 15, 2011. https://beta.companieshouse.gov.uk/company/03184319/filing-history?page=2

Connaught, plc. Form MG04 (charge No 20). Registered March 15, 2011. https://beta.companieshouse.gov.uk/company/03184319/filing-history?page=2

Connaught, plc. Form MG04 (charge No 21). Registered March 15, 2011. https://beta.companieshouse.gov.uk/company/03184319/filing-history?page=2

Connaught, plc. Form MG04 (charge No 23). Registered March 15, 2011. https://beta.companieshouse.gov.uk/company/03184319/filing-history?page=2

Connaught, plc. Form MG04 (charge No 24). Registered March 15, 2011. https://beta.companieshouse.gov.uk/company/03184319/filing-history?page=2

Connaught, plc. Form MG04 (charge No 25). Registered March 15, 2011. https://beta.companieshouse.gov.uk/company/03184319/filing-history?page=2

Connaught. AGM Statement. RNS No. 1659E Dated December 15, 2009.

Connaught. Agreement on Financing. RNS No. 1336Q Dated July 29, 2010.

Connaught. Annual Financial Report. RNS No. 3716C Dated November 12, 2009.

Connaught. Appointment of Joint Administrators. RNS Number: 3905S Dated September 8, 2010.

Connaught. Board Appointment. RNS No. 5810L Dated May 10, 2010.

Connaught. Board Change. RNS No. 3154G Dated January 29, 2010.

Connaught. Director/PDMR Shareholding. RNS No. 3352G Dated January 29, 2010.

Connaught. Director/PDMR Shareholding. RNS No. 3474G Dated January 29, 2010.

Connaught. Interim Management Statement. RNS No. 0195P Dated July 8, 2010.
Connaught. Interim Management Statement. RNS No. 1057E Dated December 15, 2009.
Connaught. Preliminary Results. RNS No. 6530A Dated October 13, 2009.
Connaught. Process of Appointment of Administrators. RNS No. 3161S Dated September 7, 2010.
Connaught. Review of Trading and Financial Performance. RNS. No. 6861Q Dated August 6, 2010.
Connaught. Statement re suspension. RNS No. 2569S Dated September 7, 2010.
Connaught. Update on Trading. RNS No. 2866O Dated June 25, 2010.
Connaught. Update. RNS No. 8809P Dated July 26, 2010.
Gray, Alistair. 2010. "Losers Count the Cost of Connaught Gamble." *Financial Times,* September 9. Accessed 13 May 2017. http://www.ft.com/cms/s/0/b4622420-bb7b-11df-a136-00144feab49a.html#axzz2iHP9WDLI
Hammond, Ed, Anoushka Sakooui, and Alistair Gray. 2010. "Connaught Calls in Administrators." *Financial Times,* September 7. Accessed 13 May 2017. http://www.ft.com/cms/s/0/fe9daee6-ba50-11df-8e5c-00144feab49a.html#axzz2oxHRo2Rs
Mackinlay, Rob. 2010. "'Unusually' High Number of Private Investors Held Connaught." *Citywire,* September 11. Accessed 30 December 2017. http://citywire.co.uk/money/unusually-high-number-of-private-investors-held-connaught/a429892

Part III

12

Insights from the Case Studies

Overview

Chapters 7 to 11 presented five in-depth case studies of companies which had experienced financial distress and ultimately insolvency. Governance issues were examined during the informal rescue stage as well as once these companies entered into administration or CVA. One company, Waterford Wedgwood plc, was placed into receivership. Since receivership is not a rescue process under English law and the company's receivership was dealt with under Irish law, its governance issues during the formal rescue process were examined in Waterford Wedgwood UK plc, the Group's principal UK subsidiary that had entered administration. This chapter draws together the discussion of governance, in a comparative analysis of the major insights that have emerged from the case studies.

The chapter concludes that whilst corporate governance is a matter of primary concern for the board of directors during financial distress, shareholders and creditors may create a peripheral governance structure which can influence the board's success or failure in achieving its objectives. The role of insolvency practitioners during administration is seen as comparable with that of the board of directors at the informal rescue stage. Insolvency practitioners in large public companies are not exempt from lenders' influence. The research also highlights the difficulties that exist in assessing the scope and impact of creditor influence during the rescue process.

Sample Companies

Table 12.1 presents an overview of the companies analysed by main subsidiaries, listing status and industry. In four out of five companies (excluding JJB Sports plc), the parent company does not have any trading activities but operates as the central decision-making body for the group. The subsidiaries do not have the independence typical of many small- or medium-sized companies.

Table 12.1 Sample overview

Company's name	Public company	Listing status	UK-based main subsidiaries	Group industry
Connaught plc	Ultimate Parent	LSE	Connaught Partnerships, Connaught Environmental Limited and Connaught Compliance	Construction & Service Supply
JJB Sports plc	Ultimate Parent	LSE	Blane Leisure Limited, Sports Division (Eireann) Limited	Retail
Stylo plc	Ultimate Parent	AIM	Stylo Barratt Shoes Limited, Stylo Barratt Properties Limited, Barratts Shoes Properties Limited, Priceless Shoes Properties Limited and Apper Limited (Formerly Shelly's Shoes Limited)	Retail & Property Development
Waterford Wedgwood plc	Ultimate Parent	LSE, Irish Stock Market	Waterford Wedgwood UK plc	Manufacturing & Retail
Woolworths Group plc	Ultimate Parent	LSE	Woolworths plc, Entertainment UK and 2Entertain Limited	Retail and entertainment

All of the parent companies in the sample are public companies. Four out of five were listed on the LSE and one company (Stylo plc) was listed on the AIM. The four companies that were listed on the LSE were formally subject to the Code whereas Stylo plc with shares traded on the AIM was not subject to the ubiquitous "comply or explain" rule. The difference in listing did not affect the disclosure of financial or more general corporate information. The boards of all of the parent companies published an Annual Report and Accounts that provided the information formally required on corporate governance and financial performance. They all also made frequent public announcements relating to trading, board changes, equity/share issue, asset sale and new debt financing/debt renegotiation.

As Table 12.1 shows, the companies in the sample had different numbers of subsidiaries. Three companies—Connaught plc, JJB Sports plc and Stylo plc—were public companies with private operating subsidiaries. Waterford Wedgwood plc and Woolworths Group plc were the principal operating companies, with at least one subsidiary operating as a public company.

Waterford Wedgwood plc was listed on two stock markets. The ultimate parent company (Waterford Wedgwood plc) was listed on the Irish Stock Exchange and the LSE. The major UK subsidiary—Waterford Wedgwood UK plc—was listed on the LSE. This dual listing did not affect the disclosure of information relating to the company. The parent company did not make any distinction between the decisions of the board of the parent company and its UK subsidiary during the informal rescue process. The author treated the informal rescue processes in the parent company and its UK subsidiary as one combined case. The collective treatment ended when the parent company entered receivership and its UK subsidiary was placed into administration.

Woolworths Group plc also had a retail subsidiary, Woolworths plc, a public company. The existence of two public companies in the Group did not affect governance issues during the informal rescue process; however, at the start of administration respective governance issues were separated in the parent company and its subsidiary as they were placed into administration separately.

Table 12.2 Analysis of the sample based on mega insolvency criteria at the start of informal rescue process

Company	Turnover	Balance sheet total (total assets)	Number of employees
Connaught plc (Sept. 2009)	£659.6 m	£470.9 m	8354
JJB Sports plc (Apr. 2008)	£811 m	£789 m	6700
Stylo plc (Feb. 2008)	£223 m	£126 m	5400
Waterford Wedgwood plc (Jan. 2008)	€671.8 m	€519.2 m	8000
Woolworths Group plc (Jan. 2008)	£2.9 bn	£2.1 bn	25,000

Table 12.2 analyses the size of the companies in the sample at the time of entry into the informal rescue process. The information in the table has been extracted from the company's last Annual Report and Accounts published prior to the start of the informal rescue process. The timing of publication of this report may not exactly match the date defined as the start of the process (one year prior to entering a formal rescue process). All of the companies qualify under the definition of mega insolvency cases described in Chap. 6. In four out of five cases, assets were largely tangible, that is, stock and properties. The valuation of stock creates a potential difficulty in determining a company's cash flow solvency, which is discussed below. Additionally in one case, Connaught plc, the balance sheet also included intangible assets including contracts, reflecting a more vulnerable position since the suspension or termination of such contracts could (and did) substantially change the company's balance sheet position, provoking a collapse into insolvency.

Corporate governance: Table 12.3 shows the size and composition of the board in the companies in the sample, including the extent of separation of the role of CEO from that of Chair, the number of non-executive and executive directors, and the extent of representation of shareholders and lenders on the board.

In four out of five cases, the composition of the board of directors was compliant with the Code, with the number of non-executive directors being more than or equal to the number of executive directors. The roles

Insights from the Case Studies   251

Table 12.3 Board size and composition

Company	Board size	Separation of the role of chief executive and non-executive chairman	Number of executive directors	Number of non-executive directors	Representation by bondholders, major shareholder or lenders on the board
Connaught plc	6	Yes	3	3	No
JJB Sports plc	7	Yes	3	4	Yes
Stylo plc	9	No	5	4	Yes
Waterford Wedgwood plc	15	Yes	6	9	Yes
Woolworths plc	10	Yes	5	5	No

of CEO and chairman were also separate in those four companies. Only one company (Stylo plc), listed on the AIM, was not obliged to comply with the governance code. In this company, the role of the CEO and the chairman was combined. Some of the non-executive directors also had family relationships with the CEO/chair.

In all of the five case studies, the parent companies had a few significant major shareholders with total shareholdings exceeding 20% of total shares. In three out of five cases—JJB Sports plc, Stylo plc and Waterford Wedgwood plc—major shareholders were represented on the board. In two companies, Connaught plc and Woolworths plc, the company had major institutional shareholders who had regular meetings with the senior management team.

Whilst all shareholders were entitled to exercise individual voting rights at shareholder meetings, in several instances it was possible to identify where major individual and institutional shareholders were able to influence the decisions of the board outside such general meetings. For instance, in one case (Waterford Wedgwood plc) preference shareholders were represented on the board alongside major individual shareholders. Those shareholders who had a presence on the board had a better chance of influencing the board's decisions than shareholders acting collectively outside of board meetings.

Debt structure: The companies in the study had different levels and types of debt. Four out of five of the companies in the sample had debt liabilities including secured debt prior to the start of the informal rescue process. Only Woolworths Group plc did not have any secured debt. All of the other companies had more than one lender. In each case the parent companies had granted security in the form of a mortgage, or other fixed and/or floating charges. In each case the secured debt was cross-guaranteed by subsidiaries making them liable for the debt owed by parent companies. The position of subsidiaries as cross-guarantors of debt has implications for the ability and scope of secured creditors to exercise their rights, and is discussed below. No detailed public information was available about the terms of secured debt which limits the level of interpretation of such terms during the rescue process.

Financial Distress and Associated Causes

Financial Distress

Table 12.4 analyses the degree of solvency of each of the companies one year prior to entering a formal rescue process.

The companies in the sample varied in terms of their solvency determined by cash flow and balance sheet tests. Three out of five companies in the

Table 12.4 Analysis of assets and liabilities (millions)

Company	Current assets	Current liabilities	Total assets	Total liabilities
Connaught plc	£218 m	£162 m	£470 m	£303 m
JJB Sports plc	£372 m	£301 m	£789 m	£424 m
Stylo plc	£41 m	£48 m	£126 m	£91 m
Waterford Wedgwood plc	€371 m	€140 m	€519 m	€839 m
Woolworths Group plc	£882 m	£800 m	£1.3 bn	£1 bn

sample, Connaught plc, JJB Sports plc and Woolworths plc, were cash flow solvent and balance sheet solvent. Stylo plc was cash flow insolvent matching the original definition of financial distress whilst Waterford Wedgwood plc was balance sheet insolvent. Under the cash flow test described in Chap. 3, only Stylo plc was technically in need of rescue. However, in three further companies—JJB Sports plc, Waterford Wedgewood UK plc and Woolworths plc—a substantial amount of assets was in the form of stock/inventory, which was not immediately realisable as cash.

Such assets are excluded in the test used by accountants in determining a company's ability to pay its short-term debt. Applying a broader commercial test, four of the companies in the sample would have been cash flow insolvent. Following the judgment in *Eurosail*, a mechanical test cannot on its own determine the degree of company's solvency and other aspects should be taken into account. All the companies were subjected to a range of external causes that were affecting the chance of survival of the business as a going concern.

It seems that the application of the legal definition of cash flow may understate the actual commercial problems that precipitate an informal rescue process. It might also reflect a more tolerant approach on the part of courts towards fixing an exact position for financial distress, allowing the company an opportunity to improve its cash flow. It is difficult from balance sheet information to determine the priority of debt in terms of when such debts become due. The cases demonstrate that a financially distressed public company that ultimately enters a formal rescue process is not always cash flow insolvent or balance sheet insolvent a year before entry, reinforcing the view that predicting the likelihood of insolvency is a difficult task even for those directors most closely associated with the business, and explaining the legal position which seems to be tolerant in terms of holding directors to account.

All but one of the companies were balance sheet solvent at the start of the informal rescue process, suggesting that they were economically strong enough to pay long-term liabilities and therefore had a high chance of recovery through the use of informal rescue options.

Internal Causes

The companies in our study share some features in terms of the internal causes of financial distress. The Cork Report identified management weakness as one of the primary contributors. Each of the case studies illustrates different examples of decisions that with the benefit of hindsight appear to have created problems for the company. These findings, suggesting mismanagement or at least poor strategic planning, are consistent with those identified by Finch and reported in Chap. 3.

For example, three companies in the sample had purchased distressed assets prior to their entry into the informal rescue process. Connaught plc had acquired the Lowe Group Ltd., certain assets of the insolvent company Predator Pest control plc, the loss-making UK Fire International Ltd. and Igrox Ltd., all of which inevitably required further investment in order to become profitable. JJB Sports plc acquired the financially distressed Original Shoe Company (OSC) in December 2007 and initially did not report that it had paid an additional £10 m as well as an initial payment of £5 m. Stylo plc purchased some assets of the distressed company Dolcis which also imposed exceptional costs on the company.

One of the companies (Woolworths plc) had for a long time persisted with an outdated merchandising strategy that was increasingly uncompetitive. Stylo plc failed to move quickly enough compared to its competitors to transfer production overseas. JJB Sports plc did not respond quickly enough to the entry of new online competitors. At the same time, wages and rents relating to leasehold retail stores remained fixed or increased, and management failed to address this problem quickly as recession took over in the immediate aftermath of the financial crisis in 2008.

External Causes

Four companies were involved in retailing and were subject to similar external factors prior to their entry into informal rescue during 2008. These external factors included the credit crunch that started in 2007 and continued throughout 2008 causing a loss of consumer confidence, and resulting in a change of shopping habits, from the purchase of nonessential to essential goods. Associated with this general downturn in the economy, lenders became more critical of existing borrowings and unwilling to extend further borrowings, consistent with Opler and Titman's conclusions (see Chap. 3).

Connaught plc was the only company in the sample that entered an informal rescue process in 2009. The company seems to have been highly reliant on receivables from councils from social housing contracts and other asset management services. The credit crunch and consequent reductions in central government funding increasingly led to delays in payments for completed work and cancellation or curtailment of existing contracts.

Informal Rescue Processes

Use of Informal Rescue Options

Table 12.5 shows the timeframe used to define when companies were subject to financial distress and the informal rescue options adopted. Using this definition, four companies entered the informal rescue process

Table 12.5 Informal rescue process: timeframe, and use of rescue options

Company's name	Timeframe	Board change	Cost reduction	Asset sale	Equity issue	Debt financing
Connaught plc	Sept 8, 2009–Sept 8, 2010	Yes	Yes	No	No	Yes
JJB Sports plc	Apr 27, 2008–Apr 27, 2009	Yes	Yes	Yes	Yes	Yes
Stylo plc	Feb 17, 2008–Feb 17, 2009	Yes	Yes	Yes	No	Yes
Waterford Wedgwood plc	Jan 5, 2008–Jan 5, 2009	Yes	Yes	Yes	Yes	Yes
Woolworths plc	Jan 27, 2008–Jan 27, 2009	Yes	Yes	Yes	No	Yes

in 2008, which ended in 2009 when they entered a formal insolvency regime. Connaught plc started its informal rescue process in 2009, which ended in 2010 when the company was placed into administration.

The companies in the sample adopted different approaches towards informal rescue. The directors in two companies, JJB Sports plc and Waterford Wedgwood plc, used all of the informal rescue options described in earlier chapters of this book. However, the outcomes were significantly different.

In all of the companies changes to the board and cost reduction seem to have met no resistance from other parties. This is to be expected since this aspect of rescue is directly under the control of the board. However the companies differed considerably in terms of the completion of the other three rescue options, that is, asset sale, equity/share issue and new debt financing/debt negotiations.

Board of Directors' Role

In practice, debt resolution strategies are typically part of more general business turnaround activities. Chapter 3 has commented on the difficulties of determining the extent of financial distress that a company may face and the extent to which management views the situation as being unique rather than part of the overall process of managing the going concern. This book focuses on debt resolution, whilst recognising that management may regard this as part of a broader range of activities designed to turn the business round. As Slatter et al. indicate, "a combination of different strategies is required, frequently requiring serious organisational change to refocus company activities" (see Chap. 3). Recent legal analysis has focused on one aspect of debt resolution, namely workout between the directors of a financially distressed company and its lenders. This book looks at a broader range of factors linked to debt resolution processes.

Board Change

Table 12.6 shows changes in executive directors and non-executive directors and the final board size during the informal rescue process. All of the companies implemented board changes in the form of new appoint-

Table 12.6 Board changes during informal rescue process

Company	Original number	Resignation	New appointments	Shift of role	Advisors	Board size
Connaught plc	6 (three executive and three non-executive)	2	1	2	4	5 (one executive director and four non-executive directors)
Stylo plc	9 (five executive directors and four non-executive directors)	2	1	1	2	8 (five executive directors and 3 non-executive directors)
JJB Sports plc	7 (three executive directors and four non-executive directors)	2	3			6 (three executive directors and three non-executive directors)
Waterford Wedgwood plc	14 (five executive directors and nine non-executive directors)	1		1		14 (five executive directors and nine non-executive directors)
Woolworths Group plc	10 (five executive directors and five non-executive directors)	4	3	1		10 (five executive directors and five non-executive directors)

ments, resignations and change of role from executive or non-executive position to executive positions in different ways and with different frequencies. However, the size of the board did not increase in any of the cases, remaining constant in Waterford Wedgwood plc and Woolworths plc and reducing in Connaught plc, JJB Sports plc and Stylo plc.

The number of executive directors did not change during the informal rescue process in four companies, although there was considerable turbulence in office holders' roles, following executive directors' exit from the company and their replacement by new external or internal appointments. Only in one case, Connaught plc, did the number of executive directors reduce.

Different patterns are evident in terms of non-executive directors. In two of the cases, Waterford Wedgwood plc and Woolworths Group plc, the number of non-executive directors remained unchanged whilst in Stylo plc and JJB Sports plc the number of non-executive directors reduced during the informal rescue process. In the case of Stylo plc, one non-executive director left the company just before it entered administration. In JJB Sports plc, the deputy chairman moved to the role of the executive chairman to fill the vacant position of the CEO. Only one company, Connaught plc, showed an increase in the number of non-executive directors during the informal rescue process.

In four out of the five cases the CEO exited the company at some time during the informal rescue process. They were temporarily replaced in each case by the chairman or an executive director from the parent company or subsidiaries. The only company where the CEO did not exit was Stylo plc where the CEO also held the role of chairman. The results may indicate that the CEO comes under pressure when the company is unable to resolve its debt problem during the informal rescue process, and replacement is potentially a sign to lenders and markets that positive changes are planned. The CEO may also be seen as a scapegoat for company problems. Board change also appears to be designed to compensate for any potential lack of perceived expertise that boards of directors have in dealing with debt problems. As Connaught plc and Stylo plc show, the board may also employ specialised advisors to support the existing board.

Cost Reduction

All of the companies in the sample attempted to reduce costs during the informal rescue process. This is an obvious way that a company can reduce its exposure to debt. In Connaught plc, the board of directors focused on the centralisation and rationalisation of support to fulfil service contracts, allowing them to bid at lower prices for new contracts, resulting in more successful bids, particularly for social housing contracts. It also reduced the variety of services offered in the same subsidiary and deferred some of its contracts. Simultaneously however, it expanded its business by purchasing a distressed firm which was counterproductive to any cost-reduction strategy. It might be that the board was not really concerned about financial distress and regarded it as a temporary situation.

JJB Sports plc focused on effective stock management (reducing inventory and fixing new terms with suppliers) at a very late stage in the informal rescue process whilst at the same time expanding by launching a new line of business—a new brand of fitness club-superstore and acquiring a distressed fashion footwear business. The results of this strategy cannot be assessed; however, a reduction in stockholding could potentially have led to an inability to meet customer demand, and the new fitness superstore and acquisition would have increased immediate costs even if the new ventures were potentially successful in the long run.

In Stylo plc, the board sourced new (cheaper) suppliers, disposed of unprofitable assets and reduced stock levels. In Waterford Wedgwood plc, the board used staff redundancies in the UK, closed unprofitable units and outsourced services to take advantage of cheaper labour. In Woolworths Group plc, the board focused on reductions in the range and quantity of stock held in its retail subsidiary Woolworths plc. However, costs were increased through the recruitment of 5,000 temporary staff for a Christmas sale prior to the retail subsidiary being placed into administration.

In all of the companies, cost reduction was limited and implemented as part of the company's activities as a going concern; therefore, no approval was required or obtained from shareholders or lenders. The companies varied in their cost-reduction initiatives. All four retailing companies made attempts to decrease stock whilst only one company, Waterford Wedgwood plc, used staff redundancies. Limited cost-reduction strategies may indicate the boards' views of the degree of financial distress. The application of a simple cash flow test indicates that none of them (with the exception of Stylo plc) was in urgent need of cost reduction to increase cash flow. Therefore the directors in each case may have believed that the company did not need an aggressive cost-reduction plan. Such a perception certainly appears to be the case in two companies, Connaught plc and JJB Sports plc, where the directors followed parallel business expansion strategies.

Asset Sale

Four companies used asset sale as part of the informal rescue process. Connaught plc did not use this rescue option, lacking substantial tangible assets. Its main assets, shown in the balance sheets of subsidiaries, were contracts that were vulnerable to suspension or termination by clients. Stylo plc's main assets included intangible assets in the form of brands, property and inventory. It sold one of its brands and two properties to raise cash. JJB Sports plc's assets included leasehold interests in stores, and freehold interests in fitness clubs. It assigned its leasehold stores retaining 205 leasehold stores out of 409. It also agreed to sell its 49 fitness clubs.

Waterford Wedgwood plc was the ultimate parent company in the Waterford/Wedgwood group, with subsidiaries which owned and managed individual brands. Although it tried to sell its German subsidiary Rosenthal AG, the attempt failed due to the business weakness of the subsidiary.

Woolworths Group plc's subsidiaries managed the brands Woolworth and Ladybird and 800 leasehold stores. It also had a minority stake in a subsidiary, 2entertainment, with BBC Worldwide. The board assigned 13 leasehold stores and attempted to sell its retail subsidiary. However, the business sale of 2entertainment was not successful due to a failure to get the agreement of lenders.

The companies varied in the extent of the use of asset sale. Three companies in the sample sold assets piecemeal, whilst one company JJB Sports plc appears to have used this strategy on a more substantial and co-ordinated basis. Since executive directors had regular meetings with institutional shareholders, and in some instances major shareholders were also board members, it would be reasonable to believe that institutional and other major shareholders might have influenced the boards' final decision, although there is no hard evidence of such influence. The boards of directors might also have regarded substantial asset sale as a signal of their failure to maximise shareholder wealth and therefore have been reluctant to adopt asset sale as a major strategy.

In JJB Sports plc, asset sale was achieved without the need for obtaining shareholder collective approval, since the company directors were able to demonstrate that substantial asset sale was the best option for financing to meet interests of the company and there was no time to obtain shareholder approval; however, existing security interests over Group assets meant that obtaining the consent of lenders was critical. In Woolworths Group plc, the board of directors failed to obtain the lenders' agreement over the sale of its retail subsidiary—Woolworths plc—resulting in the commencement of administration.

Companies differed in terms of the involvement of external professional advisors in the sale process. Two companies in the sample used consultants and advisors, which seems to be in compliance with statutory requirements relating to independent valuation of non-cash assets prior to their sale. JJB Sports plc involved Lazard & Co as sales negotiators and Waterford Wedgwood plc involved JP Morgan Cazenove. In these two companies, the sale focused on part of the business, requiring professional evaluation and marketing to avoid any harm to shareholder interests. Although Waterford Wedgwood plc ultimately did not sell any assets, the role of the external advisor continued when the parent company entered receivership, resulting in its UK major subsidiary Waterford Wedgwood UK plc entering administration. Both external advisors continued to provide services when the companies entered formal rescue procedures.

In some cases the purchasers were not always external parties. David Whelan Sports Ltd.—a company owned by JJB's original founder and previous major shareholder—bought the fitness clubs from JJB Sports plc. Sports Direct Ltd., the company's only significant competitor in the UK, bought a number of its retail stores. The original founder did not have any shareholding in the company at the time of sale. In Stylo plc's case, the company's intellectual property (Shellys brand) was bought by an overseas footwear supplier—Eternal Best Industries Limited of Hong King—whilst in Woolworths Group plc, the leases on retail stores were assigned to Tesco or Waitrose, each being major business rivals.

Equity/Share Issue

The companies varied in terms of their use of equity issue. Two companies, JJB Sports plc and Waterford Wedgwood plc, used equity issue as an informal rescue option. The option may not have been a realistic one in 2008 at a time when financial markets were turbulent, share prices were falling heavily and investors were cautious. JJB Sports plc did make a successful private placement accepting an offer from its rival Sports Direct International plc of £3.4 m in return for 238 k ordinary shares. The success of the JJB Sports plc offer appears to have been due to its balance sheet solvency and its position as the second major sports retailer in the UK. Waterford Wedgwood plc's offer failed to attract external investors. This appears to have been linked to its balance sheet insolvency which posed a substantial potential risk for external investors.

Connaught plc had successfully completed a private placement in August 2009 prior to the start of the informal rescue process and the board might have been unwilling or unable to repeat the option, and further dilute the value of shareholdings. Stylo plc did not operate on the LSE and its shares were mainly owned by family members of the board, who were perhaps unwilling to share ownership with new investors. In the case of Woolworths Group plc, the directors seem to have been reluctant to give up their positions when they faced a takeover offer from Baugur, an Icelandic private investment group. They dismissed a takeover offer reasoning that the offer undermined the pension scheme that was already in place for retired and existing staff. Their approach was also supported by a major individual shareholder who also gave his public support to the board's decisions.

New Debt Financing/Debt Renegotiation

All of the companies used debt financing and renegotiation as a way of injecting new cash into the company. In Connaught plc's case, debt financing followed a profit warning and institutional shareholder exit. Debt renegotiation was lengthy, taking place over the last three months of the informal rescue process, prior to entering administration, perhaps as a last-resort strategy. The result was a short-term standstill agreement and short-term overdraft facility. A standstill agreement would have allowed company directors to suspend or defer performance of the company's contractual obligations relating to payment of interest and the periodic repayment of debt for a period of time agreed with lenders. The failure to obtain a substantial long-term debt facility resulted in the commencement of administration.

In JJB Sports plc, the company used debt financing as the last option, five months after the start of the informal rescue process. The process was lengthy, involving a syndicate of lenders. The company used KPMG LLP and Lazard Co as external advisors for asset valuation and marketing as part of the debt financing process. This seems to have followed lenders' demand for the company to clarify the level of risk involved. It ultimately obtained £20 m from further lending followed by a standstill agreement allowing the deferment of repayment on a principal loan that was extended on two further occasions. The company also committed itself to reach a CVA as a requirement of the standstill agreement and the extension of further credit facilities.

In Stylo plc, the board of directors obtained lenders' approval to extend the time of its secured debt and increase the amount under terms and conditions that were confidential and not disclosed. There is no information as to the exact time of the initial debt financing but the company renewed the maturity date of its debenture stock three months before it entered administration.

In Waterford Wedgwood plc, the board sought debt financing before asset sale and equity issue, so it was not a case of using debt refinancing as a last resort. The attempt to refinance the company was a lengthy process over a nine-month period that was ultimately unsuccessful. Directors initially tried to obtain a €200 m multi-currency credit facility but only managed to obtain €15 m. They also obtained a short-term agreement for a two-week standstill which was extended by another 20 days, immediately prior to being placed into receivership by lenders following a failure to raise funds through equity/share issue.

In Woolworths Group plc, the company used debt financing as its primary source of cash generation. It obtained a loan exceeding £350 m over four years in return for granting fixed and floating charges over the assets of subsidiaries. The company also granted a deed of charge over its credit balances in favour of Barclays Bank plc. The details are not available.

All of the companies used debt financing and renegotiation of their existing debt. Three companies Connaught plc, JJB Sports plc and Waterford Wedgwood plc obtained standstill agreements prior to entry into a formal rescue process reflecting their failure to obtain further long-term loans. JJB Sports plc and Woolworths plc were able to obtain substantial loans, whereas Waterford Wedgwood Group plc and Connaught plc were able to obtain only short-term credit facilities. JJB Sports plc and Woolworths Group plc were both in the position where assets were substantially unsecured, making it relatively easier for directors to raise new finance through further borrowing and granting security. The amount of loans secured by Woolworths Group plc was substantial, reflecting its overall balance sheet position whereas the total facilities obtained by JJB Sports plc seem to have been far less.

In Connaught plc, Stylo plc and JJB Sports plc, debt financing involved more than one lender, each obtaining security interests over the assets. In Waterford Wedgwood plc and Woolworths Group plc, a security trustee acted on behalf of a group of lenders in each case. The involvement of more than one lender may reflect the risk involved in financing the financially distressed companies. It may also reflect the difficulty that directors may have faced in persuading individual lenders to take all of the potential risks in providing further credit or loan facilities.

Shareholder Influence

Shareholder influence can be seen in their approval of board decisions relating to the grant of equity securities. In Connaught plc, shareholders authorised directors to allot equity securities and dis-apply their pre-emption rights. This suggests that existing shareholders were not interested in exercising their rights to invest in the company's ordinary shares. In JJB Sports plc, shareholders supported the directors' informal rescue plan, approving all director appointments and re-appointments and authorising directors to allot equity securities. In Stylo plc, shareholders approved all director appointments and re-appointments, authorised directors' allotment of equity securities and limited market purchase of the company's shares. They also approved prospective business transactions between company directors and the company. In Waterford Wedgwood UK plc, shareholders approved an increase in share capital from £215 m to £5 bn, and authorised changes in share income units through subdivision, consolidation and re-designation. They also approved dis-application of their pre-emptive rights on share issues. In Woolworths Group plc, shareholders also authorised company directors to allot equity securities and/or buy back their own shares at a market price of up to £18 m. A new major shareholder also gave public support to the board's rejection of a takeover proposal.

In all of the companies in the sample, shareholders authorised directors to allot equity securities. Shareholder approval indicates their collective support for the grant of security interests on corporate assets and further investment in the company and their delegation of powers to company directors. The potential individual influence of institutional shareholders and major shareholders remains unknown; however, it is likely that an agreement would have been reached between institutional shareholders and senior management before any resolution was proposed or approved because of the former's large shareholdings and ability to influence decisions.

Stylo plc was the only company where directors proposed a resolution to shareholders relating to conflict of interests. The use of shareholder meetings for approving decisions where there are potential conflicts of interest between directors and the company may be designed to protect company directors. In Stylo's case the company was listed on the AIM, and major shareholders may already have been aware of the intention to resolve the company's debt problem through a pre-packaged sale in advance of the formal rescue proposal.

Creditor Influence

In none of the companies was detailed information available about the role of secured and unsecured creditor influence on directors' decisions during informal rescue. But we can gauge some idea of their involvement in the whole rescue process from some of the actions that were taken.

In Connaught plc, secured creditors refused to provide further financial facilities requested by its directors, resulting in the appointment of joint administrators by company directors. In JJB Sports plc, lenders agreed to extend a standstill agreement subject to the successful sale of fitness clubs, formulation and approval of a CVA, and improvement of its trading performance. In Stylo plc, a representative of Barclays Bank, the company's major lender, joined the board of directors as a non-executive director with a specific task of implementing a recovery plan. In Waterford Wedgwood plc, two representatives of Lazard Investment LLC, the company's major preference shareholder, were represented on the board at the start of the informal rescue process. They were also involved in the equity issue process and they were beneficiaries of the equity issue. Lenders invoked their security interests resulting in the Irish parent company and its non-UK companies entering receivership, and its UK subsidiary Waterford Wedgwood UK plc being placed into administration. In Woolworths Group plc, the lenders who had provided a syndicated loan disagreed with the sale of the retail subsidiary Woolworths plc, resulting in the appointment of joint administrators.

In all of the cases lenders appear to have played an active role in at least one of the informal rescue options. There were differences in the way that secured creditors influenced the informal rescue process. Connaught plc, Waterford Wedgwood plc and Woolworths Group plc are comparable since lenders declined the request for further financing facilities and this resulted in the appointment of joint administrators. In Stylo plc secured creditors were represented on the board of directors and therefore were likely to have influenced the board's decision. The JJB Sports plc case shows the greatest influence of lenders on the use of equity issue and planning a CVA through debt financing.

The lack of any fiduciary duty between directors and creditors requires that secured creditors safeguard their own interests by monitoring the performance of the company and its board against its contractual obligations. Grant of security interests will often allow secured creditors to influence any informal rescue option either explicitly or indirectly. Grant of security interests over the assets of the company and its subsidiaries will also usually require lenders' consent before any asset sale or new secured debt financing arrangements can be made. Existing security interest reduces the directors' discretion over the use of assets, and directors are legally prevented from making any decisions that affect the security interests of lenders. Lenders are not interested in asset sale if this results in exposure to further risks. Lenders monitor the company's compliance with contractual obligations and protect their own interests. Whilst the data available to this researcher provided considerable insights into the role of such lenders, the confidential nature of negotiations and security contracts makes it difficult to get a clear picture of their influence during the informal rescue process.

Formal Rescue Processes

Four companies in the sample entered administration. One company—JJB Sports plc—entered two separate CVAs in 2009 and 2011 with strong support from its lenders and unsecured creditors.

Administrator's Role

Management of Business as a Going Concern

Four companies that entered administration attempted to maintain the business as a going concern. In Connaught plc, the parent company was the main party to service contracts, delivered by two solvent subsidiaries to clients. The joint administrators had to maintain the parent company's business as a going concern on a temporary basis to avoid disruption of trading activities, until all services were transferred to the relevant subsidiaries. In Stylo plc, the parent company did not have any trading activities; the pre-packaged administration that was put in place did not result in any change of control and the going concern nature of the trading subsidiaries remained almost unchanged. In Waterford Wedgwood UK plc, the joint administrators focused on the going concern of the companies within the UK subsidiary and tried to maintain business operations because the sale of the business and the assets of the subsidiaries in the Group was the lenders' priority. The joint administrators successfully managed the going concern of the business, making arrangements with suppliers who had retention of title over large volumes of stock in the subsidiaries. Similar agreements were made with landlords and haulier companies. The management of the business as a going concern continued for at least five months until the business sale was completed. In Woolworths Group plc, the parent company did not have any trading activities but its retail subsidiary Woolworths plc had a large volume of stock. The joint administrators focused on reaching an agreement with the landlords of retail stores and the suppliers who retained title over the stock. They also retained most of the staff to expedite sales.

These companies share the common feature that their continuation as a going concern was dependent on maintaining a commercial link between the business activities of the parent company and the trading activities of the subsidiaries. In those parent companies where subsidiaries were trading, the joint administrators had to maintain the going concern until asset sale or business sale was agreed and finalised. The joint administrators' focus on maximisation of the proceeds of asset sale required them to maintain the companies as a going concern. It might be argued that the joint administrators' management of the going concern in Waterford Wedgwood UK plc and Woolworths plc may have required an agreement with unsecured creditors that allowed the latter to recover some of the losses suffered prior to administration. However, lack of any detailed information makes it difficult to substantiate the argument.

Companies in the sample that were subject to administration can be contrasted with JJB Sports plc in the sense that the joint administrators in the former companies had to manage the company as a going concern on a temporary basis until the business sale was achieved or assets were sold. In contrast, in the case of JJB Sports plc which was subject to two CVAs, the company directors continued their management of the going concern whilst they were also involved in the formulation and implementation of the CVA with the assistance of the insolvency practitioners.

Asset Sale and Recovery

In all of the companies, the primary focus of the joint administrators was on achieving substantial asset sale in a co-ordinated way at market value rather than piecemeal sale whilst they carried on the companies' businesses. However, three companies, Connaught plc, Stylo plc and Woolworths Group plc, were the ultimate parent companies without trading activities. Their main assets were held by subsidiary companies, leading administrators to focus on the sale of the subsidiaries.

In all of the companies, business sale or substantial asset sale was finalised in the first six months of administration whilst piecemeal sale of assets continued throughout administration. In Connaught plc, the business sale involved the sale of contracts owned by Connaught Partnerships, the sale of non-profitable parts of Connaught Compliance and the ultimate sale of Connaught Environmental. The buyers of assets were all external with the exception of Connaught Environmental, which was bought by its lenders.

In Stylo plc, the sale of the business to its former directors was agreed two days after administration and the buyers took immediate control. In Waterford Wedgwood UK plc, the business sale was finalised as part of the sale of the companies owned by Waterford Wedgwood plc, three days after commencement of administration. In Woolworths Group plc, assets were not substantial because the parent company did not have any trading activities. In its retail subsidiary Woolworths plc, the assets consisted mainly of stock that was sold within the first six weeks of entering administration, whilst the company maintained its going concern nature.

The ability of the joint administrators to sell assets quickly may be partly linked to the nature of such assets. In Connaught plc, the assets were mainly contracts whilst in the other companies assets consisted of stock that could lose value over time. Where assets were mainly stock this placed the joint administrators under pressure to achieve a quick sale to fulfil their duties to creditors.

Joint administrator asset sale can be differentiated from directors' sale of assets during financial distress, in the sense that the priority of directors, at least from the evidence of these cases, appears to have been on piecemeal asset sale. This seems to be aligned with attempts to keep the remaining part of the company going as a viable commercial enterprise consistent with maintaining shareholder value. This contrasts with administration where the joint administrators' focus in the cases was on business sale or substantial asset sale with the objective of paying creditors through disposal of assets at market value to directors, lenders or third parties, leading to a fundamental change in the commercial nature and value of the company.

In all five companies, business sales required the involvement of a range of legal and professional advisors as well as marketing and valuation agents. The former company directors also played a part, providing an informed perspective of the prospective business to potential buyers. The sale of assets subject to charges cannot legally take place without the consent of secured creditors where security interests are spread over the assets of parent companies and subsidiaries unless the courts are involved. Since none of the cases involved asset sale through judicial intervention obtaining leave to sell, it appears that any consents were obtained as part of the sales process.

The joint administrators' use of professional advisors during asset sale parallels that of director deployment of lawyers, financial advisors and restructuring experts during the informal rescue process. In both cases financial distress and insolvency require professional advisors who can ensure that no harm is done to the company's interests. Joint administrators rely on such advisors to compensate for their lack of specialist expertise in those areas of formal rescue that are beyond their knowledge as insolvency practitioners. Using such expertise also protects them from any potential personal liability from creditors.

Distribution to Secured Creditors

In Connaught plc, secured creditors enforced their security interests and took over the business operated by one subsidiary valued at £55 m. They also recovered 30% of the total £221 m that they were owed by the Group in cash. In JJB Sports plc, secured creditors' interests were outside the scope of the CVA, which allowed company directors to treat their claims outside the ordinary course of business. In Stylo plc, secured creditors were paid £36 m out of £43 m debt and part of their operating assets was transferred to the new company. In Waterford Wedgwood UK plc, lenders were owed €181 m whilst preference shareholders were owed €166 m and their interests were ranked after those of lenders. Preference shareholders are not paid if the company is insolvent in overall terms. The total distribution made to lenders during administration totalled £35.3 m with the possibility of recovering another €25 m. It was suggested that lenders would also recover an unspecified amount of money from other subsidiaries but there is no information as to the actual total amount recovered. In Woolworths Group plc, secured creditors recouped £324.9 m that they were originally owed by the Group, including interest accrued and fees.

Distribution to Unsecured Creditors

Table 12.7 shows the total claims owed to unsecured creditors at parent company level, unsecured creditors' share of proceeds of asset sale under priority ranking, their entitlement to dividends under the prescribed part and the final repayment of their claims during administration, for each of the companies.

Table 12.7 shows that none of the unsecured creditor groups were entitled to any share of assets (excluding the prescribed part). The recovery rate of claims for unsecured creditors is primarily determined by the statutory priority ranking that places such creditors after preferential creditors and holders of security interests. Since unsecured creditors are ranked last after preferential creditors and floating charge holders, the

Table 12.7 Payment to unsecured creditors

Company	Total claims	Right to dividends from asset realisations	Right to dividends under prescribed part	Any dividends paid during administration
Connaught plc	£34.9 m	No	Denied because of costs	No
Stylo plc	£32 k	No	No	No
Waterford Wedgwood UK plc	£1.4 m	No	Yes	No
Woolworths Group plc	£16 m	No	Yes	No
Woolworths plc	£699.2 m	No	Denied because of costs	No

joint administrators do not have any obligation or power to focus on unsecured creditor interests ahead of other creditors.

The zero recovery rate of unsecured creditors' claims is not affected by the total amount of claims, nor individual creditor claims. The zero recovery rate is determined by the total value arising from the realisation of assets of the parent company, not the total assets of individual companies in the group. This is based on individual contractual relationships between parent companies and their subsidiaries and unsecured creditors. This approach has been adopted by the joint administrators in identifying the prescribed part for unsecured creditors. The approach appears to consider each member company within a group as an independent legal entity, ignoring the fact that the parent company has a group of subsidiary companies with consolidated assets. The separate entity nature of subsidiary companies prevents unsecured creditors from extending their claims from the parent company to subsidiaries. They must rely on their contractual relationship with the parent company with which they have contracted prior to administration. This principle also applies to unsecured creditors of the subsidiaries preventing them from bringing their claims against other subsidiaries or the parent company.

In contrast, secured creditors can extend their claims to the assets of the subsidiaries where the parent company has interests and has granted security interests to lenders. Since insolvency law treats unsecured creditor claims collectively, they all receive the same treatment. No specific mechanism has been developed to allow unsecured creditors to improve their collective bargaining powers.

Collective treatment of unsecured creditor claims does not prevent unsecured creditors from reaching individual agreements with the joint administrators. Such agreements are possible only if the insolvent company or its subsidiary remains a going concern during administration and some or all of the existing unsecured creditors continue to provide support. Lack of any statutory provision that requires unsecured creditors to continue to fulfil their contracts allows them to make independent decisions post-administration about whether and how they continue to trade with the insolvent company. After administration commences, they would be paid as administration expenses and get a form of priority.

On the other hand, the joint administrators have to reach an agreement over the interim supply of products and services, where, in order to maximise the realisation of assets including stock and contracts, the company needs to be maintained as a going concern. In two out of the five companies, Stylo plc and Woolworths Group plc, the parent companies did not have any trading activities following the commencement of administration and maintaining the going concern was not an issue. Stylo plc did not have any unsecured creditors at the start of the administration process.

Connaught plc, Waterford Wedgwood UK plc and Woolworths plc each remained as going concerns. In Connaught plc, the parent company remained a going concern to provide after-sales services without which individual subsidiaries could not maintain their business. Woolworths plc remained a going concern to sell assets (mainly stock). Waterford Wedgwood UK plc also remained a going concern since the joint administrators had planned to sell it as part of the Group sale. Since the joint administrators maintained control over the parent company and its subsidiaries, they were able to make decisions about agreements with suppliers and landlords.

There is no information about the individual agreements made between joint administrators and unsecured creditors in each parent company, which makes it difficult to comment on the bargaining powers of individual unsecured creditors. However, it is reasonable to expect that these agreements would include their individual pre-administration claims allowing them to continue their contractual relationship with or without modification of their rights.

As Table 12.7 shows, unsecured creditors received different treatment of their entitlement to dividends under the statutory prescribed part. Joint administrators in all companies excluding Stylo plc considered dividends under the prescribed part for unsecured creditors. In Stylo plc, the lender's influence can be seen in floating charges that date back to pre-September 2003. The company's Statement of affairs did not identify any unsecured creditors of the parent company. Whilst unsecured creditors in all four companies were entitled to dividends under the prescribed part, only in two companies, that is, Waterford Wedgwood UK plc and Woolworths Group plc, were such creditors entitled to dividends, as the prescribed part was dis-applied in the other companies because of the costs involved in paying the dividends.[1]

In Connaught plc and Woolworths plc the costs of distribution operated as a deterring factor, resulting in no dividends for collective groups of creditors. However, those companies that offered dividends under the prescribed part did not make any payment during administration and their claims were rolled over into liquidation. Therefore, it appears that administration does not necessarily provide any automatic right for unsecured creditors to claim their dividends. In large public companies, the number and dispersion of unsecured creditors may prevent the payment of any prescribed part due to the costs of distribution. There is no mandate for joint administrators to pay dividends during administration as the priority ranking requires primary focus on lenders' claims.

The recovery rate for unsecured creditors in companies that were subject to administration can be distinguished from the recovery rate for unsecured creditors in CVA cases. JJB Sports plc entered two different CVAs. In contrast to the situation that would have occurred in administration, payments to unsecured creditors were not affected by payments to secured creditors and employees. The main factor was the continued going concern of the company and creditors' agreements with the terms of the CVA proposal, determining the way in which their claims were to be paid. The successful completion of a CVA in 2010 allowed unsecured creditors to be paid at a rate previously proposed by company directors.

The second CVA did not result in the payment of dividends to unsecured creditors and the company entered administration.

Investigation into Directors' Conduct

There was no public disclosure of information in administrators' reports concerning directors' conduct. However, it is possible to interpret the outcome of such reports based on the time of their submission and directors' involvement in administration. In Stylo plc, the administrator reports were finalised and submitted within the first six months of administration. However, the joint administrators' consent to the business sale to the company's directors may demonstrate that their conduct was legal and approved. In Waterford Wedgwood UK plc, no information was disclosed on directors' conduct. In summary, it could be argued that company directors in each of the five case studies may not have been subject to any personal liability because they acted in an informed manner advised by both internal and external legal and financial professionals.

Creditor Influence

Secured Creditor Influence

The case studies in the sample demonstrate different patterns of influence by secured creditors during administration. Their influence can be seen in the appointment of administrators, the financing of administration, asset sale, agreement and payment of fees and expenses and the extension of the period of administration.

Appointment of administrators: Lender influence can be identified in the appointment of joint administrators. In Connaught plc, Stylo plc, Woolworths Group plc and Woolworths plc the joint administrators were appointed by company directors. In Connaught plc, three administrators from KPMG were appointed by directors, but the lender's influence can be traced back to their nomination as advisors prior to administration. In Stylo plc, three administrators were appointed from

Deloitte LLP by directors. The directors subsequently bought the business back through a pre-packaged administration, making it difficult to trace the lender's influence on joint administrators' appointments. In Woolworths Group plc, the joint administrators from Deloitte LLP were initially nominated by lenders to provide advice and support to the company directors before administration. They were subsequently appointed as joint administrators through an application made by company directors to the High Court as the company was served with winding-up orders.

In Waterford UK plc, the Irish parent company and non-UK subsidiaries were placed into receivership and only the UK subsidiary entered administration. The lenders appointed four administrators from Deloitte LLP, the same firm acting as receivers for the Irish parent company and its non-UK subsidiaries. Whilst lenders may not play a direct formal role in appointing joint administrators, they may exercise an influence through involving a potential administrator in an advisory capacity prior to administration. Even if the appointment is made by the company, a substantial charge holder has a potential veto on the appointment.

Prior to formal insolvency, administrators' prospective involvement helps them to obtain insider knowledge and influence rescue strategies that may require substantial time to implement. Lender influence on the involvement and the formal appointment of administrators also prevents any legal challenge by secured creditors against company directors, who are ultimately responsible for appointing the joint administrators. Lenders may also be able to influence the number of joint administrators that are appointed, and therefore the costs of administration, since there are no explicit criteria to determine how many should be appointed. Since these costs are deducted from the proceeds of asset sale subject to floating charge, this is potentially of direct benefit to such lenders.

Financing administration: The role of secured creditors can be seen in financing administration costs. Only one company, Connaught plc, received funding from lenders in the form of a non-recoverable fund to support the costs of administration. In the other four companies, sufficient funds were available in the parent company or its subsidiaries to fund the costs of administration.

This area has not been addressed in statutory law. If the holding company and each subsidiary are treated as separate financial entities during administration, using funds from elsewhere in the group to fund administration of the parent company is effectively an intercompany loan which requires the consent of the joint administrators and the implicit consent of secured lenders with security interests spread over the parent company and all its other subsidiaries.

Financing the administration of the parent company may not be an issue where it is possible to use funds from subsidiary companies in the group as a source of funding. However, where no funds are available, administration costs may be funded by lenders with a financial stake in the speedy release of funds through asset sale. Any such further funding increases the lender's potential influence on the direction and outcome of the administration process.

Management of going concern and asset sale: In Connaught plc, the lender's influence can be seen in their initial plan to acquire the business of two solvent subsidiaries as a partial discharge of their claims. This was later modified to one subsidiary. The influence and involvement of lenders is most evident in Stylo plc which was subject to a pre-packaged sale. In this case the lenders agreed the transfer of operating assets to the new company established by members of the previous board of directors. The terms and conditions of this agreement remain confidential. In Waterford UK plc, the lenders assisted the buyer of the business with financing under a confidential agreement.

Since secured creditors had fixed and floating charges in all of the companies that were subject to administration, they had the right to choose between acquiring the secured assets, or overseeing or facilitating their sale to interested third parties through an administrator. In three companies—Waterford UK plc, Woolworths Group plc and Woolworths plc—lenders appear to have decided that administrators should seek asset sale to other parties whilst in Connaught plc and Stylo plc, they exercised their rights more aggressively.

Setting administrator fees and expenses: Lender influence on administrator fees can be exercised when unsecured creditors do not exercise their statutory rights to have a creditors' meeting. Three out of five companies—Connaught plc, Stylo plc and Woolworths Group plc—did not hold any creditors' meetings which therefore effectively required lenders' approval of the joint administrators' fee proposals.[2] In Connaught plc, the lenders initially approved the administrators' proposals for time-based fees but as administrators released details of their fees and expenses, the lenders negotiated with them, resulting in fixing the total administration fees for the whole period of administration excluding their investigation into directors' conduct, and in the process obtaining a substantial discount for the company. In Stylo plc lenders approved administrators' hourly-based fees. In Woolworths Group plc, lenders did not have exclusive rights to approve joint administrator fees. Preferential creditors whose debt exceeded 50% of the total preferential debt also had an entitlement to approve fees. There is no information as to whether this shared right was actually exercised during administration in any of the cases.

In Waterford Wedgwood UK plc and Woolworths plc, the responsibility of fixing administrator fees was left to creditors' meetings. In Waterford Wedgwood UK plc, administrators used the creditors' meeting to obtain the approval of the unsecured creditors to draw their fees and expenses on a monthly basis. Updates on payment were given to creditors in their six-monthly progress report. In Woolworths plc, the joint administrator fees were fixed by a creditors' committee.

Extension of period of administration: In four companies the lenders' consent was not sought to extend the period of administration. In Stylo plc, the period of administration was extended by the joint administrators following their application to the court. In Woolworths Group plc, administration ended after one year—the period of administration was not extended. In Woolworths plc, the period of administration was extended by the court following an application from the joint administrators. Connaught plc was different in that its joint administrators sought the lenders' consent to extend the period of administration. This appears to be because the lenders were financing the administration costs directly although the administrators could go to the court if the lenders resisted an extension. The power of appointment that lenders have in many insolvency cases and the harm that a lengthy court battle may do to their interests seem to prevent administrators from challenging lenders' decisions. Lenders appear to have little or no involvement in influencing the extension of the period of administration unless they are financing the process.

Unsecured Creditor influence

Table 12.8 shows unsecured creditor activities during administration including holding creditors' meetings and voting, modification of administrator proposals, formation of creditor committees and exercise of the right to approve administrator remuneration.

In Connaught plc, Stylo plc and Woolworths Group plc no creditor meetings were proposed for unsecured creditors since assets were insufficient to pay the claims owed to other categories of creditors. This is in line with para 52(1)(b) of Schedule B1 that does not require the joint administrators to hold a creditors' meeting where there is no dividend for unsecured creditors other than under the prescribed part. Additionally, no formal demand was made by major unsecured creditors to hold such a meeting.

The creditors' rights to have a meeting and exercise their voting right were treated differently in Waterford Wedgwood UK plc and Woolworths plc. In Waterford Wedgwood UK plc, the joint administrators initially avoided making any statements relating to recovery rates for unsecured creditors from the net realisation of asset sales and proposed a creditors' meeting that consisted of unsecured creditors of the parent company and its subsidiaries. Creditors of each company voted separately. They approved the administrators' proposals without any modification. They also approved their fee basis and monthly payments of fees and expenses.

In Woolworths plc, the joint administrators decided to hold a creditors' meeting to seek advice during administration. It is not clear whether they were asked by unsecured creditors to hold such a meeting. The administrators proposed the creditors' meeting to fulfil their statutory duties in relation to achieving creditor approval on their proposals. There is no further information on why this approach was adopted. It could be that the unsecured creditor stake was substantially higher than that of lenders and the administrators wanted to avoid further challenges.

Table 12.8 Unsecured creditor influence during administration

Unsecured creditor Influence	Connaught plc	Stylo plc	Waterford Wedgwood	Woolworths Group plc	Woolworths plc
Creditors meeting held	No	No	Yes	No	Yes
Right to vote on administrators' proposals	No	No	Yes	No	Yes
Right to modify administrators' proposals	No	No	Yes but not exercised	No	Yes but not exercised
Formation of creditors committee for individual subsidiaries	No	No	Yes (one committee and five meetings held)	No	Yes (one committee and five meetings held)
Right to approve administrators fees and payments	No	No	Yes	No	Yes

In the three companies where no creditor meetings were held, further influence over administrator decisions was frustrated. Lack of any challenge by unsecured creditors of administrator decisions reflected the passive approach of unsecured creditors. No formal request for holding creditor meetings was formally made. Even in the companies where creditor meetings were held, joint administrator proposals were approved without modification.

In these cases at least, creditors' meetings do not appear to provide any dynamic context for active involvement and influence by unsecured creditors on administrators' proposals. This may be a function of the incomplete knowledge that unsecured creditors have of the company's financial structure and any contractual relationships between the insolvent company and lenders which remains confidential during administration. Their inactivity could also be driven by the further costs and losses that their active involvement might create. Lack of a disclosure framework that requires the joint administrators to disclose relevant information to unsecured creditors prevents unsecured creditors from informed decision-making. Unsecured creditors also lack any collective structure that helps them challenge the administrators' proposals during the creditors' meeting. Their position is in stark contrast to the position of shareholders in solvent companies.

Where creditors' meetings were held in Waterford Wedgwood UK plc and Woolworths plc, the creditors showed a degree of influence on administration by approving the formation of a creditors' committee. However, the two companies differ in the way the administrators obtained their support for the formation of a creditors' committee. In Waterford Wedgwood UK plc, one creditors' committee was formed from the creditors of its subsidiary Josiah Wedgwood. This committee had no role in overseeing creditor interests at the parent company and other subsidiaries. The creditors' committee was small including HMRC and Unite—representing employees' non-preferential interests.

In Woolworths plc, creditor voting and the formation of a creditors' committee complied with statutory requirements. Its creditors' committee consisted of six members including HMRC and USDAW—representing workforce interests. Lack of any detailed information about the interaction between the creditors' committee and the joint administrators in both Waterford Wedgwood UK plc and Woolworths plc makes it difficult to analyse their influence over administrators' decisions. It seems that they avoided a confrontational approach in relation to the joint administrators, approving their initial fees and their subsequent payment.

In JJB Sports plc, the unsecured creditors approved directors' proposed CVA plans, resulting in the adoption and implementation of CVA plans in 2009 and 2011. Unsecured creditors consisted of landlords, suppliers and trade creditors, and HMRC, and only those whose claims were accepted by the chairman of the meeting had the right to vote. A vote at a creditor meeting was required to approve the CVA proposal. The first creditor meeting asked all unsecured creditors to vote on a CVA proposal which focused on the modification and payment of landlords' claims over a fixed time schedule. The same approach was adopted in 2010 when the company proposed a similar CVA proposal, again focusing on landlords' claims and resulting in the implementation of a second CVA.

Unsecured creditors did not play any role during the implementation of the CVA proposal. Neither did they have any influence in fixing the fees and costs relating to implementation of the CVA. No modification of the CVA proposal was proposed by unsecured creditors. All unsecured creditors other than landlords were entitled to continue or terminate their contractual relationships with the company, outside the terms of the CVA proposal.

Conclusions

The variety and volume of information that is available on the informal rescue options in five case studies demonstrates that boards may become involved in a range of activities including board change, cost reduction, asset sale, equity issue/share issue and new debt financing/debt renegotiation without formally describing such actions as resolving financial distress. Each of these subtly changes the nature of direction and control of the company.

Shareholders typically indicate their support through voting on management resolutions at the AGM and any EGM. Institutional shareholder influence on formulating such decisions is not clear from the case studies. As the companies examined in this research have moved closer to formal insolvency, the interests of shareholders as the dominant influence on the behaviour of directors are eroded. Asset sale, equity issue and new debt financing can all significantly reduce the degree of control and value that shareholders have in the business.

Lender influence on management decision-making may take place through syndicated lending, where one lender co-ordinates the views of other lenders and brings pressure to bear on the management team. Where lenders disagree with the directors' plans as was the case with Waterford Wedgwood plc, Woolworths Group plc and Connaught plc, administration can quickly follow.

Once in administration, the direction and control of the resources of the business pass to the administrator who is legally responsible for realising the assets of the business to pay creditor claims. Administrator actions are not typically focused on the continuation of the business as a going concern, with the exception of the example of the pre-packaged sale of Stylo plc to existing company directors.

The motivation of individual directors can only be inferred from their actions, and there is more information about some of the companies than others. In the case of Waterford Wedgewood, the high levels of shareholding of individual board members, connected by family ties, appear to have influenced the approach. Close connections between individual members of the company and the Irish financial establishment may have allowed the board to access funding to preserve the company as a significant going concern for a considerable period of informal financial distress, until one lender (Bank of America) finally refused further extension of borrowing. In the case of case of Stylo plc, members of the family had prominent roles on the board, with significant levels of shareholding and were able to influence the policies and direction of the company. Close working relationships with the professional advisors brought in when the company's financial problems worsened and CVA proposals failed allowed the directors to propose and implement a pre-packaged sale of the company to its previous directors.

The research described in this chapter and Chaps. 7 to 11 has generated insight into the evolving nature of governance in practice as companies enter financial distress and apply informal and formal rescue mechanisms. The empirical research has complemented the analysis presented in the earlier chapters. The next and final chapter revisits the original aim of this book and reviews the extent to which its objectives have been realised.

Notes

1. IA 1986, s 176(A).
2. In Woolworths Group plc, preferential creditors' approval was also sought.

Bibliography

Finch, Vanessa. 2002. *Corporate Insolvency Law: Perspectives and Principles*. Cambridge: Cambridge University Press.

Opler, Tim C. and Sheridan Titman. 1994. "Financial Distress and Corporate Performance." *Journal of Finance* 49(3): 1015–1040.

United Kingdom: Cork Review Committee. 1982. *Insolvency Law and Practice: Report of the Review Committee*. Cmnd 8558. London: HMSO

Legislation

Insolvency Act 1986.
Insolvency Rules 1986.

13

Conclusions

Overview

Chapter 1 of this book introduced the central question that became the focus of the research, namely "how does financial distress in general and insolvency in particular impact on the corporate governance of public companies?" The book has addressed the question raised in Chap. 1 in a variety of different and complementary ways. It has applied theoretical and doctrinal approaches to examine the existing literature and legal interpretation. It has also used a narrative and interpretive case study approach to examine what the boards of directors in public companies do in practice to resolve financial distress, and the joint administrators' treatment of corporate assets and payment of creditors' claims. This final chapter reviews the extent to which the original aims of this research have been met.

Comments on the Extent to Which the Aims Have Been Realised

Treatment of Financial Distress in UK Law and Corporate Governance Codes

The book began by defining corporate governance as "the systems and processes by which companies are directed and influenced". It was proposed that financial distress and insolvency may result in the formation of different governance patterns from those of solvent non-distressed companies. Chapter 2 provided an overview of the underlying principles of corporate governance and examined the economic and legal frameworks that influence and formulate the relationship between control holders, investors and the company in solvent non-distressed companies. The economic framework of corporate governance is founded on the concept of the theoretical divorce of ownership and control, a concept derived from the study of large American public companies with large numbers of dispersed shareholders. However, the reality of many UK public companies is that ownership may actually be concentrated, with institutional shareholders or significant private investors with majority shareholdings (particularly companies with a history of family ownership). In such circumstances both types of shareholders may have significant influence and control over the operations of the company.

The economics literature assumes an agency-principal relationship between shareholders and senior executives that gives directors the right to make independent decisions on the direction of the company, subject to them continuing to focus on wealth generation for shareholders. In such a context, the firm (company) can be considered as an interlinked set of contracts, and its existence continues until such contracts are terminated.

The legal perspective provides a different view of the company, defining it as a separate legal entity with limited liability. The implied consequence is that shareholders cannot be held liable for corporate debt greater than their shareholding commitment. Additionally, company directors are not deemed to be personally liable if they have acted lawfully. The separate legal concept allows company directors to exclude their personal financial interests from exposure to corporate liabilities. Liability may not be a problem for company directors when the company is solvent, non-distressed and profitable. However, it may become a matter of concern when a public company is financially distressed and its ability to repay debt is challenged.

Directors have a general duty to promote the success of the company for the benefit of its members—an exclusive corporate objective emphasised in academic legal discussion. Individual shareholders have a limited role within shareholder meetings, voting on decisions proposed by the board, without an individual right to formulate or influence such strategies unless they have substantial individual shareholding. Derivative actions are rarely used to address alleged breaches of duty in large public companies. Major institutional shareholders may choose to take an active role in influencing management decisions and ultimately the proposals that are put to a vote at formal shareholder meetings. Additionally, the presence of non-executive directors may safeguard shareholder interests.

From the review of the literature in Chap. 2 the Code appears to remain silent on financial distress. The nature and quality of relationships between directors and shareholders is assumed to remain the same regardless of changes in the company's solvency. It appears to be a code that has been largely written for solvent companies, where responsibilities to shareholders remain the primary concern of directors. The Code does not provide any specific guidelines on modification to the relationship between shareholders and directors, nor on the changing balance of influence over director decisions from shareholders to creditors in situations of financial distress where there may be potential conflicts of interest. The existing UK governance model also remains silent on how shareholders should respond to financial distress when they are asked to exercise their voting rights, and particularly the responsibilities and influence of major institutional shareholders.

There is no specific guidance in either company law or the current governance code for company directors on how they should pursue the best interests of the company when the company is in financial distress and needs to generate cash. In such circumstances directors are faced with alternative choices that can change the relative position of shareholders and lenders in terms of control of the company, and potentially damage the interests of unsecured creditors.

Chapter 3 provided an overview of the concept of financial distress and insolvency and the rescue mechanisms that are available, both within and outside the framework of insolvency regimes. Distress was defined in terms of a range of financial tests including the ratio of assets to liabilities, the type of assets and profitability of the company. Each of these tests gives a different perspective on the company's ability to repay short-, medium- and long-term debt. The Companies Act 2006 requires the board of directors of companies (excluding small companies) to review the company's performance for the previous financial year as part of the company's annual report. Disclosure rules formulated by the Financial Reporting Council implicitly require the board to address potential financial distress by reporting on the company's ability to access the funds required to stay in business in the next financial year. In large public companies, financial distress is a problem that may be shared across a group of associated companies, and the board of directors' decisions are likely to be influenced by the trading relationship between these companies, and intercompany assets and debt.

Financial distress differs from insolvency. English law has deliberately avoided a precise definition of financial distress, regarding this largely as a commercial matter. It provides only limited guidelines for company directors as they attempt to resolve debt problems to avoid a formal insolvency regime. Insolvency is defined in the UK Insolvency Act 1986 as the insufficiency of total assets to repay total liabilities, thus subjecting the company to the threat of a formal insolvency regime. In practice, fixing the precise point at which a large public company becomes insolvent is very difficult to determine, given the large and complex nature of assets and liabilities in such a company.

Directors' Duties to Exercise Commercial Judgment in Financial Distress

Chapter 4 identified some ambiguity in directors' duties at the time of financial distress. The potential threat of personal liability that they may face should they ignore severe financial distress, and the need to inject cash into the company to ensure its survival clearly influence the speed

Conclusions

and extent to which the board may choose to implement different informal rescue options. Rescue options may include board change, cost reduction, asset sale, equity/share issue and new debt financing/debt renegotiation. Adoption and implementation of these options may ultimately help the board rebalance the company's assets and liabilities. Each option may require a different level of involvement from existing shareholders and prospective investors, including new shareholders and creditors, in effect resulting in the formation of new governance patterns. As Chap. 4 illustrated, company directors are legally bound to consider the interests of creditors when the company is in financial difficulty; otherwise they might be held to be personally liable for losses suffered by creditors if they are found liable for wrongful trading.

The individual case studies discussed in Chaps. 7 to 11 and analysed collectively in Chap. 12 provide a detailed examination of changing patterns of governance in five large public companies that entered a period of financial distress. Each of the case studies presents a rich analysis of the changing position of directors, shareholders and creditors, especially secured creditors, prior to and during administration.

Board changes create an adjustment of skills, expertise and expectations amongst members of the board. The evidence from the case studies of large public companies indicates that board changes are likely to vary in scope and focus from company to company, and may be used at any stage during the informal rescue process to secure better performance. The JJB Sports plc and Connaught plc case studies provide examples of changes to board structures, one of the most common early responses to financial distress. Board changes may also provide an opportunity for closer monitoring of the performance of the company by secured creditors, if they can obtain representation on the board. The Stylo plc and Waterford Wedgwood plc case studies provide examples of such changes.

The monitoring role of non-executive directors, a "hands-off" approach, and lack of involvement in executive decisions may change. Whereas previously decisions were concentrated amongst the executive team, especially the Chief Executive Officer (CEO), Managing Director (UK) and Chief Financial Officer (CFO) or Financial Director (UK), in situations of financial distress, non-executive directors may play a more active role.

Shareholder and Creditor Influence on Informal Business Rescue

The different rescue options adopted by the case study companies involved different levels of involvement of shareholders and creditors. The potential role of major shareholders is more pronounced in those companies where major shareholders are already executive members of the board and do not choose to delegate power or demit their role. Since there is no specific external structure through which the behaviour of major shareholders—private or institutional—is reported, it is difficult to identify their actual influence on the decisions of the board regarding rescue options, although it seems that shareholders were generally supportive of the board's decisions in each company.

Whilst shareholders may continue to support the decisions of the board, there are no guidelines to limit or extend the relationship that they have with the board during financial distress. Similarly, there are no rules to modify the powers of creditors especially lenders during financial distress and, therefore, lenders are likely to seek a prime position which allows them to secure their interests at the expense of shareholders and unsecured creditors.

Cost reduction as a response to financial distress can be implemented through a series of measures including reducing inventories, staff redundancies and the closure or rationalisation of business activity. Such measures could be expected to realise cash savings and reduce risk. The role of shareholders and creditors is less evident where cost reduction is the primary strategy, perhaps reflecting the tendency to view the exercise of this option as a continuation of normal business activity, rather than an "emergency" business measure—until the extent of financial distress becomes obvious to external parties. When such activities reach a threshold level of change greater involvement of shareholders and creditors might be expected. Further empirical research in this area could usefully focus on when, where and why such thresholds are reached.

Asset sale may also be an option for the board provided that the assets involved are not subject to security interests. In large public companies, assets are likely to be spread across operating subsidiaries. Lenders will not have any influence on sale if there are no security interests and no new secured debt financing is sought. Any future influence may be gained through new debt financing/debt renegotiation. The ways in which lenders secure and exercise such rights in large distressed companies appear to have been neglected in the literature and are also a potential area for future research.

The board may also be reluctant to consider substantial asset sale because it reduces long-term borrowing power, restricts the future trading of companies in some circumstances and changes the balance sheet of the company, in effect influencing the company's size. In the case studies shareholders appear to have had little or no opportunity to get involved or influence the process of asset sale. However, the cases do illustrate situations where the substantial sale of corporate assets that are subject to security interests may become a controversial matter between the board and lenders, and the lenders' refusal to agree to the sale may contribute to the company's entry into administration (e.g. Woolworths plc).

The board's success in bringing new financing through equity issue depends initially on the support of existing shareholders since their interests are diluted by any increase in the number of shares. Lenders may influence the process by proposing that the board implements such a strategy as a condition of further financing. Where institutional shareholders remain passive or indifferent to equity issue, the board's use of proxies may allow such a strategy to be implemented. The success of such a strategy will depend on the response of the market to any such offer. As the case studies showed, fresh investment from external parties may be more likely to be successful when the board seeks new investors through private placement (e.g. JJB Sports plc).

Different boards appear to give new debt financing different levels of priority. The success of new debt financing depends on the ability of the board to persuade lenders of the value of the equity in company assets. Where this is successful, this may provide a quick solution to cash flow problems before they resort to other cash-generating options. Shareholder approval is necessary for such financing. However, the case studies confirm that shareholders are likely to provide unconditional support for such proposals, authorising the board to grant equity securities by disapplying their pre-emption rights without demanding any terms or conditions (e.g. JJB Sports plc).

Lenders exercise their influence in a variety of ways through the amount of finance they are prepared to provide, the type of finance, that is, loan or credit facilities, and the deferment of principal debt payments or interest charges under so-called standstill agreements. Secured debt financing enhances lender influence on the ultimate disposition of corporate assets and limits the independent decision-making of the board. The confidential and complex nature of debt negotiations means that it is difficult to analyse the actual influence and decision-making of lenders on the overall informal rescue process, or in relation to the reasons why re-financing is rejected. In two cases reported in this book (Waterford Wedgewood plc and Woolworths Group plc), lender unwillingness to finance further debt led to administration.

Debt negotiation may also impose further obligations on the company, with higher borrowing costs. The lenders' influence can also be seen in the appointment of specific insolvency practitioners as advisors to the board, prior to administration. There are no legal prescriptions on how such appointments should be made or the accountability of such advisors, raising questions about the conduct and allegiances of such advisors during financial distress. Where lenders have been involved in the appointment of advisors, this may provide an opportunity for them to influence the rescue process to their own advantage. Their pre-insolvency presence is typically necessary in large public companies because of the complexity of the assets and liabilities and the scale of business operations (e.g. Waterford Wedgwood plc).

Such an appointment is comparable with the involvement of insolvency practitioners in the preparation of a CVA proposal. Typically such involvement begins before the practitioner is appointed as a nominee, and again may be influenced by lenders, as the JJB Sports plc case demonstrated.

The Role of Insolvency Practitioners

On their formal appointment, administrators take over director duties to the company and creditors. Their obligation is to achieve the most appropriate statutory rescue objective, defined in scope by para 52(1) of the

Insolvency Act, 1986. This may result in the company's entry into a formal insolvency regime such as liquidation where rescue is not possible. There is no parallel duty for an insolvency practitioner who accepts the role of nominee in a CVA. The insolvency practitioner in these circumstances does not replace the company directors.

The length of appointment of the administrator is limited in the first instance to one year with the possibility of extension, subject to court or creditor approval. Typically it would be expected that the administrator would make decisions on the future of the business within a much shorter timescale. In such circumstances the responsibilities of the administrator do not include management of the company as a going concern beyond the time required to achieve a business sale or asset sale (inventory). In large public companies, decisions on whether to continue to operate individual companies may be taken separately, subject to their business viability and solvency (e.g. Connaught plc).

In large public companies that typically involve a group of subsidiaries, a CVA does not provide such discretion for the insolvency practitioner, as the board of directors maintains its control over management of all group companies. During financial distress, the board of directors implements informal rescue options with the aim of prolonging the business life of the group although their rescue options may change the scale of business operations of the subsidiaries.

The statutory duty of the administrator is to pay creditor claims through asset sale. In large public companies, business sales or substantial asset sales are typically a priority for administrators to achieve a rapid rescue process. Piecemeal asset sale becomes inevitable when a sale of the business as a whole is not possible. In large public companies, asset sale in subsidiaries is typically the primary focus of administrators, since parent companies are unlikely to have any significant business activity in their own right (e.g. Connaught plc).

A CVA does not provide power of sale for the insolvency practitioner. Power of sale remains with the board of directors. Typically the board of directors seem to focus on piecemeal asset sale due to the existence of security interests preventing them from a sale of more substantial core business(es) without obtaining lenders' consent.

The administrators' statutory duty to distribute the proceeds of asset sale amongst creditors is delayed until assets are liquidated in part or in total. Payment of secured creditors can be achieved only when asset sales are realised, and the proceeds are secured. Neither priority ranking nor the prescribed part provides a mandate for administrators to pay unsecured creditors during administration if liquidation is planned. In a CVA, the supervisory role of the insolvency practitioner limits his distribution powers to unsecured creditors, as the CVA and the terms of the CVA proposal dictate when and how they should be paid. The distribution role of the supervisor of the CVA fund can begin only when funds become available. No distribution powers can be invoked if a CVA is terminated with no funds before the proposed time limit and therefore no payment can been made (e.g. CVA2 in JJB Sports plc).

In financially distressed companies, the initiation and implementation of the informal rescue process does not exempt the company from liability to pay creditors' contractual claims when they become due. The board of directors is obliged to ensure both categories of creditors (secured and unsecured) are paid on time unless separate agreements are made with each creditor. The board's failure to pay unsecured creditors may result in winding-up petitions but commencement of administration can suspend these petitions. An automatic stay will result in all claims being frozen.

The administrators' statutory duty to investigate directors' conduct seems to be less important than their role in asset sale and the distribution of proceeds amongst creditors. Confidentiality of the administrator's report in each of the case studies prevented gaining any insight into their approach to director liability. The rarity of reported cases dealing with director liability in large public companies may indicate administrators' general acceptance of directors' approach to creditor interests prior to administration. It may also reflect the degree of difficulty in establishing where wrongful or inappropriate trading has taken place. Since joint administrators are likely to be involved in decisions made by company directors during financial distress, questions remain as to the extent of the contribution that they make and its impact on directors' personal liability.

In contrast, the supervisor of a CVA fund does not have such investigative powers since a CVA does not result in automatic discharge of company directors from their role. Perhaps the nominee's agreement to be involved in the CVA may indicate his implicit endorsement of the directors' approach to debt problems. In financially distressed companies, board change allows the termination or suspension of existing members of the board of directors without mandatory disclosure of information over their conduct.

The influence of unsecured creditors can be seen in administration where management of the going concern in the short term is planned and inventory supply and delivery is crucial (e.g. with Woolworths plc, Wedgwood plc and Connaught plc). Unsecured creditors may seek some degree of settlement for their pre-administration claims as a condition for continuing their short-term business with the company. A CVA allows unsecured creditors to continue their business relationship with the company without any modifications, only if their interests are not subject to the terms of the CVA proposal. In financially distressed companies, unsecured creditors are under no statutory obligation to continue their relationship with the company and may terminate their business if the company loses its creditworthiness.

The role of unsecured creditors in asset sales is insignificant during administration. This is due to the lack of any proprietary right to influence such sales. Lender influence on asset sale may be demonstrated by their decision to enforce their security interests and acquire the business run by a particular subsidiary or part of the assets as a partial discharge of their claims. They may also agree to a partial transfer of their security interests if the assets subject to security are sold as part of a pre-packaged administration or leave administrators to dispose of assets and provide them with the proceeds of sale. Since the valuation of assets can have a direct impact on their total recovery, they might be interested in influencing the valuation process—a potential area for further research. In a CVA, unsecured creditors or lenders do not have a specific role in asset sale.

Any influence from unsecured creditors over financing administration or controlling the costs of administration is dependent on their share of assets under the prescribed part. In large public companies, unsecured creditor influence is limited by the contracts they have with the parent company and/or its subsidiaries. Where unsecured creditors do receive a dividend from the sale of assets other than the prescribed part, they can then decide whether to form a creditor committee and potentially influence administration and financing costs.

Contribution to Knowledge

Analysis of Changes to Corporate Governance During Insolvency

There are comparatively few studies of the impact of insolvency on corporate governance, particularly in terms of the interaction between governance codes and legal practice. This book has contributed to our understanding of the complexity of the issue and the range of influences on the behaviour of the parties involved. The role of lenders and their increasing importance during financial distress has become particularly apparent and is highlighted during the research.

Identification and Analysis of Multiple Influences and a Holistic Approach

This research has taken a holistic approach to analysis seeking to identify multiple influences on the process of governance over time, rather than examining one factor (such as the replacement of directors) during financial distress. It has combined theoretical analysis with the collection of detailed case information. The resultant case studies and interpretation against the literature background present a rich picture of decision-making processes and influences which help to interpret the relative importance of legal influences and the governance code on directors' actions during financial distress.

Innovative Approach to Data Collection

To date there are comparatively few reported studies that have taken a longitudinal perspective of decision-making in individual companies during informal and formal rescue processes. A detailed forensic analysis of statutory filings, company announcements, company reports and accounts, and other media comment was used to develop five case studies of large UK companies that experienced financial distress and insolvency between 2008 and 2013. This approach is an innovative way of researching this area and one of the few ways in which the research questions and aims could have been addressed.

Research Implications

Different parties have varying levels of involvement at different stages as a company moves from profitable healthy trading (solvent non-distressed) to insolvency, illustrating changes to governance structures. This research suggests the addition of the stage of financial distress between solvent non-distressed situations and insolvency. Using these distinctions it is possible to identify a range of influences on decision-making over time, and identify and classify some of the most important decisions during informal and formal rescue processes.

The study emphasises the importance of understanding the changing relationship between lenders and directors in solvent and distressed circumstances. There is little reported research on the influence of lenders on director decision-making in the area of debt re-financing. This research has provided instances where lenders have taken an active role in promoting asset sale or business rationalisation as a condition of further lending. Compared with lenders, unsecured creditors appear to operate in a "hands-off" way with little direct involvement in the decisions of the debtor's business. The criteria that are applied by such creditors to continue business relationships seem to include the viability of the debtor's business and the extent to which the creditor is commercially dependent on that business for survival, illustrated graphically in Woolworths plc, Stylo plc and Connaught plc.

During informal rescue governance structures might be improved by the early formation of a creditors' committee that could represent the interests of different classes of creditors, operating as a new monitoring body, to work with management to resolve the distress situation. Currently they act collectively at the formal stage, after the business has closed and the dividends of unsecured creditors are often limited to the prescribed part. There is no involvement in the business planning that might have led to a better outcome. Unlike lenders with security interests unsecured creditors are currently not empowered to become involved at an earlier stage, and only appear to do so on an individual basis. The degree to which such involvement might be exercised depends on the perceived commercial importance of the debtor's business, as well as the extent of commitment of the debtor company to take this option.

The current legal system remains silent as to the duties that insolvency practitioners should have prior to administration or CVA when providing advice to the directors or secured creditors of companies that are experiencing financial strife. This research has demonstrated cases where an insolvency practitioner has been involved prior to administration to provide advice to directors. A new governance structure might require that such pre-insolvency appointments are given office-holder status to ensure that the interests of different parties are balanced.

Further Research

Potential development of this research could include:

- Extension of the number of case studies to explore the usefulness of the methodology to a more broadly based quantified analysis of informal and formal rescue processes in a wider range of companies
- UK-US comparisons, exploring the availability and usefulness of comparable data sources and case development for an American sample of companies
- Further exploration of the role of the administrator in the informal rescue process
- Exploration of the role and influence of institutional shareholders and lenders, building on the insights from this research.

Concluding Remarks

This book set out to examine the impact of financial distress and insolvency on the governance of large public companies. In completing this study it became clear that current governance codes have not yet evolved to cover situations of financial distress and the potential influencing roles of shareholders and creditors on governance. Equally, the law does not appear to have provided clear guidelines for director-creditor relationships and director-shareholder relationships as companies enter periods of financial distress, becoming involved only when distress turns into insolvency. Assuming that business failure remains a characteristic of the UK economy for the foreseeable future, then further work by legislators, and those responsible for the formation and dissemination of new governance codes, may help to bridge an apparent gap between business practice and the current legal and regulatory systems.

Index[1]

A

Accountancy Age, 134
Administration, 5, 9, 43, 55–59, 73, 95, 123, 145, 163, 185, 203, 223, 247, 289
Administrator, 10, 51, 124, 173, 186, 194–196, 203, 230, 275, 285
Advisor, 18, 69–71, 104, 149, 150, 166, 168, 169, 171, 189, 190, 203, 207, 208, 217, 227, 228, 258, 261, 263, 270, 275, 283, 292
Agency theory, 11, 32
Annual general meeting (AGM), 20, 26, 27, 29, 137, 138, 152, 171, 174, 176, 190, 210, 229, 230, 282

Appointment, 10, 17–20, 27, 30, 33, 51, 56, 68, 71, 75, 89, 96, 102, 103, 107, 111–112, 129, 131, 134, 136, 139, 150, 153–155, 173, 175, 176, 207, 212, 213, 217, 227, 228, 231–233, 256–258, 265, 266, 275, 278, 292, 293, 298
Asset, 6, 21, 44, 69, 98, 129, 145, 165, 187, 203, 223, 225, 250, 285
Asset sale, 4, 8, 10, 50, 66, 69, 75, 76, 79, 89, 97, 103–105, 108, 113–114, 117, 132, 133, 138–141, 148, 150, 155–156, 163, 166, 176, 188–190, 193–196, 203,

---

[1] Note: Page numbers followed by 'n' refer to notes.

Index

Asset sale (*cont.*)
 208, 210, 213–214, 217, 229, 232, 249, 256, 260, 263, 267–269, 271, 275–277, 279, 282, 289–291, 293–295, 297

Balance sheet, 44–47, 49, 72, 79, 83, 84, 103, 130, 147, 148, 151, 164–166, 168, 179, 186–188, 190, 194, 198, 205, 224, 225, 229, 250, 252, 253, 260, 262, 264, 291
Bank, 6, 15, 22, 45, 46, 55, 71, 72, 77, 80, 82, 85, 87, 111, 112, 114, 147, 149, 150, 154, 166, 170, 178, 187, 191, 193, 196, 210, 224, 226, 230, 234, 264, 266
Bankruptcy, 45, 46, 52, 53, 56, 123
Berle, Adolf A., 10
Board change, 10, 66, 67, 79, 132, 133, 136, 148–150, 166–167, 172, 175–176, 185, 186, 188–189, 206–207, 226–228, 249, 257, 282, 289, 295
Board composition, 18, 19
Board of directors, 3, 6, 8, 13, 14, 29, 34, 48–50, 66–75, 77, 89, 96–97, 132, 145–151, 159, 164–170, 186, 188, 189, 191, 197, 204, 206–210, 224, 226–227, 230, 247, 250, 256, 259, 261, 263, 266, 277, 288, 290, 293–295

British Gas, 227, 228, 233
British Home Stores (BHS), 5, 22
Business failure, 3, 5, 8, 22, 53, 54, 126, 299
Business Insider, 134

Cadbury Report, 12, 16, 21
Capital markets, 6, 34
Carillion plc, 5, 22, 49
Cash flow, 4, 44–46, 68, 72, 80, 83, 85, 87, 89, 99, 148, 163, 165, 169, 171, 172, 187, 188, 193, 198, 205, 223, 225, 250, 252, 253, 260, 291
Chairman, 59, 68, 74, 147, 149, 154, 164, 166, 170, 172, 174–176, 178, 186, 224, 227, 228, 230, 233, 251, 258, 281
Charge, 46, 51, 52, 56–58, 69, 72, 73, 75–77, 84, 89n1, 89n3, 107, 111, 112, 114, 135, 138, 140, 154, 157, 165–167, 169, 170, 177, 187, 194, 196, 209, 210, 214, 215, 224, 234, 235, 237, 239n1, 252, 264, 270, 271, 274, 276, 277, 292
Chief executive officer (CEO), 188, 227
Circulating assets, 73
Claim, 7, 21, 26, 30–32, 35, 44, 53–59, 77, 79, 83, 86, 95, 97–104, 106–108, 110, 113–117, 131, 147, 154, 156, 157, 159, 163,

173–175, 178, 192, 196,
212–216, 233, 234, 236,
238, 271–274, 277, 279,
281, 285, 293–295
Coase, R.H., 11
Comet plc, 5
Common law, 3, 6, 9, 14, 22–26,
30, 31, 35, 45, 53, 77, 81,
82, 85, 109, 123
Companies Act 2006, 3, 12, 15, 22,
23, 25–27, 30, 35, 67,
69, 129, 130, 134, 170,
230, 288
Companies House, 5, 19, 22, 78,
130, 131, 133–138,
140, 141
Company, 4–12, 14–16, 18, 20–25,
44, 66, 95, 145, 163, 185,
203, 224, 247
  Company Law Review Steering
  Group (CLRSG), 23
  Company voluntary arrangement
  (CVA), 5, 8, 10, 11, 43, 52,
  55, 57–59, 95–101, 126,
  131, 133, 134, 139, 141,
  145, 148, 152–154, 163,
  165, 170–178, 247, 253,
  263, 266, 267, 269, 271,
  274, 275, 281–283,
  292–295, 298
    CVA proposal, 99, 100, 139,
    145, 153, 170, 173–175,
    177, 178, 274, 281–283,
    292, 294, 295
Compliance, 10, 12, 16, 20, 22, 32,
70, 140, 164, 195, 223,
224, 228, 233, 234, 261,
267, 269

Compulsory liquidation, 5, 204, 217
Connaught Environmental, 114,
223, 224, 233, 234, 236,
238, 239n2, 269
Connaught plc, 49, 103, 105–107,
113–115, 223–239,
248–260, 262–264, 266,
267, 269, 271–279, 282,
289, 293, 295, 297
Contract, 10, 11, 22, 34, 47, 54, 57,
58, 68, 74, 76, 77, 79–81,
83, 87, 96, 99, 104, 136,
152, 198, 203, 223–226,
228, 229, 233, 236, 250,
255, 259, 260, 267, 269,
270, 273, 286, 295
Cork Report, 48, 53, 55, 101,
130, 254
Corporate governance, 3, 6–35, 50,
60, 65–89, 95–117,
123–141, 145–147, 164,
167, 185, 186, 204–205,
223, 224, 227, 247, 249,
250, 285–288, 296
  governance code, 4, 6, 7, 10, 16,
  18, 22, 26, 67, 75, 224,
  251, 287, 296, 299
  UK Corporate Governance Code,
  12, 14, 18, 36n1, 146, 186,
  249, 286–288
Cost reduction, 4, 8, 10, 50, 66, 68,
75, 132, 137, 150,
167–168, 189, 205, 207,
226–228, 256, 259, 282,
289, 290
Court order, 31, 45, 49–52, 56,
108, 109, 113, 116, 215,
217, 218

Creditor
  influence, 7, 11, 69, 74–80,
    98–101, 111–117, 138,
    140, 141, 152, 158–159,
    171–172, 174, 179,
    193–194, 197–198,
    215–217, 248, 266,
    275, 279, 280,
    290–292, 295
  interest, 88, 107, 163, 271
  Creditors' meeting, 52, 57, 58,
    96, 99, 100, 105, 114–117,
    133, 139, 153, 158, 174,
    175, 197, 216, 235–237,
    277–281
  Creditors' voluntary liquidation,
    5, 134, 140, 185, 204, 217
Credit rating agencies (CRA), 7, 9,
    10, 13, 14, 34, 35
Customer, 11, 15, 24, 46, 48, 195,
    224, 238, 259

D

Debenture, 51, 56, 77, 89n3, 137,
    147, 151, 154, 157, 169,
    171, 187, 209, 263
Debt
  financing, 4, 8, 10, 50, 66, 72,
    76, 78, 114, 129, 132, 133,
    138, 140, 148, 151, 163,
    166, 169–170, 177, 179,
    188, 191–193, 203, 206,
    209–211, 226, 227,
    229–230, 255, 256, 263,
    264, 266, 267, 282, 289,
    291, 292
  renegotiation, 4, 8, 10, 50, 66,
    72, 132, 138, 151,
    169–170, 177, 191–192,
    209–210, 229–230, 263,
    282, 289, 291
  structure, 8, 11, 135, 141, 147,
    164, 187, 205, 224, 252
Deloitte, 102, 112, 153, 155, 156,
    191, 194, 212–214, 233, 276
Derivative claim, 26, 30–32, 35
Director, 3, 9, 11, 47, 65, 95, 123,
    145, 163, 195, 204, 228,
    250, 286
Disclosure, 6, 7, 10, 28, 30, 33, 47,
    70, 74, 76, 83, 88, 105,
    107–108, 116, 140, 141,
    175, 249, 275, 280, 288, 295
Dispersed shareholders, 26, 28, 74,
    149, 224, 286
Dissolution, 52, 57, 104, 134, 140,
    153, 159, 232
Distress, *see* Financial distress
Dividend, 22, 27, 30, 33, 46, 47, 59,
    69, 107, 115, 147, 151,
    152, 157–159, 171, 178,
    187, 191, 192, 196, 197,
    210, 215, 218, 235, 237,
    238, 271, 272, 274, 275,
    279, 296, 298
Doctrinal, 4, 7–9, 123, 131, 285

E

Empirical research, 6–35, 123, 124,
    128, 283, 290
Employee, 6, 9, 15, 22, 24, 48, 54,
    68, 83, 105, 107, 108, 114,
    130, 133, 146, 147, 159,
    189, 204, 224, 236, 250,
    274, 281
Enterprise Act 2002, 51, 55, 56, 117

Equity, 4, 8, 10, 30, 50, 66, 69–71, 73, 79, 80, 89, 114, 129, 132, 133, 137, 138, 149, 151, 166, 169, 171, 176–177, 185, 187, 188, 190–192, 195, 209, 210, 229, 255, 256, 262–266, 282, 289, 291

Equity issue, *see* Share issue

Executive director, 68, 87, 109, 110, 147, 149, 150, 164, 166, 167, 171, 175, 186–189, 204, 207, 224, 228, 250, 251, 256, 258, 261

External cause, 8, 148, 165, 188, 206, 226, 253, 254

Extraordinary general meeting (EGM), 20, 26, 28, 138, 190, 192, 282

F

FE Investegate, 133

Fiduciary duty, 66, 69, 75, 80, 81, 267

Financial Conduct Authority (FCA), 32, 261

Financial distress, 3, 4, 7–35, 43–60, 65–89, 100, 105, 123–126, 130, 132, 135, 141, 145, 147–148, 151, 152, 165, 168, 172, 187–188, 193, 203, 205–206, 210, 225–226, 247, 252, 255, 256, 259, 260, 270, 282, 283, 285–290, 292–294, 296, 297, 299

Financial markets, 14, 32, 35, 49, 148, 226, 262

The Financial Times, 134

Fixed charge, 52, 73, 76, 77, 111, 114, 177, 209, 210

Floating charge, 51, 55–57, 69, 73, 75, 77, 102, 106, 107, 111, 112, 114, 135, 154, 157, 169, 187, 194, 196, 209, 224, 234, 252, 264, 271, 274, 276, 277

Formal non-rescue procedure, 50–53, 140

Formal rescue, 10, 11, 43, 53–55, 57, 76, 79, 96, 116, 126–128, 130–134, 136, 139–141, 145, 146, 152–153, 172–177, 179, 185, 194–199, 203, 204, 212–217, 223, 231–235, 238, 247, 250, 252, 253, 264, 265, 267, 283, 296, 298

G

Going concern, 25, 45, 49, 54, 57, 68, 70, 80, 83, 87, 96, 97, 101, 104, 108, 112–114, 116, 117, 132, 137–139, 145–148, 154–155, 159, 166, 172, 189, 193–195, 205, 207–209, 213, 230–232, 236, 253, 256, 259, 267, 269, 273, 274, 277, 282, 283, 293, 295

The Guardian, 134

H

Harvard Law School (HLS), 125
Hedge fund, 26
HMRC, 99, 117, 174, 175, 236, 281
HMV Group plc, 5

I

Informal rescue, 6, 10, 50, 66–80, 97, 146, 165, 188–192, 226–227, 249, 289
Insolvency, 4, 9, 26, 43–60, 73, 95–117, 124, 173, 187, 205, 231, 250, 286
Insolvency Act 1986, Schedule B1, 56, 102, 113, 154, 212, 232
Insolvency Rules 1986, 134
The Insolvency Service, 5, 109
Institutional shareholder, 6, 7, 25, 27, 33, 35, 70, 74, 89, 100, 166, 192, 204, 208, 211, 224, 227, 231, 251, 261, 263, 265, 282, 286, 287, 291, 298
Investment, 6, 46, 71, 72, 76, 87, 130, 138, 146, 151, 169, 187, 191, 192, 204, 225, 254, 262, 265, 291

J

Jensen, M.C., 11
JJB Sports plc, 5, 67, 71, 98, 131, 163–179, 248–254, 256, 258–269, 271, 274, 281, 289, 291, 292, 294

Joint administrators, 102, 103, 133, 152–159, 186, 194–198, 203, 212–218, 231–233, 266, 267, 275–281, 285, 294
Joint Stock Companies Act 1844, 51

L

Langdell, Christopher, 124
Lender, 6, 14, 69, 98, 135, 147, 166, 187, 227, 250, 287
Liabilities, 6, 13, 24–27, 34, 44–47, 49, 50, 65, 74, 80–88, 101, 102, 110, 114, 147, 148, 152, 165, 176, 187, 194, 195, 197, 205, 208, 215, 225, 233, 235, 237, 252, 253, 270, 275, 286, 288, 289, 292, 294
Lien, 72, 89n1, 194, 213
Limited liability, 24, 286
Liquidation, 5, 8, 43, 45, 51, 52, 57, 59, 75, 84, 85, 88, 99, 104, 106, 132, 134, 154, 171, 185, 194, 198, 204, 212, 215, 217, 232, 237, 238, 274, 293, 294
Loan, 6, 46, 47, 73, 76, 77, 86, 147, 152, 154, 164, 170, 173, 177, 192, 209, 210, 224, 225, 227, 229–231, 263, 264, 266, 277, 292
The London Stock Exchange (LSE), 12, 16, 18, 20, 32, 33, 133, 164, 186, 190, 204, 209, 223, 229, 248, 249, 262

M

Markets, 6, 7, 9–11, 13, 14, 29, 32–35, 48, 49, 57, 70, 71, 78, 148, 164, 165, 206, 209–211, 226, 249, 256, 258, 262, 265, 269, 270, 291
Maturity, 45, 47, 72, 164, 177, 263
Maxwell, Robert, 12
Means, G.C., 10
Meckling, W.H., 11
Mega-bankruptcy case, 130
Mega-insolvency, 130, 131, 164, 186, 224, 250
Minority shareholder, 26, 31, 35
Models of corporate governance, 14–16
Mortgage, 49, 72, 73, 89n1, 111, 114, 138, 140, 147, 154, 177, 252
Mutual fund, 26

N

Non-executive director, 9, 17–20, 66–68, 87, 109, 110, 124, 147, 149, 150, 152, 164, 166, 167, 171, 172, 175, 186, 187, 189, 204, 206, 207, 224, 228, 250, 251, 256, 258, 266, 287, 289

O

The Office of Fair Trading (OFT), 101, 111, 112, 134, 138, 167, 169, 176
Ordinary share, 33, 69, 147, 169, 204, 210, 224, 262, 265
Ownership, 9–11, 14, 15, 23, 26, 72, 73, 79, 89n1, 124, 135, 145, 146, 151, 152, 164, 187, 192, 210, 234, 262, 286

P

Parent company, 99, 128, 146, 164, 186, 204, 224, 248, 293
Pari passu, 54, 107
Pension fund, 6, 26, 210
Polly Peck, 12
Preferential creditors, 73, 75, 81, 84, 98, 106, 116, 174, 215, 235, 237, 271, 278, 283n2
Pre-packaged administration, 57, 101, 105, 145, 152–155, 159, 268, 276, 295
Priority ranking, 54, 55, 57, 73, 106, 140, 271, 274, 294
Private companies, 9, 10, 23, 128, 129, 166, 214
Progress report, 20–21, 97, 108, 134, 139, 140, 155–159, 195, 196, 198, 213–215, 232, 234–237, 278
Proquest, 134
Proxy voting, 26, 28
Public companies, 3, 5, 9–35, 50, 67, 70, 76, 78, 80, 83, 88, 98, 99, 104, 105, 110–112, 114, 123, 126, 128, 129, 131, 133, 140, 145, 146, 163, 185, 204, 223, 247, 249, 253, 274, 285–290, 292–295, 299
Public offering, 23, 70, 71, 176

Index

R

Receivership, 5, 8, 9, 43, 51, 52, 55, 111, 123, 185, 186, 194, 197, 199, 247, 249, 261, 264, 266, 276
The Regulatory News Service (RNS), 133
Restructuring, 67, 68, 149, 166, 167, 175, 189, 208, 270
Royal Bank of Scotland, 224

S

Secondary data, 125, 127, 128, 130
Secured creditor, 7, 8, 35, 50, 51, 53–55, 65, 66, 72–76, 78, 79, 81, 89, 95, 96, 98–99, 104–108, 111–117, 138–140, 152, 156–158, 163, 171, 173, 174, 179, 193, 196, 197, 208, 212, 214–216, 231, 233–235, 237, 238, 252, 266, 267, 270–272, 274–277, 289, 294, 298
Security interest, 54, 72–78, 95, 98, 111–114, 135, 138, 139, 141, 157, 164, 169–171, 176, 187, 209, 210, 214, 229, 261, 264–267, 271, 272, 277, 290, 291, 293, 295
Senior management, 17, 29, 68, 251, 265
Separation of ownership and control, 10, 11, 187
The Serious Fraud Office (SFO), 134, 167

Share capital, 69, 70, 137, 171, 176, 177, 190, 192, 265
Shareholder, 3, 9, 46, 65, 95, 123, 146, 164, 185, 204, 224, 247, 286
 shareholder influence, 11, 26–30, 74, 100–101, 151–152, 171, 192, 210, 230–231, 264, 282
 shareholder meeting, 27, 29, 74, 115, 137, 174, 251, 265, 287
 shareholder voting, 16, 27, 116, 205
Share issue, 4, 8, 10, 50, 66, 69–71, 74, 97, 132, 133, 137, 149, 151, 163, 169, 172, 176–177, 190–192, 209, 211, 229, 262, 264, 265, 282, 289
Stakeholders, 9, 12, 13, 15, 22–25, 48, 66, 83, 170, 230
Standstill agreement, 170, 191, 193, 210, 230, 263, 264, 266, 292
Statement of affairs, 110, 134, 139, 154, 157, 158, 235, 274
Statement of proposals, 195, 213, 236
Statute, 3, 6, 9, 14, 22, 35, 44
Statutory, 4, 7, 10, 14, 15, 22–26, 30, 31, 35, 44, 55, 70, 81, 82, 88, 96, 97, 102–106, 108, 109, 114–116, 127, 130–132, 139, 154, 178, 194, 198, 212, 215, 217, 229, 232, 261, 271, 273, 274, 277, 279, 281, 292–295, 297

Stock market, 10, 32, 70, 164, 209, 249
Stylo plc, 68, 75, 102, 131, 145–159, 248–254, 258–260, 262–266, 268, 269, 271–275, 277–280, 282, 283, 289, 297
Sub-committee, 19–22
Sub-contractor, 6, 231

U

Unsecured creditor, 7, 51, 73, 95, 128, 147, 171, 193, 203, 231, 287

W

Winding up, 44, 50, 52, 57, 59, 79, 211, 212, 216, 217, 276, 294
Woolworths Group plc, 5, 67–69, 102, 113, 203–218, 249, 250, 252, 258–262, 264–266, 268, 269, 271, 273–279, 282, 292
Wrongful trading, 81, 84–88, 132, 215, 237, 289

Y

Yin, Robert K., 126, 131, 132

CPSIA information can be obtained
at www.ICGtesting.com
Printed in the USA
LVHW08*2356080918
589572LV00013B/260/P